In the Shadow of the Cold War

This book offers a bold reinterpretation of the prevailing narrative that US foreign policy after the Cold War was a failure. In chapters that retell and reargue the key episodes of the post–Cold War years, Lynch argues that the Cold War cast a shadow on the presidents that came after it and that success came more from adapting to that shadow than in attempts to escape it. When strategic lessons of the Cold War were applied, presidents fared better; when they were forgotten, they fared worse. This book tells the story not of a revolution in American foreign policy, but of its essentially continuous character from one era to the next. While there were many setbacks between the fall of Soviet communism and the opening years of the Trump administration, from Rwanda to 9/11 and Iraq to Syria, Lynch demonstrates that the United States remained the world's dominant power.

TIMOTHY J. LYNCH is Associate Professor in American Politics at the University of Melbourne. He is an award-winning author and editor of several important books on foreign policy, including *Turf War: The Clinton Administration and Northern Ireland* (Ashgate, 2004) and *US Foreign Policy and Democracy Promotion* (coeditor, Routledge, 2013), *After Bush: The Case for Continuity in American Foreign Policy* (coauthor, Cambridge, 2008), and the two-volume *Oxford Encyclopedia of American Military and Diplomatic History* (2013).

Cambridge Essential Histories

Cambridge Essential Histories is devoted to introducing critical events, periods, or individuals in history to students. Volumes in this series emphasize narrative as a means of familiarizing students with historical analysis. In this series, leading scholars focus on topics in European, American, Asian, Latin American, Middle Eastern, African, and World History through thesis-driven, concise volumes designed for survey and upper-division undergraduate history courses. The books contain an introduction that acquaints readers with the historical event and reveals the book's thesis; narrative chapters that cover the chronology of the event or problem; and a concluding summary that provides the historical interpretation and analysis.

General Editor

Donald T. Critchlow, Arizona State University

Other books in the series:

Calvin Schermerhorn, *Unrequited Toil: A History of United States Slavery*
Michael G. Kort, *The Vietnam War Reexamined*
Maura Jane Farrelly, *Anti-Catholicism in America, 1620–1860*
David M. Wrobel, *America's West: A History, 1890–1950*
Mark E. Neely, Jr., *Lincoln and the Democrats: The Politics of Opposition in the Civil War*
Howard Brick and Christopher Phelps, *Radicals in America: The U.S. Left since the Second World War*
W. J. Rorabaugh, *American Hippies*
Sean P. Cunningham, *American Politics in the Postwar Sunbelt*
Jason Scott Smith, *A Concise History of the New Deal*
Stanley G. Payne, *The Spanish Civil War*
J. C. A. Stagg, *The War of 1812: Conflict for a Continent*
Ian Dowbiggin, *The Quest for Mental Health: A Tale of Science, Medicine, Scandal, Sorrow, and Mass Society*
Wilson D. Miscamble, *The Most Controversial Decision: Truman, the Atomic Bombs, and the Defeat of Japan*
Edward D. Berkowitz, *Mass Appeal: The Formative Age of the Movies, Radio, and TV*
Charles H. Parker, *Global Interactions in the Early Modern Age, 1400–1800*
John Lauritz Larson, *The Market Revolution in America: Liberty, Ambition, and the Eclipse of the Common Good*
James H. Hutson, *Church and State in America: The First Two Centuries*
Maury Klein, *The Genesis of Industrial America, 1870–1920*
John Earl Haynes and Harvey Klehr, *Early Cold War Spies: The Espionage Trials that Shaped American Politics*

In the Shadow of the Cold War

American Foreign Policy from George Bush Sr. to Donald Trump

TIMOTHY J. LYNCH

University of Melbourne

CAMBRIDGE
UNIVERSITY PRESS

CAMBRIDGE
UNIVERSITY PRESS

University Printing House, Cambridge CB2 8BS, United Kingdom

One Liberty Plaza, 20th Floor, New York, NY 10006, USA

477 Williamstown Road, Port Melbourne, VIC 3207, Australia

314–321, 3rd Floor, Plot 3, Splendor Forum, Jasola District Centre,
New Delhi – 110025, India

79 Anson Road, #06–04/06, Singapore 079906

Cambridge University Press is part of the University of Cambridge.

It furthers the University's mission by disseminating knowledge in the pursuit of
education, learning, and research at the highest international levels of excellence.

www.cambridge.org
Information on this title: www.cambridge.org/9780521199872
DOI: 10.1017/9781139027120

© Timothy J. Lynch 2020

First published 2020

Printed in the United Kingdom by TJ International Ltd, Padstow Cornwall

A catalogue record for this publication is available from the British Library.

ISBN 978-0-521-19987-2 Hardback
ISBN 978-0-521-13676-1 Paperback

To Michael Lynch, my father

Contents

Acknowledgments

I have enjoyed debating the arguments of the book with many people over several years. These include my students and colleagues at the universities of Leicester, London, and Melbourne. Much of the final writing was done while teaching at Renmin University, China, which allowed me to test some ideas in a different setting.

Donald Critchlow invited me to write this book and waited patiently for its completion. Lewis Bateman and Deborah Gershenowitz, as my successive editors at Cambridge University Press, and Rachel Blaifeder, as editorial assistant, were helpful and patient, in equal measure. I would also like to thank Lisa Carter and Shaheer Husanne for their efforts in getting the book through production.

I am grateful to the anonymous readers of the original proposal and of the finished manuscript. Isabel Stein did a remarkable job of copyediting the work. Others who read sections (some the whole thing) and gave important feedback include Charles Edel, James Goldgeier, Bruce Jentleson, Melvyn Leffler, David Milne, and Kumuda Simpson-Gray. Mel Leffler's brilliant Miegunyah Lecture on George W. Bush's foreign policy, delivered at the University of Melbourne in 2016, was a significant spur to my own thinking.

My participation at the Bridging the Gap International Policy Summer Institute (2018) at American University, under the stimulating direction of Jim Goldgeier and Bruce Jentleson, helped refine, clarify, and amend several of the approaches I have taken in the book.

Important inspiration was provided by conferences at the Clements Center for National Security at the University of Texas, Austin; the John Goodwin Tower Center for Political Studies at Southern Methodist

University; and the School of Historical, Philosophical and Religious Studies at Arizona State University. Several sections of the book were presented at the European Consortium for Political Research annual conferences (in Montreal and Oslo), at the British International Studies Association U.S. Foreign Policy Working Group Conference (at the London School of Economics and at City University), and at the Oceanic Conference on International Studies (Melbourne). The Australian Department of Foreign Affairs and Trade invited me to teach a week-long course to its new diplomats in 2014. The Australian Institute for International Affairs offered me a platform to present on Trump's foreign policy in 2017. I would like to thank those who critiqued my arguments in those forums.

My terrific colleagues in the School of Social and Political Sciences at Melbourne provided important responses on the penultimate draft. Other people who played a role in the writing of this book (whether they realized it or not) include Trevor Burnard, Andrea Carson, Gabrielle Connellan, Mick Cox, Marty Cupp, Glyn Davis, John Dumbrell, Robyn Eckersley, Adam Hannah, Alexandra Homolar, Jonathan Kolieb, Marc Landy, Robert Lieber, Stephen Lynch, David Malet, Michael Mandelbaum, Daniel McCarthy, Jim McCormick, Iwan Morgan, John Murphy, Brendon O'Connor, Raymond Orr, Avery Poole, George Rennie, Robin Simcox, Joseph Siracusa, Ed Smith, Pradeep Taneja, and Andrew Walter.

I would like to thank Mark Considine, Karen Farquharson, and Adrian Little at the University of Melbourne for finding me sufficient research leave to get the book finished. The external relations team in the Faculty of Arts, led by Fiona Abud, set up several diverse international audiences where I tested and refined some of my arguments – and, I hope, drew some students toward Melbourne in the process. These included Jawaharlal Nehru University (New Delhi), Renmin University (Beijing), and Universitas Indonesia (Jakarta).

On the theme of patience, Heather and Peerson Lynch showed much, some of it skeptical, all of it supportive, as they waited for me to finish the book. I have dedicated the book to my father, Michael Lynch. He writes books in half the time and at twice the quality.

All errors of fact and interpretation are my own.

Introduction

History is not ... a cookbook offering pretested recipes. It teaches by analogy, not by maxims. It can illuminate the consequences of actions in comparable situations, yet each generation must discover for itself what situations are in fact comparable.

—*Henry Kissinger, 1979*[1]

The Cold War ended not with a bang but with a picnic. On August 19, 1989, Miklós Németh, the Hungarian prime minister, opened his nation's border with Austria – for a few hours, he thought. The supposed "pan-European picnic" at Sopron, Hungary that afternoon led to the exodus of hundreds of East Germans into Austria and thus into the free West. When Soviet troops stationed in Hungary did not deploy to prevent this – as Németh feared they might – the Cold War was over. Within three months the Berlin Wall had fallen; within fourteen months the two Germanys were reunited; within three years of the picnic, the Soviet Union itself ceased to exist.[2]

Since that afternoon in 1989, the world has resisted easy labeling. Most of the twentieth century can be neatly parceled into distinct eras: World War I, the interwar years, the Great Depression, World War II, the nuclear era, the Cold War. Labels provide a reassuring terrain for students of history; compartmentalizing the world is often a necessary

[1] Henry Kissinger, *White House Years* (Boston, MA: Little, Brown and Company, 1979), p. 54.
[2] The story of the picnic is told by Victor Sebestyen, *Revolution 1989: The Fall of the Soviet Empire* (London: Phoenix, 2010), pp. 311–314.

first step to comprehending it. At the end of the Cold War, however, the labels for what came next became more various but less reliable. Despite efforts to craft a "new world order" after the formal collapse of America's great enemy, the Soviet Union in December 1991, no label describing that order has stuck. We still define the era in which we live now against the era that preceded it: the *post–Cold War world*.

This might seem like a subject for mere academic debate. But it also lends credibility to the thesis that because the world entered a new era of complexity, the tools of American power, supposedly more successful in simpler times, have been inadequate to meet it. Whereas the great wars of the last century were decisively turned by the intervention of the United States, since the end of the Cold War, American interventions – military, economic, or diplomatic – have had, according to several accounts, rather more mixed impacts. Increasing global complexities make foreign policy more difficult. This, according to the argument, goes some way to explaining the patchy performance of US presidents in foreign affairs for over three decades. None seemed to grasp that the world had shifted. Each devised a label for the world he inherited; none succeeded in making it permanent. The most obvious example, examined in this book, is the War on Terror. Invented by President George W. Bush in response to an event of unambiguous clarity even if of disputed meaning – the terrorist attacks of September 11, 2001 – the label itself has never commanded a consensus: "too reductive ... war cannot be made on a tactic ... too easily construed as a war on Islam ... paints a grey world in black and white...." President Barack Obama never spoke of a War on Terror even as he continued to wage it, killing more terrorists than his predecessor. Thus, we find ourselves in a distinct historical moment, the parameters of which are fluid and disputed. How, this book asks, did America cope with such a world?

The short answer is "not badly." The contention in what follows is neither a paean to American greatness nor to the perfection of its foreign policy. Claims of greatness and perfection in any human activity should be treated with caution. Rather, the book casts a sympathetically critical eye over American engagement with the world from the fall of Soviet communism through the opening years of the Trump administration. In this period there were calamitous failures resulting in the diminution of US power and/ or the loss of lives, American and non-American. There were damning failures of political will, as in Rwanda, and of military hubris, as in Iraq. The attacks of 9/11 and the intelligence failings that led to them highlight myriad deficiencies. Two decades after the Cold War ended, American capitalism looked far from triumphant, as the Great Recession, which took hold in 2008, was evidence. And yet, potentially disastrous as these and other episodes were, the United States remained the world's preeminent power, indebted, certainly, but still preeminent and indispensable. This, I argue, is more because of American foreign policy than despite it.

Readers should not, therefore, expect a blanket defense of US power in the modern era, but an accounting that recognizes its durability, elasticity, and popularity – *not* its infallibility. Its durability is the subject of much academic debate. In the 1970s, predictions of US decline were commonplace and yet it was the Soviet Union that died. In the decades after 9/11, a similar debate had "declinists" again prophesying America's replacement by more ancient powers – like China and India. However, the election of Barack Obama in 2008 and of Donald Trump in 2016 were at least suggestive of an American capacity to remake the terms of international debate and query predictions of imminent decline.

American "elasticity," as Lawrence Freedman has argued, continued to account for much of its foreign policy success:

American power is based on alliances rather than colonies and is associated with an ideology that is flexible, potentially universal and inherently subversive of alternative ideological forms. Together they provide a core of relationships and values to which America can return even after it has overextended itself in a particular area or decided that intervention in a particular conflict was imprudent and that withdrawal is necessary.[3]

By any number of measures – from immigration levels to popular culture – American popularity increased in the post–Cold War decades. Despite a rise in anti-Americanism in the early 2000s and late 2010s – much of it focused on the perceived character flaws of George W. Bush and Donald Trump – the nation remained the number-one destination for foreign students. Twenty-four percent of the world's emigrants, according to a 2010 Gallup Poll, wanted to move there. Seventy percent of immigrants in the United States still believe in the American dream.[4] In 2016, the United States issued over one million green cards; China issued 1,576.[5] Apart from a few outlier states, there were no nations who had a vested interest

[3] Lawrence Freedman, A Subversive on a Hill, *National Interest* [online], May 7, 2009; nationalinterest.org/article/a-subversive-on-a-hill-3096.
[4] David Brooks, The East Germans of the 21st Century, *New York Times*, January 29, 2018.
[5] See Mike Ives, China Wants to Attract More Foreigners (of a Certain Kind), *New York Times*, February 23, 2017.

in the waning of American influence in the decades after 1989. India and China moved toward the American model rather than away. Warring parties, from Israel/Palestine to Northern Ireland, invariably wanted Washington in their corner. American diplomatic and military might have remained popular, even essential, commodities – as regime change in Libya in 2011 proved. America's most infamous enemies became loose credit and jihadi terrorists.

THE ARGUMENT OF THE BOOK

In telling the story of the post–Cold War years, this book makes two related arguments. First, the Cold War cast a shadow on the presidents that came after it. They did not always have to be aware of operating within that shadow – indeed, several claimed to have moved beyond it – but it nevertheless conditioned how they made foreign policy the way they did, and why. That shadow was the cause of considerable continuity of foreign policy from one era to the next and of continuity in the post–Cold War years themselves. The end of the Cold War was not a decisive turning point, and neither was 9/11. Second, success came more from adapting to that shadow than from attempts to escape it. When the strategic lessons of the Cold War were applied, presidents fared better. When they were forgotten, they fared worse. These arguments are made in chapters that retell and reargue the central episodes of US foreign policy from the fall of the Berlin Wall in 1989 to the opening years of the Trump administration after 2017.

Despite the initial rhetoric of George H. W. Bush, president at the end of the Cold War, his foreign policy ultimately failed to transcend that conflict. Similarly, Bill Clinton's efforts to abandon what he called the "old think" of the Cold War were short-lived. He came to rely on Cold War strategies – like containment, in the case of Iraq, and institutions like North Atlantic Treaty Organization (NATO) – to craft his foreign policy legacy. George W. Bush, despite the drama of 9/11, waged a War on Terror with powerful analogies to the war on communism. Barack Obama, born in 1961, matured personally and politically, like his successor, in a world divided along Cold War lines. Donald Trump, like so many presidents before him, made Russia central to his foreign policy and was determined to contain Chinese power; articles in *Foreign Affairs* urged him to apply Cold War strategies to his contemporary predicaments – not to forget them.[6] It would

---

[6] See Michael Mandelbaum, The New Containment: Handling Russia, China, and Iran, *Foreign Affairs* 98, 2 (March/April 2019): 123–131.

be remarkable were these leaders, nurtured in the Cold War, not susceptible to its strategic lessons. It is more remarkable still to suppose that
the foreign policy establishment and personnel of the American government could as quickly forget them.[7] As Henry Kissinger argued, "the
convictions that leaders have formed before reaching high office are the
intellectual capital they will consume as long as they continue in office."[8]

This book represents an effort to tell the story not of a revolution in
American foreign policy but of its essentially continuous character from
one era to the next. While the world was in many ways different after the
collapse of the Soviet Union, the response of the United States to this
"new world order" – for both good and ill – was essentially unaltered.
Further, rather than a turning point, 9/11 caused President Bush to
refashion but not to revolutionize an approach basic to every president
since Harry S Truman. It is an approach that endured into the Obama
years and has unfolded since, if somewhat disjointedly, in Donald
Trump's. To understand US foreign policy after the Cold War, our
essential lens is the Cold War itself.

This theme of continuity, which provides one part of the book's thesis,
is complemented by a second, which argues that, given the challenges
facing it after the Cold War, US foreign policy was not a study in
failure. Rather, during this period, American power grew; its supposed
challengers did not emerge; states like China and India wanted to be on
the American side; despite its enormous power and purported arrogance,
the United States earned very few enemies in the post–Cold War years;
Russia, its Cold War opponent, was unable to secure many new friends;
dictators anathema to US interests and values were toppled; European
allies preferred an engaged America to a detached one. Such successes, the
book argues, are owed to the adaptation, not abandonment, of Cold War
thinking in this supposedly new world.

WHAT WAS THE COLD WAR AND WHY HAS ITS SHADOW BEEN SO LONG?

Since its beginning, academic debate about the Cold War has been fierce.
We can identify four key approaches to the cause and nature of the
conflict. Traditional or orthodox scholars find fault in Soviet behavior.

---

[7] See Patrick Porter, Why America's Grand Strategy Has Not Changed: Power, Habit, and
the U.S. Foreign Policy Establishment, *International Security* 42, 4 (Spring 2018): 9–46.
[8] Kissinger, *White House Years*, p. 54.

It was the power ambitions of the Kremlin, informed by a mixture of ideological and geostrategic imperatives, that obliged Washington to contain them. Arthur Schlesinger Jr. argued this in the 1940s and 1950s. Richard Pipes and Robert Conquest maintained this position throughout the course of the conflict. Their bogeymen were, among others, Joseph Stalin, Nikita Khrushchev, and Fidel Castro. Once the USSR ceased to act on these impulses, and loosened its grip at home and abroad, in the last decade of its existence, the Cold War was essentially over. John Mueller has argued this persuasively.[9]

Revisionist scholars reverse this characterization. For them, the Cold War was the product of American aggression and imperialism. William Appleman Williams, most impressively, posited this interpretation of the conflict in *The Tragedy of American Diplomacy* (1959).[10] His bogeymen, among many others, were Harry Truman, Richard Nixon, and John Foster Dulles (Eisenhower's dour secretary of state). The Soviet Union, though not blameless, acted to negate American economic expansionism. Rather than the Cold War being the product of communist ideology, it was the result of American wars of imperial domination, most notably in Vietnam. American ideology, claimed revisionists, was to blame.

Postrevisionism, a phenomenon of the later Cold War, sought to balance the orthodox and revisionist interpretations. Rather than the Cold War being the fault of one side or the other, it was misunderstanding and miscommunication between them that heightened tension. If relations had been better managed, a drawn-out conflict might have been avoided. The United States and the USSR had, after all, been allies in World War II. John Lewis Gaddis was a leader of this "post-revisionist synthesis," as it was called, until he moved to a more neo-orthodox position in the 1990s. He did so because access to previously secret Russian documents revealed the ideological motivation behind much Soviet behavior. Gaddis's *Now We Know: Rethinking Cold War History* (1998) is a masterful accounting of the new evidence, though many scholars dispute his conclusions.

[9] Arthur Schlesinger Jr., *The Vital Center: The Politics of Freedom* (Boston: Houghton Mifflin, 1949); Richard Pipes, *Communism: A History* (New York: Random House, 2001); Robert Conquest, *The Dragons of Expectation: Reality and Delusion in the Course of History* (New York: W. W. Norton, 2004); John Mueller, What Was the Cold War About? Evidence from Its Ending, *Political Science Quarterly* 119, 4 (Winter 2004/05): 609–631.

[10] William Appleman Williams, *The Tragedy of American Diplomacy*, 50th anniversary edition (New York: W. W. Norton, 2009).

His post–Cold War writing is indicative of the fourth approach to the conflict, grounded in access to Soviet sources – not all of it in agreement with Gaddis (see the work of Melvyn Leffler and Marc Trachtenberg, for example).[11]

All wars, of course, are subject to academic debate. The Cold War, however, is especially problematic because it was not a "normal" war. These tend to be short and hot; the Cold War was long and mostly cold. It has no precise beginning or end. While occasionally violent, it never descended into a military conflagration between its two protagonists, the United States of America and the Union of Soviet Socialist Republics. Instead, proxies in Latin American, Africa, and Asia did most of the killing and dying on behalf of Washington or Moscow. The international historians Odd Arne Westad and Paul Chamberlin document this impressively.[12] In World War II, two sides fought a bloody war until the capitals of one lay in ruins and its leaders were dead or captured. When this was achieved, the war ended. While it saw each side plan and plot the destruction of the other – with nuclear weapons more than able to accomplish this objective – the Cold War never actually saw it happen. When the USSR "lost," it was not under American occupation, but was dependent on Western aid. Its leader, Mikhail Gorbachev, did not commit suicide or face a criminal trial but, rather, was fired by the men who had originally hired him (his fate thereafter was to earn millions on lucrative lecture tours in the West).

The United States, by the same token, found it had won without ever really having to kill Russians, as it had Germans and Japanese between 1941 and 1945. There were no victory parades to mark the end of the Cold War as there had been to mark victory in 1945. George Kennan, the architect of America's containment strategy in the Cold War, was amazed. It was, he said, "hard to think of any event more strange and startling, and at first glance inexplicable, than the sudden and total disintegration and disappearance … of the great power known

---

[11] John Lewis Gaddis, *Now We Know: Rethinking Cold War History* (Oxford: Oxford University Press, 1998); Melvyn Leffler, *For the Soul of Mankind: The United States, the Soviet Union, and the Cold War* (New York: Hill and Wang, 2007); Marc Trachtenberg, *The Cold War and After: History, Theory, and the Logic of International Politics* (Princeton, NJ: Princeton University Press, 2012).

[12] See Odd Arne Westad, *The Cold War: A World History* (New York: Penguin, 2018), and Paul Thomas Chamberlin, *The Cold War's Killing Fields: Rethinking the Long Peace* (New York: HarperCollins, 2018).

successively as the Russian Empire and then the Soviet Union."[13] The
USSR "went 'poof' like the Wicked Witch in *The Wizard of Oz*,"
observed Walter McDougall,"or Sauron in *The Lord of the Rings*."[14]
The historian John Lukacs, a native Hungarian, contrasts the demise of
fascism with that of communism:

> In 1945 many thousands of Germans committed suicide. Many of those who
> killed themselves were not National Socialist party leaders, some of them not even
> party members, but all of them [were] believers. But I know of not a single
> instance, in or around 1989, when a believing Communist committed suicide
> because of the collapse of Communism, in Russia or elsewhere. Dogmatic
> believers in Communism had ceased to exist long before, even as dogmatic anti-
> Communists continued to flourish.[15]

Charles Krauthammer described the end of the Cold War as "one of the
great anticlimaxes in history. Without a shot being fired, without a
revolution, without so much as a press release, the Soviet Union simply
gave up and disappeared."[16]

This going gently into the night on the part of the USSR surprised
nearly everyone who studied that state. Its permanence, as both an
ideological project and locus of power, was assumed but rarely tested.
Instead, throughout the Cold War, it was the United States whose
decline was anticipated. During the 1970s and 1980s, "declinism" was
in academic fashion, not just among Soviet apparatchiks, who were
obliged to find scientific evidence for American degeneration, but also
within Western intellectual circles. Few thought the United States could
beat the USSR, even fewer that Soviet communism could just vanish. Paul
Kennedy's *The Rise and Fall of the Great Powers*, a bestseller in 1988
(and for years after), predicted the decline of US power – for which we are
still waiting.[17]

This intellectual climate permeated the machinery of American foreign
policy too. The most important cog in that machine, the president, was a
product of the Cold War. The staff he deployed to run his diplomacy,

---

[13] In Leon Aron, Everything You Think You Know about the Collapse of the Soviet Union
Is Wrong, *Foreign Policy* [online], June 20, 2011.

[14] Walter A. McDougall, *The Tragedy of U.S. Foreign Policy: How America's Civil Religion
Betrayed the National Interest* (New Haven, CT: Yale University Press, 2016), p. 4.

[15] John Lukacs, The Poverty of Anti-Communism, *National Interest* 55 (Spring 1999):
75–85.

[16] Charles Krauthammer, *Democratic Realism* (Washington, DC: AEI Press, 2004), p. 1.

[17] Paul Kennedy, *The Rise and Fall of the Great Powers: Economic Change and Military
Conflict from 1500 to 2000* (New York: Random House, 1988).

from Brent Scowcroft (under George Bush Sr.) to Madeleine Albright (under Bill Clinton) and from Condoleezza Rice (under George Bush Jr.) to John Kerry (under Barack Obama) and John Bolton (under Donald Trump), were students in and of the conflict. The international architecture of the Cold War did not crumble along with the Soviet Union. Instead, the enlargement of NATO became the foreign policy priority of the Clinton administration, as its formation had been that of Harry Truman in the late 1940s. The newly liberated people of Eastern Europe did not rush into a lonely, communist-free autonomy but into an American embrace, seeing US power as a guarantor of their non-communist future. People rarely set aside tools that work. They might buy new ones, but only because these more efficiently replicate what the old ones did. This dictum was true of how both US foreign policy and its objects adapted to the end of the Cold War.

Despite efforts to get over the Cold War, no president has truly succeeded in doing so – because the need has always proved insufficient. The Cold War frameworks of US foreign policy – intellectual and institutional – have endured because many of them continued to work after that conflict ended. The demand to think more imaginatively did not obtain after 1989 as it did after 1945. This is not to argue that the Cold War legacy is permanent. It is to argue that it has been more present in the decades after 1989 than is often acknowledged. We live in its shadow.

WHAT IS THE POST–COLD WAR ERA?

While the Cold War generated distinct historiographical schools, post–Cold War history has not. There is a dearth of books that endow the years since 1989 with a singular character; we have come to know the era as simply "post–Cold War." Even 9/11 has failed to change this rather vague label. George W. Bush's response to those attacks is part of a longer post–Cold War narrative. Indeed, as has been argued, the response to 9/11 synchronized rather well with traditional forms of statecraft.[18] Al-Qaeda's attack did not begin a foreign policy revolution, an argument developed later in this book.

This is not to deny that admirable attempts have been made to define what was specific, new, and different about the post–1989 years. Derek Chollet and James Goldgeier present a compelling history in *America*

[18] See Timothy J. Lynch and Robert S. Singh, *After Bush: The Case for Continuity in American Foreign Policy* (New York: Cambridge University Press, 2008).

Between the Wars: from 11/9 to 9/11.[19] Their object is the peculiar intervening period, "the interregnum," "the age of anxiety/uncertainty/ fragmentation," of "great and failed expectations/disillusion (and dissolution)," from the collapse of the Berlin Wall on November 9, 1989 up to September 11, 2001. In their preface they acknowledge this as the "Age That Even Historians from Harvard Can't Name."[20] How much harder, then, to find a single label that covers the momentous decades on either side of 9/11?

Sean Wilentz, to find historical coherence, extends the period backward to 1974, in a book he calls *The Age of Reagan*, which, though significantly foreign policy–related, offers a general accounting of US history from Richard Nixon to George W. Bush.[21] William O'Neill does something similar but, again, narrows his history to what he calls the "interwar bubble" between 1989 and 2001.[22] In 2016, Michael Mandelbaum offered a synthesis of post–Cold War failure. In coming to the aid of the Kurds in 1991, he argued, the United States established a pattern that was to endure across the post–Cold War decades. It was choosing to fight wars not for realist objectives but for a humanitarian one – the protection of Muslims from bad government – that was to recur in the Balkans, the Middle East, and East and North Africa under the next four presidents. Interests had been supplanted by values, the defining feature and failure of the post–Cold War foreign policy, and constituted a revolution in US posture:

> Without announcing it, without debating it, without even fully realizing it, the goals of American foreign policy changed fundamentally ... Historically, where their foreign policies are concerned sovereign states inhabit the realm of necessity: they do what they must do to survive. The United States after the Cold War, in contrast, dwelt in the difficult-to-reach kingdom of choice.[23]

In the Cold War, the United States sought to liberate oppressed people to weaken the Soviet Union. After the Cold War, it did so because it

---

[19] Derek Chollet and James Goldgeier, *America between the Wars, 11/9 to 9/11: The Misunderstood Years between the Fall of the Berlin Wall and the Start of the War on Terror* (New York: PublicAffairs: 2008).

[20] Chollet and Goldgeier, *America between the Wars*, p. x.

[21] Sean Wilentz, *The Age of Reagan: A History 1974–2008* (New York: HarperCollins, 2008).

[22] William L. O'Neill, *A Bubble in Time: America during the Interwar Years, 1989–2001* (Chicago: Ivan R. Dee, 2009).

[23] Michael Mandelbaum, *Mission Failure: America and the World in the Post–Cold War Era* (New York: Oxford University Press, 2016), pp. 4, 368.

was the right thing to do. For Mandelbaum, this shift was the root cause of recurrent "mission failure" abroad. Instead of negating geostrategic opponents, presidents choose to propagate the bounties of American freedom.

Stephen Walt offers a more strident indictment of post–Cold War failure. Foreign policy during this period is "impossible to defend," he argues.[24] By grandiosely and condescendingly claiming to be the indispensable nation, the United States lost all sense of the actual limits of its power. Filled with a misplaced conviction that liberal democracy was the inevitable and universal system, policymakers exaggerated the ease with which democracy could be spread. By assuming wars like Afghanistan and Iraq would be cakewalks or slam dunks, the Bush administration ended up entangled in the intractable politics of the Middle East, with America's wealth squandered and thousands of its soldiers, and millions of foreigners, dead. Walt sees continuity across the Cold War era. For him, however, it was the continuity of delusion, of successive presidents believing the rest of the world shared their assumptions about human progress, about how "peace, prosperity, and justice" might be attained.[25] When these men and women encountered resistance, they invariably overreacted. The attempt to construct a liberal world order gave us the opposite, argues Walt.

Thomas Henriksen finds more nuance than Walt. In his analysis of the first four post–Cold War presidents, he observes not a delusional quest for hegemony, but a continual wrestling with the forces of engagement and disengagement. Foreign policy since 1989 has seen recurrent "cycles of international extroversion and introversion."[26] These were not forced on presidents by public opinion, or by some political ideology, but were the product of choices and changes each man made in response to events. Herein lay the continuity of the post–Cold War years: the quest to balance a tension inherent in US foreign policy for over two hundred years between doing more versus doing less in the world. Both Bushes, claims Henriksen, were "engagement-orientated" presidents – waging large wars in the Middle East – who subsequently retreated. Clinton and Obama, on the other hand, wanted a domestic focus and largely achieved this,

---

[24] Stephen M. Walt, *The Hell of Good Intentions: America's Foreign Policy Elite and the Decline of U.S. Primacy* (New York: Farrar, Straus and Giroux, 2018), p. 7.

[25] Walt, *The Hell of Good Intentions*, p. 22.

[26] Thomas H. Henriksen, *Cycles in U.S. Foreign Policy since the Cold War* (New York: Palgrave Macmillan, 2017), p. 1.

avoiding significant war abroad. All four were trapped in a cycle of in and out, of making war and making peace, that has a long historical lineage.

What Henriksen understates, and that this book argues, is that the continuity was fuller and deeper than a response to cyclical pressures. The contrasts across the five administrations were much less than the similarities. All the post–Cold War presidents came to office seeking some form of retrenchment or foreign policy humility, of doing less, not more. All ended up fighting wars on behalf of large humanitarian causes – especially the protection of Muslim populations. All posited that they were to lead in a world transformed and yet found themselves using decidedly traditional institutions of statecraft, facing the same opponents, in most of the same ways as presidents had done for decades before. Even 9/11 failed to fundamentally break this continuity. After 9/11, each president defined the number-one national security threat as the nexus of rogue states, terrorism, and weapons of mass destruction. And each made wars to preclude that threat that relied on alliances forged in the Cold War.

Much scholarship of US foreign policy from 1989 to the present tends to concentrate on specific sub-eras or administrations within this period. Hal Brands' *From Berlin to Baghdad* (2008), as the title suggests, tells the story of US diplomacy from 1989 to 2003, or the "long 1990s," as he terms it. Brands identifies an incoherence in both American foreign policy and in the study of it.[27] Despite this, as he argues in his later *American Grand Strategy in the Age of Trump* (2018), the United States has been a "Pretty Successful Superpower."[28] Unlike the Cold War period, the post–Cold War period generated no historical orthodoxy, and consequently no revisionism of it. American foreign policy became fractured and so, as a result, did the historiography of it. Large schools of interpretation, a la the Cold War, have not developed and are unlikely to. The closest we get is a vast literature observing American failure and the much smaller one making the counter-case.

In fact, the dominant texts of the post–Cold War decades (measured in sales and citations) have not been histories but prophecies – by political scientists. In 1989, Francis Fukuyama suggested history may well be ending, an argument we will explore more fully in the next chapter.

27 Hal Brands, *From Berlin to Baghdad: America's Search for Purpose in the Post–Cold War World* (Lexington: University Press of Kentucky, 2008).
28 Hal Brands, *American Grand Strategy in the Age of Trump* (Washington, DC: Brooking Institution Press, 2018), pp. 1–23.

Samuel P. Huntington disagreed.[29] While he agreed that ideological conflict would recede, "The Clash of Civilizations?" (the title of his 1993 *Foreign Affairs* article and 1996 book, with the question mark being lost along the way) would take its place. "The great divisions among humankind and the dominating source of conflict will be cultural," argued Huntington.[30] The world would become more dangerous as these differences, long suppressed by the Cold War, were let loose. His book sold well in the middle 1990s but enjoyed a further boost after the al-Qaeda attacks of September 11, 2001; his predicted clash of Christianity and Islam seemed to have come true. He observed, "For 45 years, the Iron Curtain was the central dividing line in Europe. That line has moved several hundred miles east. It is now the line separating the peoples of Western Christianity, on the one hand, from Muslim and Orthodox peoples on the other."[31]

Huntington's pessimism was shared, if for different reasons, by the Chicago professor John Mearsheimer. In 1990, he argued against the general euphoria brought about by communist collapse. Rather, we would "soon miss the Cold War ... The conditions that have made for decades of peace in the West are fast disappearing, as Europe prepares to return to the multi-polar system that, between 1648 and 1945, bred one destructive conflict after another."[32] Robert Kaplan joined this chorus of realist pessimism. In a widely debated article in the *Atlantic Monthly* he detailed "the coming anarchy."[33] These authors offered analyses betraying a fundamental nostalgia for the Cold War, a nostalgia that was soon apparent in the foreign policymaking of the Bush Sr. and Clinton administrations.

---

[29] See Francis Fukuyama, The End of History?, *National Interest* 16 (Summer 1989): 3–18; Fukuyama, *The End of History and the Last Man* (New York: Free Press, 1992); Samuel Huntington, The Clash of Civilizations? *Foreign Affairs* 72, 3 (Summer 1993): 22–49; and Huntington, *The Clash of Civilizations and the Remaking of World Order* (New York: Touchstone, 1996).

[30] Huntington, Clash of Civilizations? (1993), p. 22.

[31] Huntington, *Clash of Civilizations* (1996), p. 28.

[32] Mearsheimer, Why We Will Soon Miss the Cold War, *Atlantic Monthly* 266, 2 (August 1990): 35–50. He later indicted the "great delusion" of Western foreign policymakers in *The Great Delusion: Liberal Dreams and International Realities* (New Haven, CT: Yale University Press, 2018).

[33] Robert D. Kaplan, The Coming Anarchy: How Scarcity, Crime, Overpopulation, Tribalism, and Disease Are Rapidly Destroying the Social Fabric of Our Planet, *Atlantic Monthly* 273, 2 (February 1994): 44–77.

Despite much initial rhetoric about "a new world order" (Bush Sr.) and an era of "democratic enlargement" (Clinton), neither man was able to define the precise contours of these visions. Instead, when reality set in, both men pursued a foreign policy strikingly like those of their Cold War predecessors. If the years from 1989 to 2001 were played out in the shadow of the Cold War, the years since 2001 took place within its penumbra. They did so despite predictions by several scholars of a foreign policy revolution under Bush Jr. and of sweeping change under Barack Obama. Though the actors, issues, and crises are new (and, with the presidency of Donald Trump, unexpected), the Cold War continues to shape the international landscape in which they unfold. How this came to be is the subject and argument of this book.

George H. W. Bush

New World Order, Old World President, 1989–1992

The Cold War didn't end; it was won.

—*George H. W. Bush, 1992*[1]

George Herbert Walker Bush was the last American president born before World War II and the last president to have fought in it (he enlisted at age eighteen). His political career reached its pinnacle just as the Cold War, which gave it form, vanished. Shaped by two great global wars, World War II (1939–1945) and the Cold War (1945–1989), Bush became president just as America's longest-standing opponent, the Soviet Union, was dissolving. How did the new president adapt to this turn of events? *Cautiously* and *nostalgically* would be potential answers. As if in disbelief that America could win so easily, he remained wary of the speed at which Moscow abandoned its ideological mission and wary of the prospects for disorder of its so doing. He set about using World War II and the Cold War as basic reference points in his construction of what he called "a new world order." Rather than jettison the past, Bush made it his essential prism. His reward for this was a series of significant foreign policy successes, from regime change in Panama to the liberation of Kuwait. The price he paid was electoral defeat, in 1992, at the hands of a younger opponent who dismissed foreign policy in favor of domestic economic renewal, and who wanted to look forward, not backward. The story of Bush's international success and national failure is told in this chapter.

[1] State of the Union Address, January 28, 1992.

THE END OF HISTORY?

What was the nature of the world George Bush confronted in 1989? That summer, a young political scientist at the RAND Corporation, a California-based research organization, offered an attractive answer. Francis Fukuyama argued that the waning of the Cold War was indicative of "the end of history." In an influential article in the journal *National Interest*, extended over the next two and a half years into a bestselling book, Fukuyama claimed the world had moved into a possibly permanent, post–ideological era.[2] The collapse of ideological competition, leaving liberal democracy "as the final form of human government," meant that history had ceased. History, as Karl Marx and Friedrich Engels had predicted in the nineteenth century, was indeed directional, but toward the system of government enjoyed by the United States rather than by its opponents.

As with George Kennan's Long Telegram (1946) and X Article (1947), which were the intellectual anchors for US strategy in the Cold War, it is as difficult to prove the impact of Fukuyama's ideas on the making of American foreign policy as it is difficult to divorce them from it.[3] Neither President Bush nor his successors declared the end of history. But in his diplomacy each man seemed to have imbibed the logic and to have exaggerated the optimism of Fukuyama's work. There was actually much pessimism and little of the triumphant in his writing – without ideas to contend over, men would become timid and "without chests." However, to find oneself on the right side of history was no doubt enormously reassuring. The task for the post–Cold War presidents, unlike for their predecessors, who had the job of containing something bad, was to help spread something good – and inevitable, according to Fukuyama. The big question of which ideological system would inherit the earth had been answered in America's favor; its foreign policy could thus become a tidying-up operation. Washington would content itself with nudging along an inexorable process – "encouraging, guiding, and managing change without provoking backlash and crackdown," was how Bush

[2] Francis Fukuyama, The End of History?, *National Interest* 16 (Summer 1989): 3–18; Fukuyama, *The End of History and the Last Man* (New York: Free Press, 1992).

[3] George F. Kennan, *American Diplomacy: Sixtieth-Anniversary Expanded Edition* (Walgreen Foundation Lectures) (Chicago: University of Chicago Press, 2012).

described it.[4] If, for Kennan, Soviet communism had been "a fluid stream ... fill[ing] every nook and cranny available to it in the basin of world power," liberal democracy was a tide with which the United States was swimming.

Universities across the United States seemed similarly caught in the wave. Theories of "democratic peace" became vogue. Did democracies really not fight wars with each other? Would the spreading of liberal democracy enlarge the zone of peace? Was war becoming obsolete? Those answering such questions in the affirmative did not map exactly the terrain laid out by Fukuyama but embraced many of the same themes and betrayed a similar bias. This undoubtedly carried over into government, entrenching a political science theory at the heart of American statecraft. While George H. W. Bush is now remembered as a foreign policy realist, his public rhetoric betrayed a belief that the world was turning decisively in an American direction and entering a small "r" republican dawn. In an address to Congress on September 11, 1990, he outlined his vision of a new world order, even as he was amassing in the Saudi Arabian desert one of the largest armies in world history:

A new era – freer from the threat of terror, stronger in the pursuit of justice and more secure in the quest for peace. An era in which the nations of the world, east and west, north and south, can prosper and live in harmony.

A hundred generations have searched for this elusive path to peace, while a thousand wars raged across the span of human endeavor, and today that new world is struggling to be born. A world quite different from the one we've known. A world where the rule of law supplants the rule of the jungle. A world in which nations recognize the shared responsibility for freedom and justice. A world where the strong respect the rights of the weak.[5]

The same month, his thesis was rejected by the conservative commentator Charles Krauthammer. 'The immediate post–Cold War world is not multipolar. It is unipolar," he wrote. "The center of world power is the unchallenged superpower, the United States, attended by its Western allies."[6] Rather than the dawn of a multilateral era, the demise of communism had left the US preeminent but, as a consequence, argued Krauthammer, it was now threatened by aggrieved "weapons states."

---

[4] George H. W. Bush and Brent Scowcroft, *A World Transformed* (New York: Random House, 1999), p. xiii.
[5] George H. W. Bush, address before a Joint Session of Congress September 11, 1990; https://bush41library.tamu.edu/archives/public-papers/2217.
[6] Charles Krauthammer, The Unipolar Moment, *Foreign Affairs* 70, 1 (Winter 1990/91): 23–33.

He cited Iraq, Libya, and North Korea as the most obvious examples. In each, "anti-Western grievances run deep" and compelled their regimes into a quest for weapons of mass destruction that they could deploy against America. This was the new national security challenge facing the United States, argued the author.

Why did President Bush not share this analysis? What had happened during his initial period in office to make him so confident that his more hopeful vision would come to pass? One answer to this question can be found in the amity between the US and USSR as the Bush administration took office.

THE GORBACHEV FACTOR

Relations with Moscow had been thawing quickly since 1985, when Mikhail Gorbachev had become Soviet leader. Ronald Reagan became very fond of "Gorby," as he referred to him in his diaries. This was passed along to his vice-president, who described the Russian's "disarming smile, warm eyes, and . . . engaging way of making an unpleasant point." As president, Bush set great store in his "good feel" for his Soviet counterpart. This was slow to gestate but became very strong.[7] Like estranged brothers reconciled when one of them is dying, broader US–Soviet relations were also very good in the final years of the USSR's life. Gorbachev's internal policies of *glasnost* (openness) and *perestroika* (restructuring) were reflected in a willingness to do business in foreign affairs. Within a month of Bush's inauguration, though hardly because of it, Soviet troops ended their sapping and futile ten-year occupation of Afghanistan, a retreat that convinced the Islamist forces to which the country was soon to be subjected that "great" powers were paper tigers and would always run away if challenged.

However, while this Soviet spring offered hope of domestic renewal, in reality Gorbachev's reforms were a final desperate effort to rescue the USSR from economic collapse. The stereotype of the Cold War as a bipolar struggle between forces of equal mass and charge belies the remarkable weakness of the Soviet Union in comparison to the United States. Since the early 1970s, Soviet citizens had become dependent on grain imports from America, the enemy they were supposed to be helping

---

[7] Bush and Scowcroft, *A World Transformed*, pp. 4–5. See also Jeffrey A. Engel, *When the World Seemed New: George H. W. Bush and the End of the Cold War* (New York: Houghton Mifflin Harcourt, 2017).

bury. In 1959, Nikita Khrushchev reassured Russians they would be present at America's funeral. He was right about a funeral taking place, except when it did the roles of mourner and corpse were reversed. In the mid-1980s, the average American male could expect to live over seven years longer than his Soviet counterpart (71.2 years v. 63.8) and to live better, enjoying a standard of living far outstripping that of the average Russian.

Shortages of basic commodities were chronic across the Warsaw Pact countries that the USSR controlled. In East Germany, the German Democratic Republic or GDR, customers wanting a shampoo often had to take their own towels to the salon. A black sense of humor provided some sort of coping mechanism for the peoples within the Soviet orbit. One joke describes a woman walking into a state-run store:

"I would like some bread, comrade," she asks.

"Sorry, comrade, we are the store that doesn't sell meat," the store assistant replies. "The store that doesn't sell bread is across the street."

In Budapest, Hungary, a smiling man was seen hopping across Palace Square in one shoe. "Why are you smiling?" an onlooker shouts, "You have lost a shoe."

"No," says the man, "I found one!"[8]

An *anekdot* well-known in Soviet Russia neatly captures the contra-dictions of life there:

> No unemployment but nobody works.
> Nobody works but productivity increases.
> Productivity increases but the shops are empty.
> The shops are empty but fridges are full.
> Fridges are full but nobody is satisfied.
> Nobody is satisfied but all vote unanimously.[9]

During its seventy-year existence, Soviet communism had mutated from being the hope of the working class to its great persecutor (extinguishing millions of lives and retarding many more), to an economic absurdity. By its end, the Eastern bloc functioned as a gigantic Ponzi scheme, accruing ever more foreign debts to pay off preexisting foreign loans.

Gorbachev was the first Soviet leader to acknowledge the enormous material imbalance between communism and capitalism. "We are

[8] In Stephen Kotkin, *Uncivil Society: 1989 and the Implosion of the Communist Establish-ment* (New York: Modern Library, 2009), p. 67.
[9] In Alena Ledeneva, *Russia's Economy of Favours: Blat, Networking and Informal Exchange* (New York: Cambridge University Press, 1998), p. 72.

encircled not by invincible armies," he declared, "but by superior economies."[10] At the 27th Communist Party Congress in 1986, an affair usually marked by long, dull, sycophantic speeches detailing Soviet superiority in all things, Gorbachev pointed out failings that were eventually to cost the USSR its life, five years later:

Difficulties began to build up in the economy in the 1970s, with rates of economic growth declining visibly. As a result, the targets for economic development set in the Communist Party Programme, and even the lower targets of the 9th and 10th 5-year plans, were not attained. Neither did we manage to carry out the social program charted for this period. A lag ensued in the material base of science and education, health protection, culture and everyday services.

Though efforts have been made of late, we have not succeeded in fully remedying the situation. There are serious lags in engineering, the oil and coal industries, the electrical engineering industry, in ferrous metals and chemicals in capital construction. Neither have the targets been met for the main indicators of efficiency and the improvement of the people's standard of living.[11]

Eduard Shevardnadze, Gorbachev's foreign minister, was more succinct: "Everything is rotten. It has to be changed."[12]

A foreign policy that paid no regard to how poor most Soviet citizens were was unsustainable. President Reagan instinctively knew this – as did Gorbachev. While it is historically blinkered to make Reagan wholly the cause of Soviet demise, without his insistence that Moscow be challenged to increase its military spending, the death of the USSR might well have taken longer. Traditionally, the Soviet Union had been able to compete on a military level with the United States, even enjoying a superiority of conventional (non-nuclear) forces in its twilight years. The results of domestic economic failure, however, combined with the demands of military competition – and, crucially, a leader willing to accept these facts – made matching the United States impossible. It was "morning in America," Ronald Reagan's catchy campaign slogan in 1984, but dusk in the USSR. George H. W. Bush had inherited a Russian triceratops, its heavy armor concealing an inner vulnerability.

Despite emerging evidence of Soviet weakness, the Bush administration remained wary of a return to a more aggressive posture by the Kremlin.

---

[10] In Melvyn Leffler, For the Soul of Mankind: The United States, the Soviet Union, and the Cold War (New York: Hill and Wang, 2007), p. 461.

[11] In Paul Kennedy, The Rise and Fall of the Great Powers (New York: Random House, 1987), pp. 632–633.

[12] Leon Aron, Everything You Think You Know about the Collapse of the Soviet Union Is Wrong, Foreign Policy [online], June 20, 2011.

Soviet history was punctuated by false dawns. The caricature of the heroic Leon Trotsky being supplanted and then murdered by Joseph Stalin is basic to sympathetic histories of the Soviet Union. Each generation threw up a new leader promising enlightenment and a return to *real* Marxism – none delivered. Nikita Khrushchev denounced Stalin in 1956 but by 1962 was deploying nuclear missiles to Cuba, almost resulting in World War III. Leonid Brezhnev seemed to have accepted the logic of détente and accommodation with the West in the early 1970s, but by 1979 had invaded Afghanistan, having spent much of the decade foisting the Soviet project onto assorted Africans and Central Americans. Despite what Bush saw as the "man-to-man sincerity" of Gorbachev, the American's diplomacy reflected a historically informed caution about the Soviet system's ability to reform.

Brent Scowcroft, Bush's national security advisor, helped to magnify his boss's wariness about where the USSR was heading. In early 1989, the hope that communism might fall was not nearly as heartening as the fear of what might follow was disturbing. "Suicidal nationalisms," warned Bush, might be worse than the communist system that held them in check. Accordingly, the new administration prepared for the worst-case scenario. Knowledge of Russian history rarely induces optimism about the Russian future. In February that year, Chris Gueffroy, a twenty-year-old waiter, was shot dead while trying to escape from East to West. As it turned out, he was the last person of some 238 to be killed crossing the Berlin Wall, but Bush could not have known this – no one could.[13]

Not anticipating the revolution that was soon to take hold, Bush adopted a traditional pattern of diplomacy in those early months. His first foreign trip as president was to Japan, in February 1989, for the funeral of Emperor Hirohito. In May, he celebrated the fortieth anniversary of the NATO in Brussels. Since 1941, the United States had regarded the Far East and Europe as central to its national security and interests. Bush continued this pattern.

Whereas Ronald Reagan commanded and continues to command the admiration of American neoconservatives and others on the right of the political spectrum, his successor was a different political animal. Bush's conception of the Soviet Union particularly and of world affairs generally was molded more by pragmatic realism than by Reaganite optimism.

---

[13] One more person died after falling from a balloon, in the last doomed attempt to reach the West. Gueffroy was the last to be killed by GDR border guards, who, after German reunification, were tried and convicted for his murder.

He was, someone once quipped, "somewhat to the center of center."[14] Born in Milton, Massachusetts, in 1924, Bush had been schooled at Andover and Yale, where, according to one historian, "he imbibed the Stimsonian ethos of hard work, modesty, competition, and public service."[15]

After service in World War II (where he was shot down over the Pacific), he made it rich in the Texas oil business. The son of the powerful Connecticut senator, Prescott Bush, his lineage and wealth marked him out for political office. He served two terms in the US House of Representatives, from 1967 to 1971, as the first Republican to represent Houston. His most significant failure, arguably, until he lost the presidency in 1992, was losing his bid to become a US Senator from Texas in 1970 (having failed initially, but less surprisingly, six years earlier). The failure was propitious. It was not until 2009 that a senator repeated John Kennedy's feat of moving directly from Capitol Hill to the White House.

From 1971 to 1981, Bush went from being ambassador at the UN to vice-president of the United States with stops along the way as chair of the Republican National Committee, envoy to China, director of the Central Intelligence Agency (CIA), and challenger for the GOP presidential nomination (in 1980). Some referred to him as the "résumé president."[16] Historian Herbert Parmet said Bush was a man with interests rather than convictions.[17] Others were even more disparaging. According to one source, Bush was the "sort of man who steps out of the shower to take a piss."[18] This safety-first attitude was reflected in the men he chose to run his foreign policy.

THE BUSH TEAM

While continuity is the hallmark of presidential transitions, there are exceptions. The active agenda of Bush's new foreign policy team was to

---

[14] In John Micklethwait and Adrian Wooldridge, *Right Nation: Why America Is Different* (New York: Penguin, 2004), p. 33.

[15] George C. Herring, *From Colony to Superpower: U.S. Foreign Relations since 1776* (Oxford: Oxford University Press, 2008), p. 900. See also Jon Meacham, *Destiny and Power: The American Odyssey of George Herbert Walker Bush* (New York: Random House, 2015).

[16] Herring, *From Colony to Superpower*, p. 900.

[17] Herbert S. Parmet, *George Bush: The Life of a Lone Star Yankee* (New York: Scribner, 1997).

[18] In Micklethwait and Wooldridge, *Right Nation*, p. 33.

replace the supposedly ideological approach of the Reagan administration with a more pragmatic centrism. Such an approach, according to the new secretary of state, James Baker, was the rule of American Cold War diplomacy that Reaganites had risked with their moral certainty and faith in victory. The Cold War was not to be won, he said, but managed. "Remember," Baker warned as he led the Bush transition, "this is *not* a friendly takeover."[19]

This conflict within the Republican party over foreign policy was to recur both in and out of office over the next thirty years. During the first and last Bush administrations, realists held sway. (The middle Bush term, 2001–2005, has a more complicated label, considered later in this book.) Realists, though no two are ever identical, share some common approaches to the world. They believe that American interests, rather than values, should drive foreign policy. Values are messy. They lead to bad liberal wars, like Vietnam, or unnecessarily antagonized opponents, as Reagan's calling the USSR "an evil empire," early in his term, had done. Realists observe the fixity of interests that states tend to have, making them skeptical that changes of regime alter anything very much. In his first month in office Bush reminded Congress: : "The fundamental facts remain that the Soviets retain a very powerful military machine in the service of objectives which are still in conflict with ours. So, let us take the new openness seriously, *but let's also be realistic.*"[20]

Two men carried forward this supposed reversion to realism: James Baker as secretary of state and Brent Scowcroft as national security advisor. While neither was a mirror image of his boss, they were his staunchest allies and closest advisors. Also, unlike the secretary–advisor relationship of the preceding decades, Baker and Scowcroft worked as teammates. Bush was determined to avoid the open warfare that had compromised US foreign policy under his predecessors – and he largely succeeded. The Rogers–Kissinger, Vance–Brzezinski, and Shultz–Weinberger personality-driven turf wars – "slugfests," Baker called them – were set aside.[21] The intrigue of Reagan's National Security Council (NSC) staff was replaced by a far more open, deliberative process, with Bush, Baker, and Scowcroft functioning as buddies.

---

[19] In David Halberstam, *War in a Time of Peace: Bush, Clinton and the Generals* (New York: Touchstone, 2002), p. 73.
[20] In Leffler, *For the Soul of Mankind*, p. 424. Emphasis added.
[21] In David Rothkopf, *Running the World: The Inside Story of the National Security Council and the Architects of American Power* (New York: PublicAffairs, 2005), p. 263.

Because the bureaucracy and focus of US foreign policy is so huge, the men and women whom the president chooses to help make sense of them are crucial. In the Cold War, Dean Acheson and Henry Kissinger were arguably as key to the making of foreign policy as their respective bosses, Harry Truman and Richard Nixon. The post–Cold War era has, so far, been denied such towering figures, but Baker and Scowcroft came close.[22] If Acheson had been present at the creation of US Cold War strategy, and Kissinger (according to him) had helped rescue it, Bush's advisors oversaw its fulfillment.[23]

Brent Scowcroft had previously been Gerald Ford's national security advisor (NSA), replacing Kissinger, who moved to Foggy Bottom (home of the State Department) full-time in 1974 (Kissinger remains the only man in US history to have been both NSA and secretary of state simultaneously.) Scowcroft's reappointment to that post in 1989 spelled a return to Kissinger-style diplomacy. What does this mean? While Kissinger was not the prophet of a new diplomatic religion, he did establish a foreign policy orthodoxy. As a matter of historical record, and as David Rothkopf tabulates convincingly, he was connected to every key foreign policymaker – "by at most two degrees" – from the 1970s to the present.[24] He has cast a long shadow. Even George W. Bush, a supposed pawn of neoconservatives, listened to Kissinger, their significant opponent. Barack Obama similarly took soundings from the German émigré. Scowcroft worked under him in the Nixon/Ford White House and for him – as vice-chair of Kissinger Associates – in his years in the private sector, 1977–1989.

Kissinger was not the amoral monster of his detractors' caricature.[25] Rather, he believed that morality was only possible in a stable world order. Unless leaders could bring order to international life, hopes of liberty were mere pie in the sky. There is no liberty without order, argued Kissinger.[26] A foreign policy that attempts to expand the zone of human

[22] See Bartholomew Sparrow, *The Strategist: Brent Scowcroft and the Call of National Security* (New York: PublicAffairs, 2015).

[23] See Dean Acheson, *Present at the Creation: My Years in the State Department* (New York: W. W. Norton, 1969).

[24] Rothkopf, *Running the World*, pp. 14–21.

[25] See Niall Ferguson, *Kissinger, 1923–1968: The Idealist* (New York: Penguin, 2015).

[26] See especially Henry Kissinger, *A World Restored: Metternich, Castlereagh and the Problems of Peace, 1812–22* (Echo Point Books: Brattleboro, VT, 2003; first published 1957) and Robert D. Kaplan, *The Coming Anarchy: Shattering the Dreams of the Post Cold War* (New York: Penguin Random House, 2001), pp. 127–156.

rights, for example, will likely make those rights less secure because the attempt will foster instability, and instability will provoke crackdown. Threaten a "bad" state and it will retrench. Offer to help it realize some of its objectives and it will be moderate in their pursuit.

Scowcroft imbibed enough of Kissinger's approach in the 1970s to reapply its central strictures – of caution, pragmatism, patience, and accommodation – as the Cold War ended. A defining experience of the Church of Jesus Christ of Latter-day Saints, to which Scowcroft belonged, was its forced migration in the 1850s. Born in much bloodshed, Mormons have valued the stability of Utah, their eventual home. Liberty needs order. The demise of communism, as viewed from the Oval Office, offered very little prospect of it. As Scowcroft's joint memoirs with President Bush attest, their abiding concern was not the death of America's enemy but what would rise in its place. In 1857, as the Mormons had fled west, war ensued. Scowcroft feared the same consequences for those Europeans heading west to escape oppression a century and a half later.

James A. Baker III was a lifelong friend of George H. W. Bush, forming a relationship "unique in the annals of the American presidency."[27] When the former president died in 2018, Baker was at his bedside. Like his boss, he was a wealthy Texan and a skilled political insider. He had served as White House chief of staff and treasury secretary under Reagan. In 1988 he led Bush's presidential campaign to a convincing victory over the hapless Michael Dukakis. It was Baker whom Bush turned to, rather more in hope than expectation, during the losing 1992 campaign, promising the electorate that he would put the respected Baker in charge of reversing economic recession. Like Bush and Scowcroft, Baker saw the world through the prism of American interests. International politics, for him, was like the oil business: an arena better suited to negotiation and deal-making than to ideology and moralizing. It was an approach carried over into his foreign policy service.

Richard "Dick" Cheney completed a triumvirate of hard-nosed, conservative realists by becoming secretary of defense, though he was only second choice for the role. John Tower had been Bush's favored nominee. As would happen to Clarence Thomas in 1991 during the incendiary hearings of Bush's second nominee to the Supreme Court, in 1989 Tower watched the Senate trawl through the minutiae of his

---

[27] Peter Baker, "I Love You, Too": George Bush's Final Days, *New York Times*, December 1, 2018.

personal habits – he was rumored to be too fond of booze and women. Unlike Thomas, however, Tower failed in his confirmation fight, leaving the door open for Cheney. The nomination battles Bush fought over Tower and Thomas highlight the enduring nature of interbranch conflict in the United States. The US Constitution established a system of competition for power. Ambition was made to counteract ambition. The Cold War, while it concentrated American minds, did not do away with political rivalry. If anything, that rivalry increased after the Cold War, reaching its zenith under Bill Clinton, whose impeachment represented a concerted Republican effort to damage him – a level of vitriol Democrats were to display toward Donald Trump decades later.

Dick Cheney, as vice-president to George W. Bush for two terms, has a central role in later chapters. At this juncture, it is important to grasp the fundamentally conservative agenda he sought to advance. Rather than the engineer of some vast imperial project, a charge he faced recurrently, Cheney was crucial to the implementation of an essentially minimalist American foreign policy. He believed, along with Colin Powell, his colleague at the Pentagon, that the US military was to be wielded solely for the purpose of American security. Nation-building and democratization were not part of Cheney's grand plan. He really had no grand plan, beyond short, sharp war – after which America was to disengage as quickly as possible. Every military intervention in which the Wyomingite had a controlling influence, especially the wars with Iraq, betrayed this conservative bias. He did not want to make the world safe for democracy. He did intend to make American democracy safe in the world. Indeed, this was a narrow, if essential, end of statecraft that was shared across the Bush team.

TIANANMEN SQUARE

The cautious conservatism of the Bush administration was first displayed in response to events in China during the summer of 1989. If a picnic was to lead to the fall of communism in Europe, a similarly peaceful, if much larger, gathering in Beijing had the opposite effect on its Chinese variant. While East European regimes collapsed with barely a whimper, the ruling Chinese Communist Party (CCP) bloodily reasserted its dominion. The response of the Bush administration to the Chinese government's massacre of between 180 and 10,454 students (estimates vary, precise numbers of dead have never been ascertained) again reveals the deeply pragmatic nature of its outlook – a response the Chinese communists expected.[28] There was a political price to be paid for Bush's conflict-avoidance strategy, which became apparent in the presidential campaign of 1992. A basic recourse in his challenger's rhetoric that year was to Bush's coddling of the "butchers of Beijing." The charge must have stung the sitting president. He had been his nation's first emissary to the People's Republic of China from 1974 to 1975, a state that had been regarded as a pariah since its creation in 1949. Bush established his diplomatic credentials as a consequence of and in the wake of Richard Nixon's remarkable opening up of the PRC, a process that arguably reached fruition in the spectacular Beijing Olympics in 2008.

In April 1989, in an initially unintentional parallel with protests stirring in communist Eastern Europe, students began to gather in Tiananmen Square, the world's largest public square in the world's most populous nation. Their ostensible purpose was to mourn the death of Hu Yaobang, a popular pro-democracy official. This provided the platform for the venting of assorted grievances over the glacial pace of political reform in China. The economic reforms begun by Deng Xiaoping after Mao's death in 1976 had succeeded in making many Chinese wealthier but fewer much freer. It has become almost a physical law in political science, only recently challenged, that economic liberalization and the exposure of a society to a free market will eventually result in demands for greater individual and hence political freedom. The Tiananmen protest seemed to be following a preordained script. Idealistic demands were made by the students. The government would condemn them. Both sides would then meet halfway.

Tragically, if not unpredictably to scholars of Chinese history, this is not how events unfolded.[29] Instead, humiliated by the presence of thousands of unwashed, moaning students during a visit of Mikhail Gorbachev to Beijing on May 15, the communist government decided to crush rather than appease the protest. During the night of June 4, tanks and soldiers of the People's Liberation Army (PLA) rolled into the square. Those students not crushed to death or shot were rounded up and taken out of circulation, many not surfacing for years afterwards, if at all. The lone man who, by facing down a PLA tank, provided the protest with its iconic image has never been traced. In the years since, China has remained at the top of Amnesty International's league of human rights abusers.

---

[28] See Mary Elise Sarotte, China's Fear of Contagion: Tiananmen Square and the Power of the European Example, *International Security* 37, 2 (Fall 2012), pp. 156–182.
[29] This story is told compellingly in Engel, *When the World Seemed New*, chap. 9.

The massacre has been expunged from official consciousness and ani-
mates few young Chinese today because they have been kept essentially
ignorant of it. Googling "Tiananmen Square" in a Chinese internet café
will reveal only tourist information and architectural histories.

What lesson did the Bush administration take from this episode? The
crackdown certainly cooled any ardor on behalf of more vociferous US
intervention when communist regimes in Eastern Europe were challenged
in the months that followed. Erich Honecker, the octogenarian leader of
the German Democratic Republic (GDR), had spoken approvingly of
"the Chinese solution" as East Germans began to stir against his regime.
Bush had good reason to believe that American interference in the Soviet
sphere could only destabilize a precarious situation, lead to a crushing of
reform and a return to Cold War tensions. Bush's public declarations,
then and afterward, again display his innate conservatism and caution.
Joining with most European nations, he suspended arms sales to China
(a penalty that has stood ever since), but not much else followed. Indeed,
Bush remained wedded to the scientific certainty of democratization.
Despite the CCP's departure from the script, Bush wanted to stick with
it: "If people have commercial incentives," he argued, "the move to
democracy becomes inexorable. For this reason, I wanted to avoid cutting
off the entire commercial relationship" with Beijing.[30] Within a month of
the massacre, Brent Scowcroft made a secret visit to the city (a tradition
begun by Henry Kissinger in the early 1970s), assuring Deng Xiaoping
that the crackdown would not derail Sino–American rapprochement.
Within 12 months, America had renewed the PRC's "most favored
nation" trade status.

Was Bush's kid-gloves stance justified? The question was to recur
twenty years later when Barack Obama earned censure for failing to
condemn with enough anger the Iranian government's crackdown on
political reformers. How cautious is too cautious? In Bush's defense, we
should remember that he was obliged to operate on the basis of Cold War
experience rather than post–Cold War optimism. As Robert Service
reminds us, "No Western or Soviet politician had expected the Cold
War to end in their working lifetimes. Everything took place as if in a
dream that unfolded with unexpected twists in the plot before people
woke up to what had occurred."[31] Recall that even in the summer of

---

[30] Bush and Scowcroft, *A World Transformed*, p. 89.
[31] Robert Service, *The End of the Cold War: 1985–1991* (London: Macmillan, 2015),
p. 497.

1989 the very notion of "post–Cold War" would have sounded fantastical, but by the winter it was a reality. But the Bush team could not know this. Thaws often lead to refreezes – and refrozen fare is much less appetizing. The appeasement charge also ignores the importance of the United States keeping China onside. This classic piece of realpolitik was designed to build US–PRC cooperation so as to stall Sino-Soviet relations and to provide less of an incentive for China to seek allies in the developing world. It was better to appease China than push it into a Russian or Middle Eastern or African embrace. Nixon and Kissinger had accepted this logic; George Bush was schooled in it.

THE OTHER 9/11: THE FALL OF THE BERLIN WALL

China was the exception to how communism was tending in 1989. The Chinese experiment in authoritarian capitalism was well under way, and starting to pay dividends, by the time Soviet satrapies in Eastern European got the message. By then, it was too late. Once the necessity for reform was conceded, communism fell like a house of cards. It was "a sandpile ready to slide," as John Lewis Gaddis put it. "All it took to make that happen were a few more grains of sand."[32] The early–Cold War American presidents had feared the domino theory, with one nation after another falling to communism. The only dominos falling during 1989's "autumn of nations" (a play on 1848's "spring of nations") were communist: Poland first, then Hungary, followed by East Germany, Czechoslovakia, Bulgaria, and Romania. In all but the latter case, where Nicolae and Elena Ceauşescu were executed and a further 1,104 died over Christmas 1989, these revolutions were bloodless, oiled by much celebratory alcohol, and cemented by democratic elections.[33] They were also fundamentally endogenous – thus minimizing any role the United States might have played – and the product less of formal opposition strategy than of informal, unorganized mobilization.[34] Without much prompting from established reform movements – outside of Poland's Solidarity there really were none in Eastern Europe – people, when their

---

[32] John Lewis Gaddis, *The Cold War: A New History* (New York: Penguin, 2005), p. 238.

[33] Between January 11–13, 1991, in Vilnius, Lithuania, and Riga, Latvia, then parts of the USSR, Soviet troops killed 14 protestors and injured 702. Gorbachev quickly disowned the killers.

[34] See Sarah B. Snyder, *Human Rights Activism and the End of the Cold War: A Transnational History of the Helsinki Network* (New York: Cambridge University Press, 2011).

governments declined to stop them, simply walked, biked, and drove to freedom.

In Poland, on June 4, 1989, ironically the same day as the Tiananmen crackdown, Solidarity was voted into office, securing *every* seat in the Polish *Sejm* (the equivalent of the US House of Representatives), and 99 out of 100 in the *Senat*. The first full electoral test of communism's popularity, as Joseph Stalin had predicted and why he avoided them, was a disastrous failure. The historian Timothy Garton Ash captured the unfolding dynamic there and across the Eastern Bloc as it then evolved:

A few kids went on the streets and threw a few words. The police beat them. The kids said: You have no right to beat us! And the rulers, the high and mighty, replied, in effect: Yes, we have no right to beat you. We have no right to preserve our rule by force. The end no longer justifies the means.[35]

Between September and November 1989, tens of thousands of East Germans gathered in Leipzig's main square. As the anticipated crackdown failed to materialize, the size and resolve of the crowd grew. On November 9, Günter Schabowski, a member of the GDR's politburo, in perhaps the greatest cock-up in Cold War history, gave a press conference. In attempting to announce a new visa system allowing East Germans to visit the West, he mistakenly blurted out, "Um, we have decided today, um, to implement a regulation that allows every citizen of the German Democratic Republic, um, to, um, to leave the GDR through any of the border crossings. That comes into effect, according to my information, immediately, without delay."[36] Within hours, partying East and West Berliners were taking chunks out of the Berlin Wall. "Just like that," as Stephen Kotkin puts it, "27 million Soviet lives lost to defeat the invading Germans and take Berlin, and then some apparatchik misspeaks at a press conference, and gone!"[37] A KGB lieutenant colonel, Vladimir Putin, stationed in the disintegrating GDR, watched with growing discomfort. Less than eleven months later, with the world's eyes then on the developing Persian Gulf crisis and agent Putin back in Leningrad, Germany was reunited.

---

[35] In Gaddis, *The Cold War*, p. 237.
[36] In Kotkin, *Uncivil Society*, p. 62. See also Mary Elise Sarotte, *The Collapse: The Accidental Opening of the Berlin Wall* (New York: Basic Books, 2014), pp. 118–119.
[37] Kotkin, *Uncivil Society*, p. 62.

PANAMA AND "HEMISPHERIC HYGIENE"

Regime change was not confined to Eastern Europe; the ending of history was a global phenomenon, as Francis Fukuyama had suggested. The release of Nelson Mandela, in February 1990, symbolized the beginning of the end of white rule in South Africa, paving the way for multiparty elections. The next month, Chilean democracy was restored for the first time since 1973. Critics on the left continue to claim that US ambivalence, if not outright connivance, kept apartheid South Africa and Augusto Pinochet's Chile alive for too long. The United States certainly had an interest in stalling the defection of these states into the Soviet camp during the Cold War – a very real possibility until the collapse of communism in Europe. Defenders of America's Cold War policy counter that South Africa and Chile endured repulsive regimes for decades but were at least spared the political and economic ruination of communism, allowing them to transition into democracy in a much healthier condition than might otherwise have been the case.[38] In 2009, Chile became the first state in history to change its status from a "developing" nation to a "developed" one. In 2010, South Africa became the first African state to host the soccer World Cup, a significant logistical undertaking. Regime change in Panama required more of a deliberate US push, and provided the first test of the US military under President Bush.

George Will, the conservative commentator, welcomed Bush's decision to topple the regime in Panama as "an act of hemispheric hygiene."[39] Latin Americans have bridled at such condescension, but few mourned the removal of Manuel Noriega from power over Christmas and New Year 1989–1990. The immediate *casus belli* were the murder by Noriega's operatives of a US Marine lieutenant in Panama City. This straw broke the camel's back. On December 20, 27,000 US troops, half of whom were already based in the Panama Canal Zone, swiftly scattered Noriega's military loyalists, though it took several weeks for the dictator himself to be arrested, after having been holed up in the Vatican embassy. A civilian government was quickly installed. *Newsday* described it as "a brilliant and violent thrust" that had proven Colin Powell's "military mettle," to be tested again in the Persian Gulf the next year.[40] Like the

---

[38] See Jeane Kirkpatrick, Dictatorships and Double Standards, *Commentary* 68 (November 1979): 34–46.
[39] George F. Will, Good Neighbor Policy, *Washington Post*, December 21, 1989, p. A29.
[40] In Karen DeYoung, *Soldier: The Life of Colin Powell* (New York: Vintage, 2007), p. 184.

interventions in Kosovo in 1999 and Iraq in 2003, the Panama invasion, codenamed Operation Just Cause, took place in the absence of a United Nations resolution. Very few military interventions undertaken by the United States since the creation of the UN in 1945 have been ordained by it. Again, this was a pattern that carried over from the Cold War to the post–Cold War era.

After recurrent and lengthy interventions in the Americas from 1898 to 1945 (and then predominately in Central rather than South America), the United States declined to commit overt military force to maintain its regional hegemony during the Cold War. The CIA knew of and chose not to stop the 1973 coup in Chile, which ended the minority government (and life) of Salvador Allende but did not order or trigger it. US sponsorship of rightist forces in Guatemala and El Salvador was conditioned not by imperialism but by fears that escalation would mean another Vietnam.[41] Reagan's "police action" in Grenada in 1983 did not lead to a lengthy occupation. The funding of the Contra rebels in Nicaragua in the 1980s was rendered illegal by an act of Congress, a root cause of the Iran–Contra scandal, which consumed much of Reagan's second term. Panama was the exception that proved the rule in this regard. Invasions of Latin America in and after the Cold War began and ended with Panama. Only Haiti, in the Caribbean, offered a further test of US hard power, but this heavily circumscribed invasion had little to do with geopolitical interest and nothing at all to do with hegemony, as we will explore in the next chapter.

United States policy toward its southern neighbors, from the Cold War to the post–Cold War era, represents a continuum. Even overtly anti-American regimes, such as that of Hugo Chavez in Venezuela, failed to excite Washington to the point where military action against them was contemplated. The Cold War presented an ambiguous lesson for foreign policymakers. The United States deployed hundreds of thousands of troops and billions of dollars of aid to Southeast Asia, only to see Cambodia, China, North Korea, and North and South Vietnam go communist. It committed, in comparison, negligible numbers of troops and inconsistent funds (much of them illegal) to Latin America in the same period, and only one small island – Cuba – went and stayed red.

---

[41] See Bob Woodward, *Veil: The Secret Wars of the CIA 1981–1987* (New York: Simon & Schuster, 1987), p. 174.

IRAQ INVADES KUWAIT

Halfway through Bush's term, the world, if not the US economy, seemed to be going the president's way. A New York businessman, Donald Trump, was interviewed in *Playboy* magazine in May 1990 to bemoan how America was being "openly screwed" by Japan and Saudi Arabia. But he garnered little attention. Then, on July 25, April Glaspie, US ambassador to Iraq, sat down for her first private conversation, after two years in the post, with Saddam Hussein. That encounter can be said to mark the first in a series of miscalculations and misunderstandings that defined the United States–Iraq relationship for the next twenty years. The inability of each side to read the nature and intentions of the other was to cost over a million lives, most of them Iraqis and many of them children, and reduce the Iraqi state to total collapse. A week after that meeting, America began a war against Iraq that it waged in both hot and cold forms under the command of four presidents, of both parties, over two decades. What did Ambassador Glaspie say to initiate the defining conflict of the post–Cold War years?

To answer this question, it is necessary to understand the course of United States–Iraq relations to this point. Created by the British in 1920, Iraq, a country about the size of California, became an important pillar of US strategy in the Middle East from the 1970s. The withdrawal of British power, in any meaningful sense, "east of Suez," in 1968 coincided with America's transition from a net exporter to a net importer of oil. The Persian Gulf, under which lay much of the world's oil, suddenly increased in importance. The Arab decision to triple oil prices during the October 1973 "Yom Kippur War" with Israel sent the United States and Europe into the worst recession since 1929. America, like Britain before it, had to work harder at finding allies in the region.

The declaration of an Islamic Republic of Iran in January 1979, the accompanying anti-Americanism by which this theocracy defined itself, and the prestige-sapping US embassy hostage crisis (lasting 444 days), which followed hard upon it, made Iraq and its oil reserves a natural ally of the United States. The old maxim that the enemy of my enemy is my friend explains the strategic alliance between Washington and Baghdad through the 1980s. In the 1970s, America had shown Tehran a similar largesse to counter Soviet influence in the Gulf.

Iraq was hardly a model state. Its leader was brutal and his ambitions disquieting, verging on the irrational. Glaspie, with no little wisdom, later observed that "we foolishly did not realize Saddam was stupid."[42] His Baath party was socialist. He had flirted with Moscow in the 1980s. He counted Joseph Stalin as a political hero. Saddam's opulent palaces were inspired by a visit he made to Uncle Joe's old dachas. But he was prepared to make war on Iran, America's new foe, and that counted for much. The Iran–Iraq War, begun by Saddam's opportunistic bid to seize an oil-rich province in southwestern Iran in 1980 and lasting eight bloody years, suited American interests, serving to check the expansionist aspirations of both regimes. "It is a shame they both can't lose," Henry Kissinger said wryly. "We didn't want either side to have the advantage," was how Representative Charlie Wilson put it. "We just wanted them to kick the shit out of each other."[43]

So long as Saddam was prepared to balance Ayatollah Khomeini, Iran's supreme leader, America was prepared to supply him with the military means to do so. However, the "paradox of Iraqi power," as Kenneth Pollack has documented, "can be put simply: any Iraq that is strong enough to balance and contain Iran will inevitably be capable of overrunning Kuwait and Saudi Arabia."[44] This concern was repressed by the Reagan administration for as long as Saddam looked east to Tehran rather than south to the oil-rich Gulf states.[45] His terrible decision to attack Iran in 1980, a campaign he had expected to last only a few weeks, against a nation three times the size of his own, was hardly assessed by US intelligence until he again invaded a neighbor ten years later.

Until then, diplomatic engagement between Washington and Baghdad had become routine. In 1983, to advance the strategic partnership between both nations, Donald Rumsfeld, the man who was to plan the 2003 invasion of Iraq, met with Saddam. An American cartoon after Saddam's capture, twenty years later, depicts him in his cell as Rumsfeld approaches. "Rummy!" shouts the former tyrant, arms outstretched. The sketch was discomfortingly close to capturing the reality of American support of a noxious regime. Some 50 percent of all the arms Iraq purchased from 1979 to 1990 were made in American factories. By 1990, those factories had helped create the most formidable military

---

[42] In David Hoffman, U.S. Envoy Conciliatory to Saddam, *Washington Post*, July 12, 1991.

[43] George Crile, *Charlie Wilson's War* (New York: Grove Press, 2003), p. 275. See also Lisa Blaydes, *State of Repression Iraq under Saddam Hussein* (Princeton, NJ: Princeton University Press, 2018), pp. 80–111.

[44] Kenneth M. Pollack, Securing the Gulf, *Foreign Affairs* 82, 4 (July/August 2003): 2–16.

[45] See Bruce W. Jentleson, *With Friends Like These: Reagan, Bush, and Saddam, 1982–1990* (New York: W. W. Norton, 1994).

power in the region. Saddam's crimes against his own people during this period – from gassing and ethnic cleansing to communal punishment and torture – were elided because of the proxy role Saddam was willing to play on America's behalf. Such charges became the basis for the criminal trial that led to his execution in 2006.

Indeed, though the pretext for the 2003 invasion that ultimately toppled Saddam relied on an erroneous assessment of his weapons capacity, that assessment was plausible, because America had been complicit in its initial creation. He must have weapons of mass destruction (WMD), ran the logic, because we gave them to him. Israel had been sufficiently impressed by his evolving nuclear capacity; in June 1981 fourteen Israeli warplanes destroyed Iraq's Osiraq reactor, near Baghdad. Twenty years later, in the wake of 9/11, the fear that Saddam had reconstituted his WMD program was enough of a reason for President George W. Bush to plot his downfall.

The further irony of America's cool embrace of Saddam was that his war against Iran, while it suited American geostrategy, was the root cause of Saddam's eventual targeting of Kuwait. The Iran–Iraq War came close to bankrupting the Iraqi state. America had sold Saddam weapons; it had not donated them. Saddam wanted compensation from his Arab neighbors for negating Persian ambitions. Containing Shia Iran was and remains a fundamental security concern of both the United States and its Sunni Arab allies, especially Saudi Arabia. Those states, little Kuwait in particular, were unwilling, however, to pay for Iraqi sacrifices. Loans Arab regimes made to Iraq during the conflict (totaling about $10 billion) were not forgiven. Kuwait, Saudi Arabia, Qatar, and the Emirates connived to keep the oil price low, increasing the pressure on Iraqi coffers. Saddam Hussein, dependent on oil revenues, saw this as an effort to sabotage his regime. He claimed the Gulf states, in league with the United States – "conspiring bastards," he called them – were part of a Zionist plot to ruin Iraq.[46] In reality, America had a vested economic interest in cheap oil, which Kuwait's overproduction made possible. Saddam's anger sought an outlet.

In July 1990, he reawakened a long-standing Iraqi claim on Kuwait. The tiny Gulf monarchy (slightly smaller than New Jersey) was historically the nineteenth province of Iraq, insisted Saddam. Its existence was an affront to Arab unity (at best a contradiction in terms), symbolic of British colonial gerrymandering, and its oil production quotas were forcing the

---

[46] In Hal Brands and David Palkki, "Conspiring Bastards": Saddam's Strategic View of the United States, *Diplomatic History* 36, 3 (June 2012): 625–659.

Iraqi people into starvation. These assorted grievances (each with some foundation) were presented to Ambassador Glaspie that afternoon. "Does the U.S. have a view?" he asked. "No," replied Glaspie, "... the issue is not associated with America." The Iraqi leader saw this statement of American ambivalence as a green light.[47] A week later, on August 2, he invaded, quickly subduing the terrified Kuwaitis, who pleaded to the international community for redress.

A larger cause of this audacious act, and one which perplexed American policymakers thereafter, was the psychology of Saddam Hussein himself. The three US presidents who made war on him had different interpretations of what made the Iraqi leader tick. In August 1990, President Bush offered a warning from history. Hussein, he said, was an Arab Adolf Hitler. "This man is evil," wrote Bush in his diary, "let him win and we rise again to fight tomorrow."[48] The analogy conditioned his response to the invasion and framed the issue for American consumption. Saddam's role model, down to the moustache, was actually Joseph Stalin, but the Nazi comparison stuck. Three days after Kuwait succumbed, in a clear (though Bush contends unplanned) reference to Munich 1938, he declared the Iraqi aggression "would not stand." A compromise short of full Iraqi withdrawal was thus rendered unrealizable from the outset. Saddam had calculated the invasion would increase his diplomatic leverage. It had not.

DESERT SHIELD

The early clarity of the American position – reinforced by the British prime minister, Margaret Thatcher, who insisted Bush not "go wobbly" on her – certainly helped him in constructing an anti-Saddam coalition, at home and abroad.[49] On August 9, President Bush reported to Congress that he had ordered "the forward deployment of substantial elements of the United States Armed Forces into the region ... to deter Iraqi aggression and to preserve the integrity of Saudi Arabia."[50]

---

[47] See Stephen M. Walt, WikiLeaks, April Glaspie, and Saddam Hussein, *Foreign Policy* [online], January 29, 2011.
[48] George H. W. Bush, *All the Best, George Bush: My Life in Letters and Other Writings* (New York: Scribner, 2013), p. 503.
[49] See Margaret Thatcher, *The Downing Street Years* (New York: HarperCollins, 1993), p. 824.
[50] George H. W. Bush, Letter to Congressional Leaders on the Deployment of United States Armed Forces to Saudi Arabia and the Middle East, August 9, 1990; at https://bush41library.tamu.edu/archives/public-papers/2152.

Bush was confronted with two options. The first one entailed an immediate air war to force Iraqi forces to withdraw. This was the president's preferred option in the opening months of the standoff. He believed it would demonstrate resolve and bring the matter to a head quickly. But it was risky. As Colin Powell warned him on September 24, an air campaign alone might be weathered by Saddam. The Iraqi leader might retaliate by tightening his grip on Kuwait, killing more of its civilians, and/or setting alight its oil fields.

The second option, favored by Powell, was more certain of success but entailed waiting. It meant a long diplomatic campaign to further isolate Iraq, gain UN support for a military solution, and, crucially, amass enormous numbers of men and hardware in Saudi Arabia, sufficient to overwhelm the 150,000 Iraqi troops it was estimated Saddam could raise to defend his quarry (in addition to his standing army of some 350,000). Waiting also left hope that the sanctions imposed on Iraq might be enough to convince Saddam to retreat before military action became unavoidable. The second option, despite misgivings from President Bush, who never felt sanctions would work, won out.

Over the next four months, Bush assembled an almighty coalition of nations. His secretary of state visited some twelve capitals in November alone. Bush succeeded in getting the UN Security Council to pass Resolution 678, which gave Saddam until January 15, 1991, to withdraw or face "all necessary means" to make him do so. Even the USSR supported the resolution, confirming, at least temporarily, that Bush's "new world order" had dawned. Some half a million soldiers, from thirty-five nations (three from the now defunct Warsaw Pact: Czechoslovakia, Hungary, and Poland), sat in the Saudi desert, waiting for Saddam to buckle. Operation Desert Shield was the largest mobilization of military force since World War II.

Despite the scale of the international coalition Bush assembled, popular support at home was not overwhelming. On January 12, 1991, after a far more rancorous debate than that which would precede the 2003 Iraq invasion, the Senate voted 52–47 and the House 250–183 in favor of war. A strong majority of Democrats in both Congress and the country were against it. Even moderates like Sam Nunn voted against the president. While liberal hawks were to become prevalent in the coming Clinton administration (Al Gore was one of only ten defecting Senate Democrats that voted for war), during the Kuwait crisis, Democrats displayed an antiwar sentiment that harked back to Vietnam and had never really gone away – and would recur in the post–9/11 years. Democrats were seemingly conditioned by the Cold War to see foreign threats as always less than the sum of their parts. The GOP was accused of threat exaggeration – as practiced by Reagan and now by Bush. The moral relativism that had condemned Reagan's labeling of the Soviet Union as "evil" (in 1983) found renewed vigor in response to Bush's denunciations of Saddam (in 1990). This Cold War echo will be heard again later in this book.

DESERT STORM

On January 16, 1991, within hours of Iraq's failure to comply with United Nations Security Council Resolution 678, Desert Shield became Desert Storm. Despite the inevitability of conflict, given the intractable positions both Bush and Hussein adopted, when hostilities commenced the drama was compelling. The US strategy was simple but stunningly effective – and much shorter and less bloody (for the US side) than even the most optimistic military planners had hoped. Its first, longer stage was an air bombardment of Baghdad, targeting centers of Baathist politico-military control. Its second, shorter phase, lasting from February 24 to 27 (approximately 100 hours in total), was a ground war to expel Iraqi troops from Kuwait, killing several thousand of them, many as they attempted to flee on the only major road back into Iraq. With America and its allies in complete mastery of the sky and desert, combat operations were "suspended."

Saddam Hussein's rule, however, was not. Indeed, the period from August 1990 to February 1991 may be said to mark the opening phase of a much longer war with Saddam. There's the rub. His hold on power strengthened in inverse proportion to the health of the nation he ruled: leader strong, his people weak. In the weeks and months following Saddam's capitulation, Bush offered a sop to the men and women America claimed to support, but essentially abandoned them for another twelve years. Why did Bush do this? Colin Powell stated the reason succinctly: "Our practical intention was to leave Baghdad enough power to survive as a threat to an Iran that remained bitterly hostile to the United States."[51]

OPERATION PROVIDE COMFORT

President Bush's refusal to topple Saddam Hussein was to have disastrous short- and long-term consequences. In the short-term, indigenous

---

[51] Colin Powell, *My American Journey* (New York: Ballantine, 1995), p. 516.

opponents of the Baathist regime found themselves dangerously exposed to the dictator's vengeance once he and they realized America was unwilling to honor its promise of military support.[52] Any coup against Saddam would have to be an entirely homegrown affair, but that coup never came.

Two long-term consequences were set in train. First, the refusal to end permanently Saddam's threat to Saudi Arabia meant US troops remained stationed in "the land of the Prophet." While a series of United States–led wars advanced Muslim interests and saved Muslim lives in the 1990s (in the Balkans especially), the "occupation" of Saudi Arabia by Western "infidels" was a root cause of Islamist rage – a "principal recruiting device,"[53] Paul Wolfowitz conceded. Some of that rage was visited upon the American homeland on September 11, 2001. Second, America began a process, approved by the United Nations, in which Iraq was reduced to penury. This was not the intention of a sanctions regime designed to weaken Saddam's resolve; it was the effect. This meant that when George W. Bush decided to end the long war with Iraq started by his father, he inherited a collapsing Iraqi state, bankrupted by twelve years of economic isolation.[54] Worse still, those betrayed by US inaction in the spring of 1991 were understandably skeptical that confronting Saddam a second time would elicit the US backing promised and then denied the first time. In 2003, the United States invaded a dying nation with essentially no support from the justifiably wary Iraqis. The countdown to that debacle began in the mountains of Iraqi Kurdistan, on the border with Turkey, in March–April 1991.

The remarkable speed of the United States' victory in January–February obscured its ambiguous nature. The Kuwaiti monarchy was restored, and Iraqi troops decisively expelled from the kingdom. But Saddam Hussein remained in power in Baghdad. Bush the moralist called for his overthrow. Bush the realist knew that if America were to wield the knife, the international coalition he had crafted to restore Kuwaiti sovereignty would break apart. The ending of the Saddam Hussein regime may have been a legitimate war aim; it was not a legal one. Bush had no international legal authority – as expressed in a UN resolution – to take his war to the streets of Baghdad. Arab states complicit in Desert Storm would not, he argued, have allowed for this mission creep. Importantly, neither would his generals. The chairman of the joint chiefs, Colin Powell, had fought in the Vietnam War as a young soldier. The Powell Doctrine

---

[52] See Blaydes, *State of Repression*, p. 87–88.   [53] In Wilentz, *Age of Reagan*, p. 302.
[54] This sorry decline is retold in Blaydes, *State of Repression*.

became a powerful deterrent to open-ended military campaigns, waged by troops with no idea of what victory might look like. Powell's commander in chief claimed to have "kicked the Vietnam syndrome once and for all," but in several respects this Cold War hangover had endured in the Iraqi theater. Or, rather, it stopped the Americans taking the war into Iraq proper. The war aims were defined as the restoration of Kuwaiti sovereignty, not the termination of Saddam's dictatorship. Bush, perhaps more in hope than in expectation, left it to the oppressed people of Iraq to do that.

And for a moment, it appeared possible. Kurds in the north of Iraq and Shia in the south, emboldened by pledges of US support and Saddam's hasty withdrawal from Kuwait, rose in rebellion. With much fervor but few arms, these rebels were quickly subdued by a dictator with a keen survival instinct and, even allowing for his defeat in Kuwait, with the most significant military capacity in the region. The figures are staggering. Some two million Kurds headed for the hills along the Turkish border or east to the relative safety of Iran. Turkey, long distrustful of Kurdish separatism within its own borders, would only take in so many. By Easter, over 300,000 Kurds found themselves abandoned in the snow-covered mountains, prey to Saddam's US- and Russian-made helicopter gunships, which coalition troops watched fly over their heads.

The moral obligation to act, as in Somalia but not in Yugoslavia in the coming months, weighed heavily upon Bush. It was the realists' realist, James Baker, who observed the unfolding catastrophe firsthand on April 8. "You've no idea of the human nightmare here," he told President Bush. "We've got to do something and do it now."[55]

That something was Operation Provide Comfort. The continuing utility of Cold War alliances was again on display. US forces were joined by troops from Britain, France, Holland, Italy, and Spain. NATO had been given a renewed purpose. The provision of aid to the refugees was eventually accompanied by the creation and imperfect maintenance by the British and American air forces of no-fly zones in the north and south of Iraq. The zones were enough to coax the terrified refugees down from the mountains and back to their homes. This was to form two sides of the infamous "box" in which Saddam was to be kept for the next twelve years, along with his several hundred thousand victims. The strength of the box was to become a key point of dispute in the countdown to war in 2002–2003.

[55] Baker, *Politics of Diplomacy*, p. 433.

START TO FINISH OF THE USSR

The developing American obsession with Saddam Hussein, with all the war and human tragedy it entailed, obscured the most remarkable event of twentieth-century history: the demise of the Union of Soviet Socialist Republics. This revolutionary empire ceased to exist on December 26, 1991. When its end came, it was not with US troops in occupation of Moscow. Rather, the deputies of the USSR voted it into oblivion. Mikhail Gorbachev did not commit suicide in a bunker. He was not removed from his post; his post was removed from him. With no Soviet Union there was no longer a need for a Soviet president. "The thing about innovations," warned Raisa Gorbachev, his wife, "is that sooner or later they turn around and destroy the innovators."[56]

The American role in this drama was unremarkable, especially when we consider that the containment of Soviet power had been the central objective of US foreign policy for nearly half a century. The Bush administration facilitated the end of the USSR and, according to some, may actually have postponed it by several months. It did not cause it. From the moment the Berlin Wall cracked on November 9, 1989 to the death of Soviet communism on December 26, 1991, Americans were keen observers rather than active participants. Indeed, President Bush remained pessimistic that such flux could end happily. At moments during the crisis, his ambition was to secure Gorbachev, his friend, in power, rather than aid the first non-communist to rule Russia since Alexander Kerensky in 1917. George Bush was a very late convert to the vodka-fueled presidency of Boris Yeltsin, who played Brutus to Gorbachev's Caesar.

Donald Trump, then a brash businessman, visited Moscow in 1990 and counseled that the Kremlin needed to apply a Tiananmen-style solution to internal unrest and noted, "they were vicious, they were horrible, but they put it down with strength. That shows you the power of strength."[57] The Soviet leader's refusal to countenance force against the people of Eastern Europe when they revolted against their Soviet-backed regimes through 1989 was a decisive act of omission. Without the implicit threat of force to hold its satellites in orbit, they quickly broke away. The Warsaw Pact, the Soviet NATO, suddenly became irrelevant. By July 1991 it was formally dissolved. Arms negotiations, the

---

[56] In Halberstam, *War in a Time of Peace*, p. 13.
[57] Glenn Plaskin, Interview with Donald Trump, *Playboy*, March 1, 1990.

punctuation marks of Cold War history since the 1970s, became less fraught. Strategic arms reductions talks with the United States succeeded, in the form of the Strategic Arms Reduction Treaty (START), to the chagrin of Moscow's cold warriors.

In August 1991, nostalgia for the pre-*glasnost* days of military strength and economic stability got the better of several senior Kremlin officials. Led by Vladimir Kryuchov, they placed Mikhail and Raisa Gorbachev under house arrest at the couple's Black Sea holiday home. A coup was underway. Desire, however, was not matched by performance. Emboldened by alcohol, but robbed by it of a capacity for strategic thinking, the plotters soon ran into trouble. The Soviet army could not be persuaded to join the plot. The extraordinary bravery of Boris Yeltsin, whose political career, unlike those of the plotters, was testament to the enabling qualities of Russian vodka, faced down wavering tanks outside the Russian parliament. The coup fizzled. President Bush, watching from a distance, was mightily relieved when Gorbachev appeared from an Aeroflot plane in Moscow, to resume his now time-limited post. His prestige never recovered, whereas Yeltsin's soared. By June 1991, Yeltsin had already assumed the presidency of a newly constituted Russian Federation. Six months later the USSR was dissolved, and Gorbachev was left to contemplate the lucrative Western lecture circuit. A coup, of sorts, had taken place, but one that consigned Soviet communism, as Reagan had predicted, to "the ash-heap of history."[58] In 1989, Dick Cheney had warned that Gorbachev would "ultimately fail" – and he was right, though perhaps not in the way he had intended. The USSR proved beyond reformation.[59]

"NO DOG IN THIS FIGHT": BUSH AND YUGOSLAVIA

The fall of communism in Eastern Europe and Russia was met with euphoria. In Yugoslavia, it was met with war. For over forty years, the Federal Republic of Yugoslavia had been held together by a paradox. To be coherent as a nation state, it needed an ideology that could subdue more ancient nationalisms, which would ultimately tear it apart, and communism fitted the bill. However, the utility of Yugoslav communism was uniquely predicated on the personality of one man: Josip Broz Tito. When he died, his regime was placed on life support. Marx said history

---

[58] In Leffler, *For the Soul of Mankind*, p. 341.   [59] In Wilentz, *Age of Reagan*, p. 291.

makes great men, not great men history, but Tito made communist Yugoslavia – without him it fell apart.

After Tito's death in 1980, Serbia, the largest nation within the union, began to assert a hegemony over the smaller. Its claim to rule, without Tito to hold such ambitions in check and, after the fall of the Berlin Wall, devoid of a communist cloak, quickly antagonized its neighbors. Slovenia, Croatia, and Bosnia–Herzegovina each feared for their survival as republics under Serbian control. One after the other they declared their independence. Croatia and Slovenia made the break simultaneously in June 1991. Slovenia was too distant from Belgrade for the Serbs to do much about it. Croatia was not. Rather than allow a large proportion of ethnic Serbs to be subsumed into the new Croat state, Serbia went to war. Croats, fearing the consequences of being trapped inside Serbia, resisted. When Bosnia made the same move, nine months later, Slobodan Milošević, the Serbian president of what was left of Yugoslavia, declared it would be "born dead." He was nearly true to his word. And the war came.

The horror was spread across Yugoslavia but concentrated in Bosnia, a federal unit of Yugoslavia about the size of West Virginia, and within Bosnia it centered on its capital city, Sarajevo – about the size of Tucson, Arizona. Starting in the spring of 1992, Serbian guns were parked on the hills surrounding this picturesque city, and fired onto it for the next three years. The siege of Sarajevo became the symbol of the war – and of Western inaction. Jacque Poos, the Luxembourg foreign minister, declared this the "hour of Europe."[60] George Bush was ambivalent; Yugoslavia gets a mere four citations in his coauthored memoir of the period.[61] America had "no dog in the fight," said James Baker, and added importantly, "We don't want to put a dog in this fight."[62] The administration was content for Europeans to end the fighting – and skeptical that they could. Lawrence Eagleburger (or "Lawrence of Serbia," as he became known as a result of Bush policy) said the inevitable European failure would "teach them to burden share."[63] It was a contention already well-formed in the mind of Donald Trump.

What all this meant was abandoning the people of the Balkans to the men with the most guns. The European Union, then called the European

---

[60] In Ivo H. Daalder, *Getting to Dayton: The Making of America's Bosnia Policy* (Washington DC: Brookings, 2000), p. 6.
[61] Bush and Scowcroft, *A World Transformed.*
[62] In Engel, *When the World Seemed New*, p. 475.
[63] In Brendan Simms, *Unfinest Hour: Britain and the Destruction of Bosnia* (London: Allen Lane, 2001), p. 54.

Community (EC), had compromised its initial response by the unilateral recognition of Slovenian and Croatian independence by Germany, a state that had itself only recently ended its Cold War separation. The United Nations compounded the woes of the Bosnian Muslims, who had access to few weapons, and advanced the cause of the Bosnian Serbs, who had many, by imposing a blanket arms embargo on all parties to the conflict. This locked in the Serb advantage; their forces controlled over ninety percent of the hardware of the Yugoslav army. Much of this was visited upon their opponents, especially those living in Sarajevo from 1992 to 1995.

The story of how America moved from a studied indifference under Bush to war on Serbia under Clinton is told in the next chapters. What the breakup of Yugoslavia confirmed was the continuing necessity for American security guarantees in Europe. The end of the Cold War prematurely raised expectations, in part advanced by Washington, that there was no longer a market for US power on that continent. With the Soviet storm now past, the Cold War security umbrella provided by the United States could be collapsed. Leaders in both Europe and America optimistically hoped so. Yugoslavia left them badly exposed. As a consequence, instead of NATO becoming a relic, it was rejuvenated, and the Balkans were made its first post–Cold War testing ground. An organization designed to win the Cold War saw its most concerted military use in the decades that followed that conflict.

The foreign policy of his son is often derided as a departure from Cold War precedent, but in Yugoslavia it was Bush Sr. that refused to countenance support of the kind his predecessors had pledged. Harry Truman's decisive intervention in the Greek civil war, from 1947 to 1949, close to the Yugoslav theater, while it cost 100,000 Greek lives, undoubtedly saved many more. Greece remained within the American camp and the line held against Soviet subversion. Truman succeeded in dampening the ambitions of communists across Europe by committing US power to Athens in the first test of American resolve in the Cold War. Bush did not try to check the ugly nationalisms that defaced Yugoslavia and thus failed a key test of US resolve after the Cold War. Even those who had applauded Desert Storm began to question the wisdom of his foreign policy. As Bush's star fell, his Democratic challenger's rose.

"IT'S THE ECONOMY, STUPID": THE 1992 ELECTION

If Harry Truman was not his role model in the Balkans, it might have been some salve to George Bush's bruised ego to recall the fate of Winston

Churchill. Having guided Great Britain to its greatest ever military victory, he was summarily dumped out of office in July 1945 by the very men and women whom for over five years he had led and inspired. The task of postwar reconstruction and the formation of the British welfare state on the back of US loans was handed to the less colorful, certainly soberer, and more domestically attuned Clement Attlee. The analogy is not unhelpful, if imperfect, when we consider Bush's fate after his victory in the Gulf War, eighteen months before his defeat to Bill Clinton in November 1992 and less than a year after the collapse of Soviet communism. It is helpful in allowing us to understand what Bush seemingly did not: that diplomatic and military success abroad cannot appease economic discontent at home. Barack Obama was to apply this lesson after 2008.

Bush faced two overriding domestic problems that he was unable and, crucially, appeared unwilling to solve. The first – economic – was less his fault than the second – political – surely was. In combination, they led to his snatching of electoral defeat from the jaws of martial victory in the fall of 1992. The latter half of the Bush presidency coincided with the worst recession since the 1970s and the longest one since the Great Depression. There is some irony in the observation that communism died during a crisis of faith in the capitalist system itself. October 13, 1989 – Black Friday – gave intimations of a downturn, which became evident in 1990–1992. This market free fall was compounded by the bill coming due for Reagan's defense spending and tax cuts in the 1980s. Bush had won election by promising "no new taxes." In his January 1990 budget he broke this promise – claiming unconvincingly that he was not creating new taxes, only authorizing "tax revenue increases" in order to begin cutting the Reagan deficit.[64] His base never forgave him.

Bush had inadvertently and unforgivably catalyzed a fracturing of the Republican party that would be exploited decades later by Donald Trump. If Bush's vision abroad was nonideological, his GOP opponents at home were. Pat Buchanan, annoyed by the will o' the wisp quality of Bush's domestic agenda and tax cut betrayal, declared a religious and cultural war. His arena for so doing was not a TV show – his mainstay in the 2000s – but the Republican National Convention, the nominating jamboree for George Bush in August 1992. Buchanan's speech became the centerpiece of the event. "There is a religious war going on in our country

---

[64] See Iwan Morgan, *The Age of Deficits: Presidents and Unbalanced Budgets from Jimmy Carter to George W. Bush* (Lawrence: University Press of Kansas, 2009), p. 139.

for the soul of America," said Buchanan. "It is a cultural war, as critical to the kind of nation we will one day be as was the Cold War itself."[65] The speech, mocked Molly Ivins, "probably sounded better in the original German."[66] Though he only captured a fifth of the delegates, it was clear, as the campaign entered its final phase, that Bush's Gulf War momentum had been all but lost. A third-party candidacy by Ross Perot's Reform party further split Republicans.

Bill Clinton, the Democratic challenger, inherited this fortuitous circumstance. Keen to divide the GOP vote further, his campaign ran hard on the deteriorating economy and the patrician Bush's lack of empathy with the plight of working families: the president had been unable to guess the price of a gallon of milk during the campaign ($2.78 in 1992) and was caught clock-watching during one of the candidate debates. Democrats, then and since, used the Senate confirmation hearings for Clarence Thomas, Bush's pick for the Supreme Court, to claim his party was institutionally sexist. Thomas had been accused of sexually harassing his coworker, Anita Hill. What Thomas, an African-American, called his "high-tech lynching" dominated US politics in 1991–1992. A record number of women were returned to Congress that November; Bush did himself no favors by stating his "hope" that "a lot of them" would lose.[67]

If pundits countered that Bush had crafted a remarkable record in foreign policy, Clinton's campaign, in one of the most infamous examples of the downgrading of American political discourse, responded that foreign policy did not matter: "It's the economy, stupid!" And so it proved. Presiding over the end of the Cold War and the creation of the world's largest military coalition helped contribute to only a 38 percent vote share (to Clinton's 43% and Perot's 19%). A man with essentially no foreign policy experience had defeated one of the greatest diplomat-presidents in modern US history.

"NO ONE SHOULD HAVE TO DIE AT CHRISTMAS": BUSH AND SOMALIA

Doing the "right thing" in each of the foreign episodes that defined the Bush presidency was much harder than doing what was realpolitik.

[65] Patrick Buchanan, speech at Republican National Convention, Houston, TX, August 17, 1992.

[66] Molly Ivins, *Nothin' but Good Times Ahead* (New York: Vintage, 1994), p. 136.

[67] The number of women went from 33 to 55 in the House and from 1 to 5 in the Senate.

Removing Saddam permanently from his Baghdad palaces was a more testing proposition than leaving him in place. It is too harsh to call Bush's late-term fascination with Somalia an exercise in displacement activity, but it is also difficult to completely exonerate him of this charge. Consider the world Bush surveyed in the fall of 1992. In Iraq, Saddam was making mincemeat of opponents Bush had called friends. In Yugoslavia, the United Nations arms embargo Bush had signed-up to risked the annihilation of Bosnia's Muslims. In Russia, Boris Yeltsin, backed too late by Bush, was facing a great battle to cement the legitimacy of the postcommunist Russian state. In China, the era of authoritarian capitalism, rather than of political liberalization, had dawned. The argument that Bush, in his final months in office, was seeking about for a small but important corrective to all this is too cynical. But Somalia did afford the departing president the opportunity to engineer a military intervention as morally pure in its aims as arguably any in US history. However, what began as an exercise in moral purpose was to become Bill Clinton's first foreign policy disaster.

The seeds of that disaster were sown in Bush's insistence that America should do as much as was necessary to prevent a man-made famine in Somalia – but no more. The absence of anything approaching a stable government, from independence in 1960 to civil war from 1991, left Somalia, a country slightly smaller than Bush's Texas, devastated. As Bush explained:

The scope of suffering there is hard to imagine. Already, over a quarter-million people . . . have died in the Somali famine . . . The people of Somalia, especially the children of Somalia, need our help. We're able to ease their suffering. We must help them live. We must give them hope. America must act . . . To the people of Somalia I promise this: We do not plan to dictate political outcomes. We respect your sovereignty and independence . . . We come to your country for one reason only, to enable the starving to be fed . . . We will not stay one day longer than is absolutely necessary.[68]

A severely compromised humanitarian aid operation was in danger of deserting the country until Bush committed US power, under the umbrella of the United Nations (Resolution 794). In a surreal scene, US Marines, part of a contingent of 26,000 American soldiers, under cover of darkness, but actually in the full glare of the world media who were waiting on the beach, crawled ashore on the night of December 4, 1992. Given its

[68] George H. W. Bush, Address to the Nation on the Situation in Somalia, December 4, 1992; https://bush41library.tamu.edu/archives/public-papers/5100.

limited if moral objective, the mission was a success. The militias that had terrorized Mogadishu, the capital, were temporarily quieted, and the starving fed. In the months that followed, the United States began to withdraw its military personnel (to about 5,000) as a new administration began to talk up the mission's aims. This mismatch was to have deadly consequences, giving Clinton his wake-up call to the world, explored in the next chapter.

CONCLUSION

Historians record that George H. W. Bush succeeded abroad but failed at home. This is not quite right. His foreign policy was not an unqualified success, just as his domestic efforts were not a complete failure. His diplomatic legacy was an ambiguous one, with which his successors struggled, his elder son and Barack Obama especially. When communist regimes fell like a pack of cards between 1989–1991, Bush was a master of caution. His diplomacy at the end of the Cold War deserves the many plaudits it has subsequently earned. Eastern Europe freed itself, the USSR collapsed, and Germany was reunited without a US shot being fired. Bush patiently nudged along these remarkable developments. He did not force their pace.

Bush was masterful in his creation of alliances. His great weakness lay in deferring to them. The most prominent example of this was the Gulf War. Never before had such an army been arrayed against a solitary aggressor. The autocrats of the Middle East all lined up with Bush. International law sanctioned his campaign. And yet the president, with both law and legitimacy on his side, refused to offend his allies and remove the regime that was to become the scourge of American foreign policy in the next century. His instinctive caution expelled Saddam from Kuwait but cemented him in Baghdad. Maintenance of a temporary alliance – assembled for reasons of utility – postponed regime change in Iraq for a disastrous twelve years. His Gulf War was a military success but a political and strategic failure.

In Yugoslavia, Bush refused to pick a side, preferring, seemingly, to wait until one side of a brutal three-sided war annihilated the other two. The cost to American prestige was significant. Bill Clinton, who invested much diplomatic capital in the enlargement of NATO, as we will see next, soon realized quieting Serbia was an essential test of the Cold War organization's post–Cold War rationale.

Bush's softly-softly treatment of Beijing in the wake of Tiananmen, while no doubt explained by a growing American acceptance that China was becoming America's banker, also called into question his commitment to democratic reform abroad. There are few presidents in US history who have prospered by ignoring the democratic claims of foreigners. The presidential greats have been defined by their democratization projects: Lincoln, Truman, FDR, and JFK. Bush's refusal to take risks in Russia, preferring the phony stability of Gorbachev over the vodka-fueled flux of Yeltsin, his appeasement of the Chinese communist party after they crushed a rebellion by students who had held aloft the Statue of Liberty, and his refusal to protect Bosnia from the Yugoslav army compromised the Bush foreign policy legacy. In all the above cases, Bush played by the rules. He observed international law and worked with the international community, as liberals demanded. He was flexible in his commitment to humanitarianism, as realists urged. It is unclear how "freer from the threat of terror, stronger in the pursuit of justice, and more secure in the quest for peace" the world was as a consequence.

2

Bill Clinton

New Think, 1993–1996

I'm tomorrow's boy, and I don't like being seen doing yesterday's business.
—*President Bill Clinton, 1993*[1]

Nothing is more difficult to handle, more doubtful of success, nor more dangerous to manage, than to put oneself at the head of introducing new orders.
—*Niccolò Machiavelli, 1532*[2]

William Jefferson Clinton was the first president since Woodrow Wilson (1913–1921) to win two presidential elections with less than 50 percent of the popular votes cast in each. He got fewer votes in 1992 than did Michael Dukakis – one of the weakest candidates ever nominated by the Democrats – four years earlier. In both victories Clinton relied on an eccentric third-party candidate to split the Republican vote. He left office, however, as one of modern America's most popular presidents. As his nation became consumed with the aftermath of 9/11 and the perceived shortcomings of George W. Bush, the president handed that emergency, nostalgia for Bill Clinton only grew. It is a cliché to refer to any president as an enigma, but Clinton was surely one. A man of great potential, perhaps the most politically attuned man to ever hold the office, but his

---

[1] In Strobe Talbott, *The Great Experiment: The Story of Ancient Empires, Modern States, and the Quest for a Global Nation* (New York: Simon & Schuster, 2008), p. 326.
[2] Niccolò Machiavelli, *The Prince*, translated by Harvey C. Mansfield (Chicago: University of Chicago Press, 1998), p. 33.

greatest test – his impeachment – was self-induced. Like Theodore Roosevelt, he felt himself worthy of a great crisis but, instead, was delivered (and claimed to have delivered) the most prosperous decade in US history and the most seemingly quiescent world for a century in which to craft it. As the first president to be born during the Cold War (in 1946) and the first to govern entirely in its aftermath (1993–2001) he expected to transcend that conflict. Instead, he found himself engaged in foreign adventures that resembled the Cold War or were the hangovers from it. "New thinking" was the style of his diplomacy; old thinking became its substance.

Clinton was a born politician, "the natural," Joe Klein called him.[3] From an early age he had the presidency in his sights. A remarkable photograph, taken in 1963, captures the sixteen-year-old Clinton shaking hands with President Kennedy at the White House. His testing ground for high office was the governorship of his native Arkansas, one of America's poorest states, a post he held from 1979 to 1981 and again, after a comeback – the *leitmotiv* of his political career – from 1983 until he became president ten years later. In 1975 he married Hillary Rodham, a partner whose own political ambitions were perhaps slower to manifest themselves but eventually became as high as her husband's. Despite – or perhaps because of –the relative obscurity of Arkansas, the couple were determined to win national power.

Bill Clinton's outlook, like that of landlocked Arkansas, was more insular than international. He had traveled very little in his pre-presidential days, especially compared to George H. W. Bush. As a Rhodes Scholar, he had studied at University College, Oxford (1968–1970), using this as a base for a series of short hops around Europe. The suspicion that he used his Oxford sojourn as a means of escaping the Vietnam draft resurfaced during the 1992 election.[4] Clinton regretted this dodge, like the later Lewinsky affair, as "a quagmire" of his own choosing.[5] Unlike so many of his predecessors, Clinton never served in the US military – though as its commander he became fond of its use,

---

[3] Joe Klein, *The Natural: The Misunderstood Presidency of Bill Clinton* (New York: Doubleday, 2002).

[4] See Michael Mandelbaum, Bill Clinton and the Draft, *New York Times*, February 12, 1992.

[5] In Nigel Hamilton, *Bill Clinton: An American Journey: Great Expectations* (London: Random House, 2003), p. 200.

deploying troops overseas on over eighty occasions.[6] His presidency was explicitly predicated on domestic renewal, not foreign adventure, though his eight years in office saw both.

At the first meeting of his National Security Council (NSC) staffers, Tony Lake, the new national security advisor, told them foreign policy was a secondary issue. A senior member of the new team, Rose Gottemoeller, sat incredulous as Lake said:

> "This is a president who wants to shine a laser light on the domestic economy. Therefore, *we are going to keep foreign policy on this side of the driveway*, on the OEOB [Old Executive Office Building side]. We are not going to trouble the president with foreign policy." And I can just remember looking around at the others and thinking, "This is never going to work."[7]

Lake's admonition reflected an early and ultimately doomed attempt to pretend that Clinton could subcontract international affairs and treat them as a branch of domestic economic policy. Clinton reinforced this by creating, in one of his earliest innovations, a National Economic Council (NEC), which he anticipated would gradually supersede and replace the NSC. It did not. Rather than supersede national security, economics became more entwined with it. The decades after the Cold War saw the rise of "intermestic" issues as the United States fought wars on such foes as drugs and terrorism, campaigns with strong *inter*national and *do*mestic dimensions.

THE FIRST CLINTON TEAM

For a while the insistence that home and abroad could be separated was maintained. Like Dwight Eisenhower in 1953, Clinton put economics at the heart of the executive bureaucracy. His campaign theme became his governing philosophy – for as long as foreigners would let it. Ike reconfigured the NSC, created by Harry Truman in 1947, to include the secretary of the treasury and the budget director.[8] Clinton, using a similar model, compelled by a similar imperative – to save money and balance the budget – created the NEC.

---

[6] Eighty-four times, according to George C. Herring, *From Colony to Superpower: U.S. Foreign Relations since 1776* (New York: Oxford University Press), p. 936.

[7] In Timothy J. Lynch, *Turf War: The Clinton Administration and Northern Ireland* (Basingstoke: Ashgate), p. 53. Emphasis added.

[8] See Melvyn P. Leffler, *For the Soul of Mankind: The United States the Soviet Union, and the Cold War* (New York: Hill and Wang, 2007), p. 113.

The primacy of economics was reflected in the creation of an economic brain trust. Bob Woodward's *The Agenda* offers a compelling description of how these officials operated in the opening months of the new administration.[9] The price paid for this was a foreign policy team of mixed competency and compatibility. The standing of the Scowcroft–Baker–Cheney troika under Bush seemed inversely proportionate to that of Lake–Christopher–Aspin under Clinton. Democratic foreign policy-makers had, after all, been out of office since the demise of the Carter administration in 1981. Unfairly or not, many of these officials labored under their connection to Carter and the Iran hostage debacle, which ended Carter's hopes of reelection. As one commentator reminds us:

When Clinton took office, there were virtually no Democrats under the age of 35 who had occupied the hallways of the State Department, Pentagon, or USAID. Democratic foreign-policy graybeards were very gray beards, and there was little in the way of a clear plan for translating their criticism of the first Bush administration's foreign-policy into a superior alternative.[10]

Tony Lake, the national security advisor, drew criticism from some officials for his obsession with grammatical precision in policy documents. Others complained that he lacked suitable political antennae to do the job well, that he was a bureaucratic infighter, Machiavellian even, but as a consequence wanted to remain hidden from public view.[11] Unlike Brent Scowcroft, Lake knew his president hardly at all – and the relationship did not blossom in power. A diplomat of long standing, Lake had a track record of steady diplomacy and independent thinking. He had resigned from Henry Kissinger's staff in 1970 in protest at the secret bombing of Cambodia. A scholar–diplomat (he has written several fascinating books on US foreign policy), Lake had a cerebral approach that often compounded Clinton's unwillingness to make decisions. Foreign policy in Clinton's first term became a series of options to be debated rather than a plan to be implemented. This rankled the ultradisciplined Colin Powell, who continued as chairman of the Joint Chiefs through Clinton's first nine months. Meetings run by Lake, he recalled, "would meander like graduate student bull sessions or think tank seminars in which many of my new colleagues had spent the last 12 years out of

[9] Bob Woodward, *The Agenda: Inside the Clinton White House* (New York: Simon & Schuster, 1994).
[10] John Norris, Four More Years ... in Exile, *Foreign Policy* [online], November 26, 2012.
[11] See Patrick J. Maney, *Bill Clinton: New Gilded Age President* (Lawrence: University Press of Kansas, 2016), p. 118.

power. I was shocked one day to hear one of Tony Lake's subordinates, who was there to take notes, argue with him in front of the rest of us ... the president was not served by the wandering deliberations he permitted."[12]

Warren Christopher, the new secretary of state, was a lawyer by training and temperament. "He *lawyers* everything to such an extreme," noted the *Washington Post*, "that there is no visible enthusiasm left when he talks about it. You get a sense that he peels so many layers off the onion that there is only a very small vegetable left at the end."[13] Clinton defended Christopher as "the most disciplined man on the planet."[14] He spent more time on airplanes than any previous holder of the post. His counsel to the young president – often long-distance – was invariably considered, the product of careful reflection, and carried weight.

This was not the case for Les Aspin, Clinton's first secretary of defense. According to historian David Halberstam, Aspin could not control the Department of Defense "because he could not control himself."[15] Aspin's feeding habits were notorious (rushed packets of potato chips with mayonnaise) and his meeting preparation questionable: hastily drafted memos on the back of envelopes. His hapless tenure lasted only ten months before he resigned. It would be unfair to blame the listless nature of US foreign policy in Clinton's opening years on Aspin. And yet there is a sense in which the ill-discipline of Clinton's initial approach was symbolized by the groping for control that marked out Aspin's brief tenancy at the Pentagon. Later in this book we will examine the control-freakery of Donald Rumsfeld in the same post as Aspin, from 2001 to 2006. With very different styles, both men were guilty of retarding US foreign policy in significant ways. Their ability to do so in both cases was compounded by poor interpersonal relations with members of their respective foreign policy teams.

GAYS IN THE MILITARY

Clinton's unsteady start was captured in his messy attempt to implement a campaign promise to legitimize the place of gay men and women in the US

---

[12] Colin Powell, *My American Journey*, p. 576.
[13] Ann Devroy and R. Jeffrey Smith, Clinton Reexamines a Foreign Policy Under Siege, *Washington Post*, October 17, 1993.
[14] Bill Clinton, *My Life* (London: Hutchinson, 2004), p. 489.
[15] David Halberstam, *War in a Time of Peace: Bush, Clinton and the General* (New York: Touchstone, 2002), p. 246.

military. For years, homosexuality had been prohibited by the Uniform Code of Military Justice. Clinton, playing to his liberal base and because he saw the issue as one of natural justice, found himself embroiled in a fight with a military establishment already skeptical of their new chief's Vietnam record and his animus toward defense spending. Clinton was ridiculed for having to take instruction on how to salute.[16] When Senator Robert Byrd reminded him that Rome's fall was precipitated by rumors of Caesar's homosexuality, Clinton pointed out that the sin did not make the Ten Commandments but that bearing false witness did, and there were plenty of liars in uniform.[17] What began as a point of principle for the new president, however, became a muddled compromise that barely appeased both sides of the issue. Personnel who happened to be gay were permitted to serve so long as they did not advertise their sexual orientation. An informal policy of "don't ask, don't tell," announced in July (and in force until Barack Obama revoked it in 2010), was not much to show for the discontent between White House and Pentagon that the issue caused. For a president about to embark on several significant military interventions, who would rely on traditional military power more than he ever imagined, it was an inauspicious start.

2/26: THE FIRST WORLD TRADE CENTER ATTACK

On February 26, 1993, in the second month of Clinton's presidency, Ramzi Yussef exploded a truck bomb underneath the north tower of the World Trade Center in New York City. With hindsight, we know that the plot, which killed eight people, was a dry run for the far more destructive attack engineered by his uncle, Khalid Sheikh Mohammed, eight years later – killing 2,753 – on September 11, 2001. Without hindsight, Yussef's barbarism appeared to be an isolated and futile strike. Clinton has been judged harshly for his failure to understand what 2/26 – a date that did not come to live in infamy – presaged. The charge is that he treated the attack as a crime rather than a declaration of war and so offered in response a criminal investigation rather than a military campaign. Instead of embarking on a martial solution to the gathering terrorist threat, the Clinton administration conducted a judicial inquiry,

---

[16] See Klein, *The Natural*, p. 71.
[17] Taylor Branch, *The Clinton Tapes: Wrestling History in the White House* (London: Simon & Schuster, 2009), p. 5.

deploying lawyers, not soldiers.[18] This argument ignores how far Clinton mimicked Reagan in his approach to terrorism. During the 1980s, attacks were regarded as law-enforcement issues. The single largest attack on US citizens after World War II and before September 11, 2001 was in Lebanon in October 1983. Two-hundred and forty-one Marines were killed in their Beirut barracks by an Islamist suicide bomber, widely speculated to have been sponsored by the Iranian and/or Syrian governments. Reagan did not declare war. He initiated an indeterminate intelligence investigation and *withdrew* American forces from the UN peacekeeping mission of which they had been a part.[19]

If Clinton copied Reagan, his counterterrorism efforts were also necessarily compromised by not having a decisive attack, of the 9/11 – or even the Beirut – kind, to offer them urgency. Given the absence of such an enabling event, is the charge that Clinton failed to take terrorism seriously valid? When Clinton learned of an Iraqi plot to assassinate George H. W. Bush in Kuwait, in June 1993, he was swift in firing Tomahawk missiles at targets in Baghdad. Such action, though, was seen by his detractors as half-hearted and unserious. Clinton was mocked for killing unfortunate cleaning staff; the strikes had happened in the middle of the night.[20] His critics apportion him much blame for failing to connect the dots of Islamist terrorism in the years before 2001. But his successor was hardly any more vociferous in his counterterrorism efforts during his first nine months in office. George W. Bush did not prioritize the fight against terrorism of global reach until after 9/11. Why, then, should we have expected Clinton to so do? Also, the climate in which counterterrorism was constructed in the Clinton years made an ad hoc approach seem sensible. The Clinton Doctrine, being worked out as the Twin Towers wobbled but did not fall in February 1993, served to relegate rather than promote fears of terrorism.

THE CLINTON DOCTRINE

Clinton's world view depended on a key assumption: that international order after the Cold War was decisively shaped by the politico-economic

[18] See Robert Patterson, *Dereliction of Duty: The Eyewitness Account of How President Bill Clinton Compromised America's Long-Term National Security* (Washington, DC: Regnery, 2003).

[19] See James D. Boys, *Clinton's War on Terror: Redefining U.S. Security Strategy, 1993–2001* (Boulder, CO: Lynne Rienner, 2018).

[20] See Henriksen, *Cycles in U.S. Foreign Policy*, p. 147.

system the United States had spent much of that conflict advancing. Francis Fukuyama argued in 1992 that in the absence of a significant alternative to liberal democracy, America found itself the predominant state at "the end of history." Its example was now universal and inevitable. It had no viable challenger. Terrorists, especially those claiming a Koranic inspiration, argued Fukuyama, were doomed to failure. Because political Islam was markedly inferior to American capitalism in its capacity to deliver material prosperity, it followed that those determined to realize a caliphate by terrorism would never achieve it.

The Clinton Doctrine, which embraced the logic of the end-of-history thesis, necessarily and rationally treated terrorism as a second-tier issue. Unlike communism in the Cold War, terrorism after it did not pose a clear and present danger to the United States. When terrorists struck, as they did with varying degrees of ferocity in the 1990s, Clinton officials saw a flickering candle rather than a gathering storm. "Democratic enlargement" and trade, they assumed, would gradually remove the sources of grievance on which terrorism fed. Until then, policing the terrorist threat was a necessary but hardly an all-consuming objective of US foreign policy.

The Clinton Doctrine, a hasty attempt to find foreign policy coherence in an era when it was elusive and potentially unnecessary, extended not much further than assertions that history was moving in an American direction and that US foreign policy should reflect this. Enlargement, said Gaddis Smith, was "banality on stilts."[21] America should tweak, prod, and promote democracy abroad to help speed up what was inevitable. Again, consistent with Clinton's domestic agenda, the doctrine had a strong economic flavor. Its enunciation can be traced to three speeches – by Clinton, Lake, and Albright – in September 1993. It was further refined into the White House's National Security Strategy of Engagement and Enlargement in July 1994.[22]

Lake's speech at Johns Hopkins University was an effort to replace containment – the label for the US Cold War strategy – with enlargement – the concept that would capture the essence of its post–Cold War strategy. Clinton's foreign policy advisors had run a "Kennan sweepstakes" in the early months of the new administration, betting on who could invent a concept that would express the simplicity of US objectives in the same way George Kennan and Harry Truman had done at the Cold War's

[21] In Devroy and Smith, Clinton Re-examines a Foreign Policy Under Siege, A1.
[22] See http://nssarchive.us/NSSR/1994.pdf.

beginning. The 90-year-old Kennan himself was even roped into the discussion, and remained skeptical of the attempt to render foreign policy a "bumper sticker."[23] Lake began by outlining the essential problem. Somehow America had to move beyond the containment of something bad to the expansion of something good. Instead of containing "the creeping expansion of that big, red blob," the United States should now promote "the enlargement of the blue areas of market democracies."[24]

That task was as attractive to contemplate as it was hard to achieve. Expanding the American model, if model it was, free from the fear of a communist counterresponse, imbued American foreign policy with a bracing optimism. What enlargement robbed it of was any precise way of measuring success. The contraction of territory held by communists during the Cold War – in Korea, Latin America, and Afghanistan – was easy to observe even if was costly to attain. What constituted a success for the United States after the Cold War was less clear. Through Clinton's first term, the Doctrine found much expression though little actual success. Events in Russia, Somalia, Haiti, Mexico, and the Balkans posed a variety of tests, few anticipated by the Clinton Doctrine. When troubles came, as they did in his first term, they came not single spies but in battalions.

RUSSIA AND THE LIMITS OF DEMOCRACY PROMOTION

Clinton set great store in his nurturing of Russian liberty. Not unlike Harry Truman's attitude toward Japan at the end of World War II, which set America's adversary on the path to a remarkable economic and political transformation, Clinton believed Russia could become the great success story of the post–Cold War era. The United States, ever magnanimous in victory, would help the vanquished remake themselves in an American image.

Russia did not, we now know, follow a Japanese trajectory. A few Russians certainly got very rich very quickly, but autocracy (euphemistically described as "one-party democracy") returned. Russia, as one commentator observed, "went from one ghastly, indefensible tyranny to a horrible Hobbesian chaos in three or four years."[25] What did Clinton get

---

[23] See John Lewis Gaddis, *George F. Kennan: An American Life* (New York: Penguin Press, 2011), p. 680.

[24] Address at the School of Advanced International Studies, Johns Hopkins University, Washington, DC, September 21, 1993.

[25] In Rachel Bailes, An interview with Peter Hitchens, *Spectator*, December 5, 2015.

wrong? Part of the explanation for his failure to deliver on his promise to aid Russia's transition from communism to liberal democracy was a misplaced faith in the efficacy of the free market. Creating any number of acronyms for trade organizations – NAFTA (the North American Free Trade Agreement) in 1994; the WTO (World Trade Organization) in 1995; and the G7 (Group of Seven nations) in 1997 – could not disguise the highly uneven path economic liberalization would take after the Cold War. Inviting states to join trade compacts did not necessarily alter their national characters or calculations of their geostrategic interests. As Tony Lake conceded, "We had too much faith in [economic] 'shock therapy,' and not enough concern for its social consequences."[26] Strobe Talbott, Clinton's Russia hand, said what Russians needed was "less shock and more therapy."[27]

The connection between Clinton's failure and Putin's rise was causal, argued Angus Roxburgh. "The West's handling of post-Soviet Russia has been just about as insensitive as it could have been."[28] The Russian government of Boris Yeltsin – a leader Clinton coddled – was keen on wealth, less so on the open society and democratic accountability that in the West went hand in hand with it. Clinton's pouring of US dollars into the Russian economy – some $24 billion was pledged in 1993 – contributed to a gangster capitalism. A black market, uncomfortably tolerated by the communists, suddenly found itself lauded as the engine of wealth creation. Oligarchs became ubiquitous, ruthlessly exploiting the oil and gas reserves under the Russian soil. "Everything the Communists told us about communism was a complete and utter lie," ran a Muscovite aphorism. "Unfortunately, everything the Communists told us about capitalism turned out to be true."[29] Democracy was condemned as *dermokratiya* ("shitocracy"). Vladimir Putin, elected in 2000, presented himself as the solution to this upheaval, moving the state from an oligarchic free-for-all to a version of autocratic capitalism – some distance from what Bill Clinton had imagined in 1993 (though what he predicted of Putin in 2000).[30]

[26] Anthony Lake, *6 Nightmares: Real Threats in a Dangerous World and How America Can Meet Them* (Boston: Little, Brown, 2000), p. 193.

[27] In Talbott, *Russia Hand* (New York: Random House, 2002), p. 106.

[28] Angus Roxburgh, *Strongman: Vladimir Putin and the Struggle for Russia* (New York: I. B. Tauris, 2012), p. 7.

[29] In Lake, *6 Nightmares*, pp. 192–193.

[30] See Roxburgh, *Strongman*, p. 6, and Karen Dawisha, *Putin's Kleptocracy: Who Owns Russia?* (New York: Simon & Schuster, 2014).

Clinton's Russia policy mimicked that of Richard Nixon: engagement with Moscow became an end in itself; the extent to which this engagement moved Russia toward liberal democracy mattered less. At Nixon's funeral in April 1994, Clinton paid tribute to the "wise counsel" on Russia the 38th president had offered him. Nixon's détente with the Soviet Union in the early 1970s had attempted to replace the ideological antagonism of the early Cold War with a cooler realism. "Our objective," wrote Henry Kissinger, its architect, "was to purge our foreign policy of all sentimentality."[31] Donald Trump was to make a similar attempt in 2017. But Clinton was nothing if not sentimental, especially when it came to humoring Boris Yeltsin. "A candidate for tough love," is how Clinton described the Russian leader.[32] His investment – political, financial, and emotional – in Yeltsin's capacity to deliver has entered diplomatic folklore.

Yeltsin was a vodka alcoholic. He was once so inebriated on a flight from Moscow that he was unable to greet the Irish prime minster at Dublin airport. During his first official overnight stay at the White House (in 1995), a privilege reserved to very few foreign leaders, the Russia leader was discovered wandering around in his underpants at 3 AM demanding, "Pizza! Pizza!"[33] "Who knows," asked Robert Cottrell sarcastically, "what Russia might be like now if Yeltsin had been left to stagger on into the night, rather than returned to his bedroom in Blair House? At that point in Russia's transition everything was still possible. In the four remaining years of Yeltsin's miserable reign the possibilities drained away, until only Putin was left."[34]

Clinton, the stepson of an alcoholic, was prepared to appease such behavior on the understanding that Yeltsin represented the best of a rather limited set of alternative leadership options. That faith was ultimately misplaced. Rather than beginning a line of Russia democrats, the idiosyncrasies of the Yeltsin years led Russia back into the more reliable autocracy of Vladimir Putin – hardly a victory for Clinton's democratic enlargement. In the interim, Clinton's interventions against Serbia, Russia's traditional ally – first in Bosnia in 1994 and again in Kosovo in 1999 – brought the relationship to new lows.

---

[31] In Gaddis, *Strategies of Containment*, p. 342.   [32] In Talbott, *Russia Hand*, p. 45.
[33] In Talbott, *Russia Hand*, p. 135.
[34] Robert Cottrell, Russia, NATO, Trump: The Shadow World, *New York Review of Books* 63, 20 (December 22, 2016).

SOMALIA: CLINTON'S BAY OF PIGS

Despite disappointment with progress in Russia, that state at least provided a testing ground for Clinton's democratic enlargement strategy. The Kremlin ruled a corrupt but functioning polity with a civil society that the citizens of Somalia could only dream about. Their lot was to inhabit not a political space bending toward democracy but a mere "geographical expression."[35] Inheriting the intervention from his predecessor, Clinton was slow to claim ownership of the Somalia problem. According to a close aide, he "took his eye off the ball."[36] What had begun as a limited humanitarian intervention began to transmogrify. Madeleine Albright, his ambassador to the United Nations (a post Clinton had upgraded to full cabinet status), applauded the conditions the US military force had crafted, sufficient, she claimed, "for the restoration of an entire country" under United Nations stewardship. The United Nations, however, was unable to quiet clan violence, concentrated in Mogadishu. The task fell to US Army Rangers. Now, in fall 1993, those Rangers were much fewer in number, and warring clans were keener to assert dominion.

Between his inauguration in January and the loss of eighteen US soldiers in a Mogadishu gun battle on October 3, President Clinton had not held a single foreign policy principals' meeting on the situation in the country – an omission repeated in the case of Rwanda early the next year. He had eighteen such meetings with his advisors on Bosnia and four on Haiti in the same period. Nancy Soderberg, the NSC staff director, later admitted that he had relied too much on "career officials" to wind down the Somali action. "He was not as engaged as he should be … Somalia was his wake-up call."[37] It was, she later wrote, "Clinton's Bay of Pigs."[38]

A newly elected President Kennedy had endured a similar baptism by fire in Cuba. Acting on a plan inherited from the Eisenhower administration, Kennedy authorized a covert invasion of Cuba by CIA-trained Cuban exiles. Assured by his military advisors that the communist regime of Fidel Castro would quickly collapse, the new president refused to

---

[35] Robert I. Rotberg, *When States Fail: Causes and Consequences* (Princeton, NJ: Princeton University Press, 2004), p. 9.
[36] Author interview with Nancy Soderberg, February 20, 2002.
[37] In Lynch, *Turf War*, p. 39.
[38] See Nancy Soderberg, *The Superpower Myth: The Use and Misuse of American Might* (Hoboken, NJ: John Wiley and Sons, 2005), pp. 37–40.

provide US air cover when the rebels found themselves under fire on the landing beach at the Bay of Pigs. Within hours, they had been routed. Trumbell Higgins, a historian of the episode, called it the "perfect failure."[39]

The analogy between Cuba 1961 and Somalia 1993 is not perfect, but each debacle served to convince the young president that deference to "expert" advice – military and diplomatic – should be a highly rationed commodity. Optimistic assumptions about the efficacy of military force made JFK highly skeptical of such arguments during the Cuban Missile Crisis. Clinton, while he went on to use troops on many different occasions, took two important lessons from Somalia. First, military advice is not necessarily superior. Military actions are highly subject to the contingencies of the theater in which they take place. Second, faith in the capacity of the United Nations to keep peace without significant US involvement was misplaced. Thereafter, the United States acted in support of the United Nations or acted without it. A pattern that had become established in the Cold War – of using the United Nations hardly at all – continued after Somalia. Ensuing military interventions, before and after 9/11, as we will see later, either commenced without UN approval (as in Kosovo under Clinton and in Iraq under Bush) or went beyond the objective mandated by the United Nations (such as Obama's role in regime change in Libya).

HAITI

If Somalia was a debacle, forcing the US military to turn tail and quit the country soon after the Black Hawk Down incident, it was at least a long way from home and could, in part, be blamed on UN failings. Haiti, less than 700 miles from the Florida coast, was uncomfortably close. One of the world's poorest states, Haiti has been subjected to alternating periods of instability and brutality throughout its history. The United States had occupied the former French colony from 1915 to 1934, but not so long that American habits of democracy, or even basic infrastructure, physical and institutional, could take root. In 1991, a coup led by General Raoul Cedras removed Jean-Bertrand Aristide, the first democratically elected president in the country's history. The repression that followed was disapproved of in Washington. United Nations sanctions were passed.

---

[39] Trumbell Higgins, *The Perfect Failure: Eisenhower, Kennedy, and the CIA at the Bay of Pigs* (New York: W. W. Norton, 1987).

As in the former Yugoslavia, as we will see, sanctions made an already desperate situation worse. Haitians, the hemisphere's poorest people, were rendered poorer still. Thousands took to the Caribbean Sea in rickety boats and truck tire inner tubes with the aim of reaching the United States. Repression inside Haiti and sanctions from the outside combined to produce a humanitarian disaster.

Clinton confronted a number of pressures as a result. The most graphic was the refugee crisis. For how long could Americans watch on their TVs desperate boat people without their government acting to stem the flow? The Congressional Black Caucus was especially vocal in persuading Clinton to contemplate the restoration of democracy by force. On October 11, 1993, barely a week after the firefight in Mogadishu, the USS *Harlan County* sailed into Port-au-Prince. To greets its American and Canadian troops at the dockside was a mob of Cedras supporters. Waiving machetes and pitchforks, they chanted "Somalia! Somalia!"[40] Fearing a bloodbath, the *Harlan County* was ordered to turn around. Tony Lake later described the affair as "a total fuckup."[41] American unipolarity was exposed as a sham; it did not even hold dominion in its own hemisphere. Unchecked by the fear of a Soviet counterresponse, the United States was seemingly incapable of projecting even limited military power into its own backyard. Osama bin Laden was watching all this from Somalia, plotting its exploitation. His conception of the United States as a paper tiger, as a weak horse, was rendered plausible.[42] In Baghdad, Saddam's resolve to dig in and defy US pressure was strengthened – after all, his assassination attempt on former President Bush had provoked only a limited military response from President Clinton. If American power was resisted, it would retreat.

Even without the benefit of post–9/11 hindsight, this initial American refusal to countenance bloodshed in defense of democratic enlargement called into question the central tenets of Clinton's doctrine. If a few protestors could derail the first military intervention of his presidency, what message did that send to more entrenched and distant opponents? Clinton made amends – but it took almost a year. On September 19, 1994, having suffered the indignity of a "sanctimonious" and "freelancing" Jimmy Carter (adjectives chosen by members of Clinton's team) brokering a deal with the Haitian junta (as the former president had also

---

[40] Halberstam, *War in a Time of Peace*, p. 271.   [41] In Klein, *The Natural*, p. 73.
[42] See Lawrence Wright, *The Looming Tower: al Qaeda's Road to 9/11* (London: Penguin, 2007), pp. 187–188.

done to calm a nuclear standoff with North Korea in June), Clinton ordered what has been called an "immaculate invasion" of Haiti.[43] Some 22,000 US troops, with contributions from twenty-eight other nations, confident they would not be targeted, invaded "for the express purpose of protecting themselves."[44] Democracy was restored. Saddam Hussein was hardly cowed by the example. The next month he deployed some 80,000 troops to the Kuwaiti border. Clinton, fearing a second invasion of the tiny kingdom, countered with 50,000 of his own. This recurrent cat-and-mouse game became basic to US Iraq policy for the next ten years.

RWANDAN GENOCIDE

The American timidity exposed in these episodes was magnified in Rwanda. In April 1994, the small East African state (about the size of Maryland) endured "the fastest, most efficient killing spree of the twentieth century."[45] Its speed caught the world by surprise. In May, 2,500 journalists descended on South Africa to celebrate the formal end to white rule; a mere 15 (at most) were in Rwanda during the height of the killing (April–June).[46] The Congressional Black Caucus, so vocal over Haiti, was strangely mute over Rwanda.[47] Within a matter of weeks, members of the Hutu majority, armed largely with machetes, killed some 800,000 of the Tutsi minority (or about 20 percent of Rwanda's population). The United Nations managed to extricate most foreigners from the scene, but could do little to slow the rapidity of the killing.[48] The United States, chastened by the debacles of Somalia and Haiti – which even in combination hardly approached the horrors of Rwanda – chose to turn away. It was a sin of omission for which Bill Clinton later apologized. On weaker humanitarian grounds, his successors chose to use military force in Afghanistan, Iraq, Libya, Syria, and Uganda. The speed of killing in Rwanda was greater than in all these conflicts.

[43] See Bob Shacochis, *The Immaculate Invasion* (New York: Grove Press, 1999), and Chollet and Goldgeier, *America between the Wars*, p. 94.
[44] Shacochis, *Immaculate Invasion*, p. 254.
[45] Samantha Power, Bystanders to Genocide, *Atlantic Monthly* (September 2001), p. 84.
[46] See Samantha Power, *"A Problem from Hell": America and the Age of Genocide* (New York: Basic Books, 2002), p. 375.
[47] Power makes this pointed observation in *A Problem from Hell*, p. 376.
[48] Searing accounts of the genocide include Philip Gourevitch, *We Wish to Inform You That Tomorrow We Will Be Killed with Our Families: Stories from Rwanda* (New York: Picador, 1998); and Roméo Dallaire, *Shake Hands with the Devil: the Failure of Humanity in Rwanda* (New York: Carroll and Graff, 2004).

That America avoided such a conflict in 1994 served to reconfirm a narrative held by its foes: the United States had not escaped its Vietnam syndrome. It would prefer the death of myriad men and women in the developing world over the costs to American blood and treasure of saving them. It had no stomach for war, let alone for the long occupations that inevitably follow. This was an interpretation of US character not without credibility. Clinton had talked tough on North Korean nuclear proliferation, for example, but ultimately, in the summer of 1994 chose to buy Pyongyang's cooperation with technological and economic assistance – much as Kennedy had done with Moscow to resolve the Cuban Missile Crisis.[49] Those plotting to reduce US global power could point to far more examples of underkill than overkill. As Osama bin Laden observed about America after Somalia: "[You] left the area carrying disappointment, humiliation, defeat, and your dead with you."[50] He had justifiable confidence, thereafter, that the United States would quit the Middle East as it had Africa, that American resolve could and should be tested because it would be found wanting.

REPUBLICAN MIDTERM GAINS

By the time of the November 1994 midterm elections, Bill Clinton's foreign policy was failing. Victory in the Cold War had, within a matter of two years, dissipated into a series of botched military campaigns, as in Haiti and Somalia; failed economic reconstructions, as in Russia; and an avoidance of moral tests, as in Rwanda and North Korea. Though this does not account exclusively for the drubbing his party received in November, it does help establish the diplomatic context Clinton occupied in 1995–1997, years that many assumed would be his last in the White House.

The wave that swept Republicans back into control of both houses of Congress for the first time since 1947 was only partially about foreign policy. Of ten specific legislative pledges made by GOP candidates (their "Contract with America"), only one concerned national security.[51] What losing Congress presaged, it seemed certain at the time, was the slow

---

[49] In 1962, a public pledge not to invade Cuba and a secret pledge to withdraw US missiles from Turkey appeased Soviet demands.
[50] In the 9/11 Commission Report, p. 48.
[51] See 141 Cong. Rec. H1747 – The National Security Restoration Act in *Congressional Record* 141, 29 (February 14, 1995).

death of any sort of foreign policy coherency on Clinton's part; he would lack the power at home to be innovative abroad. This is not how things transpired. In several respects, in terms of both domestic and foreign policy, losing Congress gave the president a foil denied to him when his own party controlled Capitol Hill. Failure, after 1994, could now be blamed on "partisan" opponents, politicians animated by electoral expediency rather than by the national interest. It was a tactic Clinton mined ruthlessly as he set about remaking his foreign policy. His own party had hardly been helpful in supporting his agenda abroad – only 102 House Democrats had voted in favor of the North American Free Trade Agreement (NAFTA) a year earlier – so all the better to have avowed opponents to define one's statesmanship against. Clinton became blessed with adversaries disabled by their loathing of him – a blessing Donald Trump was later to also prosper by.

This battle with a GOP-led Congress put Clinton in good company. Despite losing Capitol Hill in 1947 and enduring the profound vilification of his opponents in both parties, Harry Truman laid the foundation for US Cold War strategy for the next four decades. His victory in the 1948 presidential election, not unlike Clinton's in 1996, was all the sweeter, given the political obituaries being written after the midterms. After 1994, Clinton cemented his reputation as "the comeback kid."

NAFTA AND THE MEXICAN BAILOUT

Clinton was able to shift the foreign policy debate onto terrain more to his liking soon after the midterm defeat. Somalia, Haiti, and Rwanda showed a president uneasy with the use of military force; the dynamics of hemi-spheric trade were more his speed. Clinton was at heart an economic determinist. Give people an economic stake in society, he reasoned, and you help make them free. Freedom, in turn, would make allies of former rivals. Clinton's first foreign policy speech, in February 1993, was about the North American Free Trade Agreement. He would use NAFTA throughout his term in office to forge his "globalization presidency." In January 1995, this economic faith was tested. His decision to bail out the Mexican peso was, according to the journalist Thomas Friedman, "the least popular, least understood, but most important foreign policy decision of the Clinton presidency." Clinton conceded, "He might have been right."[52]

[52] In Clinton, *My Life*, p. 645.

Mexico was America's third-largest trading partner. Despite this, the country has, throughout its history, failed to build the legal and economic infrastructure necessary to maintain investor confidence. A convenient solution was to peg the Mexican peso to the US dollar – much as Greece used the euro currency to create a façade of economic strength in the 2000s – so banks would continue to lend to the Mexican government. The rot set in when civil unrest, including the assassination of a presidential candidate, caused investors to flee. Borrowing money became prohibitively expensive; banks did not believe loans would be repaid. To meet the hiked interest payments, Mexico was forced to abandon parity with the dollar and devalue its currency, an act of fiscal desperation (denied to Greece while it remained in the euro zone), which, in turn, caused more investors to abandon it. The possible collapse of a neighbor so woven into the fabric of the US economy – a situation NAFTA had intensified, much as Greek fiscal collapse in 2012 was both caused by and intensified by the European Union – was likely to stymie America's recovery from the Bush recession. Plus, the stream of Mexican refugees fleeing economic collapse would make the exodus from Haiti seem trivial.

Just as Germany's bailing out of Athens after 2011 was unpopular with Germans, so too was Clinton's Mexican bailout with Americans; some 80 percent were opposed. "If this fails," warned Sandy Berger, Clinton's new national security advisor, "you'll be accused of pissing millions of dollars down a Mexican rathole."[53] If persuading the American public were not hard enough, Clinton faced having to convince a now Republican-controlled Congress to release the funds; the Mexican crisis inconveniently coincided with the swearing in of the 104th Congress.

The difference between the European Union and NAFTA cases is instructive. Transnationalism, regionalism, and globalization have become fashionable areas of academic study, each variously contending that the state is withering away. In its place has arisen a supposedly more mature architecture of international law and governance where states pool their sovereignty. Both the European Union and NAFTA have been used as examples of this emerging world order. However, this reading of post–Cold War history exaggerates the decline of the nation state and is especially faulty in its understanding of the United States and its reasons for creating a trade area with its two neighbors. Clinton did not envisage NAFTA as the first step in the creation of a new nation, as French and

---

[53] In Derek Chollet and James Goldgeier, *America between the Wars*, p. 165.

German presidents did the European Union. Similarly, war was hardly likely among the nations of North America in the absence of the agreement, whereas avoiding war was a repeated rationale for the deepening of European integration.[54] Rather, NAFTA was a means to enhance US economic interests – not to dilute Washington's sovereignty and make it politically indistinguishable from Ottawa and Mexico City. Indeed, Donald Trump, as we shall see, was to subsequently revise the agreement in 2018, to make it compatible with his own version of economic nationalism.[55]

During the Cold War, the United States worked with international institutions – founding the key ones, such as the United Nations, NATO, and GATT (the General Agreement on Tariffs and Trade) – but was never subject to their authority in a legally binding sense. If membership enhanced national interests, presidents and Congress would abide by their terms. If such "international law" were considered detrimental to those interests, then national law was supreme. This reasoning has remained basic to how US leaders navigate the complex tapestry of international regimes – signing up to some, like NAFTA, and refusing to ratify or even vote on the ratification of others, like the Kyoto Protocol and the International Criminal Court. And largely this has worked. The United States went from a reluctant international player in the 1910s and 1920s to the most powerful state in world history a generation later. It did so without reforming its Constitution or parceling out its competences to foreign institutions. Americans have prospered because of their constitutionalism. Their nationalism is equated with and contributed to global power and rising prosperity. European nationalisms, alternatively, between 1914 and 1945, brought the continent to the brink of destruction.

Clinton's marriage to NAFTA was not shotgun, and the Mexican bailout he reasoned it demanded was entirely synchronous with American statecraft in the Cold War. Clinton was able to engineer a rescue package totaling some $50 billion. Nearly half of this was pledged by the International Monetary Fund. Unable to convince Republicans to authorize US funds, Clinton simply circumvented them. In a canny, if brazen, act of executive fiat, he tapped the Exchange Stabilization Fund for $20 billion. This emergency reserve, designed in the 1930s, could be spent without

---

[54] See Angela Merkel's speech to the German parliament, October 26, 2011, and Emmanuel Macron's speech in Paris, November 11, 2018.
[55] See Stewart Patrick, *The Sovereignty Wars: Reconciling America with the World* (Washington, DC: Brookings Institution, 2018).

prior Congressional approval. Mexico and its peso stabilized through 1995. Clinton had won his first victory over his GOP opponents. Intimations of a braver, more politically savvy foreign policy were evident. Newt Gingrich, the new Republican speaker of the House, had called the peso "the first crisis of the twenty-first century." And yet it was President Clinton, as Chollet and Goldgeier observe pointedly, who fixed it "well before the end of the twentieth."[56]

THE BALKANS AND NATO CREDIBILITY

Two further foreign policy breakthroughs followed the Mexican bailout. In Northern Ireland, despite setbacks, Clinton's diplomacy was an important ingredient in making a peace process work. In the Balkans, his use of US troops made Bosnia viable and ultimately led to the demise of its chief tormentor, Slobodan Milošević, after the Kosovo War in 1999. Because a Muslim state was viewed as unnatural in Europe, some European Union leaders were content to see Bosnia expunged from the map. (A similar bias against Turkey provides one explanation why its application for European Union membership is recurrently denied.) Clinton was never comfortable with this reasoning.[57] His diplomacy, slow to form, made an independent Bosnian state possible, and later, that of Kosovo too.

Two factors made President Clinton reluctant to act in the former Yugoslavia. First, he had inherited a decidedly noninterventionist position from George H. W. Bush. The United States had no dog in the fight. Of what interest was the victory of one ethnic nationalism over another in southeastern Europe? This indifference was not transformed by Clinton's election, despite some limited campaign rhetoric in 1992 indicting it. Second, he read *Balkan Ghosts* by Robert Kaplan. This 1993 book argued that the enmities of the Balkan peoples were so deep, no amount of US action could mend them.[58] The sheer human plight, however, was difficult to ignore. The siege of Sarajevo was intense as Clinton was sworn in. The grim reality of life under Serb bombardment was punctuated by especially gratuitous attacks – on town squares and markets, libraries and hospitals. Consistent with how Clinton had seen the international

---

[56] Chollet and Goldgeier, *America between the Wars*, p. 167.
[57] See Clinton, *My Life*, p. 513.
[58] Robert D. Kaplan, *Balkan Ghosts: A Journey through History* (New York: St. Martin's Press, 1993).

community malfunction in Somalia and Rwanda, in Bosnia the United Nations had made the situation worse through its supposed egalitarianism. The United Nations Security Council in September 1991 had imposed an arms embargo on all sides. Serbs, who controlled over 90 percent of Yugoslavian army hardware, had their superiority enshrined in international law. The Bosnians lacked all protection and were denied the legal means to find any.

One of Clinton's greatest regrets was his failure to lift the UN arms embargo soon after he came to office – he did not do so until 1995.[59] It offended natural justice, he said. John Major, the British prime minister, was sanguine; Serb victory would at least end the war. This cynical realism represented, according to historian Brendan Simms, Britain's "unfinest hour."[60] More predictably, perhaps, the Russian government argued for the maintenance of the embargo, masking its defense of Serbia with the argument that more arms meant more war. America's closest Cold War ally and its greatest Cold War opponent were thus united in resisting international intervention, beyond a token UN force.

Given these constraints, getting involved was all the more remarkable. Clinton had inherited a Western policy toward Bosnia that was "in complete disarray."[61] Lawrence Freedman describes the failures of the wider international community in telling terms:

Since June 1991, the Security Council has adopted more than 60 resolutions and experimented with almost every available form of coercion short of war in an attempt to influence Serbia and protect its victims. Diplomatic isolation, high-level conferences and prominent mediators, expulsion from multilateral organizations, loss of sporting and cultural links, arms embargoes, economic embargoes (ranging from oil products to all trade), naval blockade, air-exclusion zones, air and land humanitarian relief corridors, control of artillery pieces, ceasefire lines, traditional peacekeeping operations, preventive deployments, the establishment of "safe areas" – all have been tried.[62]

The vacillations contributed to "Europe's worst massacre since World War II."[63] In Srebrenica, in July 1995, over 7,000 Muslim men and boys

[59] See Branch, *Clinton Tapes*, p. 9.
[60] Brendan Simms, *Unfinest Hour: Britain and the Destruction of Bosnia* (London: Allen Lane, 2001).
[61] Ivo H. Daalder, *Getting to Dayton: The Making of America's Bosnia Policy* (Washington, DC: Brookings, 2000), p. 5.
[62] Lawrence Freedman, Why the West Failed, *Foreign Policy* 97 (Winter 1994/95): 53–69.
[63] See David Rohde, *Endgame: The Betrayal and Fall of Srebrenica, Europe's Worst Massacre since World War II* (Boulder, CO: Westview Press, 1998).

were murdered by Bosnian Serbs. The enclave within Serb-dominated territory had been designated a UN "safe area" the previous April. Instead of assuring safety, the 750-strong UN contingent – mainly Canadian and Dutch – symbolized the ambivalence of a half-hearted international relief effort. Lacking a clear mandate to fight Serb forces, the UN peacekeepers found themselves witness to the ethnic cleansing of the town, as coaches packed with Muslims were driven past them. The vehicles' occupants were never to be seen again. "Bosnian Serbs," said Clinton, "had made a mockery of the UN."[64]

The massacre was a tipping point in Clinton's approach to the war. European leaders had recurrently and – for Clinton and his team – frustratingly hesitated over whether to allow the sustained air-bombing of Serbian positions by NATO forces.[65] Such hesitation was compounded by the UN secretary general, Boutros Boutros-Ghali, who wanted a seemingly impossible unanimity on the Security Council before agreeing to air strikes. After Srebrenica, however, American hawks had the upper hand. Richard Holbrooke, chief among them, used a Cold War analogy in describing American perceptions. In 1954, the French had capitulated to Vietnamese communists at Dien Bien Phu. The ensuing division of Vietnam into a communist North and noncommunist South shifted President Eisenhower's assessment of what was at stake. If the United States toed the French line and acquiesced in further Western withdrawal from the theater and the abandonment of the South, soon Southeast Asia would follow China and North Korea and go communist. The credibility of the American Cold War project would be tested in tiny Vietnam, reasoned Eisenhower and his successors. In Bosnia, according to Holbrooke, Clinton had faced his "Dien Bien Goražde."[66] The Muslim enclave of Goražde would be next in line, after Srebrenica, to fall to the Serbs unless firmer resistance, ignoring European qualms, was offered.

Eisenhower had referred to the French after their capitulation in 1954 as "a hopeless, helpless mass of protoplasm." (George W. Bush later adapted the insult, bemoaning that "the French are always there when they need you."[67]) Clinton was more diplomatic in 1995 but believed, like Ike, that unless he acted his European counterparts would

---

[64] Clinton, *My Life*, p. 666.
[65] See Warren Christopher, *Chances of a Lifetime: A Memoir* (New York: Scribner, 2001), p. 254.
[66] In Daalder, *Getting to Dayton*, p. 72.
[67] Eisenhower in Fredrik Logevall, *The Origins of the Vietnam War* (London: Longman, 2001), p. 21; Bush in *Daily Telegraph*, January 20, 2010.

not. Goražde would be no repeat of Srebrenica, said Clinton, but, rather, "a line in the sand ... from then on, NATO would be much more assertive."[68] Using a similar logic as presidents Johnson and Nixon in Vietnam, Clinton determined that "diplomacy could not succeed until the Serbs had sustained some serious losses on the ground."[69]

NATO air strikes against Serbian positions had the desired effect. By November, each party to the conflict recognized that US intervention had changed fundamentally what they could achieve by fighting. In the "charming small Ohio city" of Dayton, Clinton essentially locked in the former Yugoslavia's warring leaders until a peace accord was signed.[70] It took almost three weeks (during which time Clinton began a series of sexual encounters with a young White House intern that was to have significant consequences in his second term). Ohioans, as Holbrooke records, embraced their tenure as the "temporary center of international peace."[71] Warren Christopher, whose patience and diligence were key to the progress of the negotiations, was given a standing ovation in a local restaurant. The Dayton Accords were highly imperfect but did forge a viable peace.

While Clinton saw Serb aggression as morally beyond the pale, this alone is not enough to explain his decision to use military force in southeastern Europe. After all, Hutu attacks on Tutsis in Rwanda represented an even greater scale of inhumanity than the three-sided Balkans War and yet elicited barely a White House discussion. Bosnia, however, implicated the enlargement of NATO – a key plank of Clinton's foreign policy – and thus US intervention there is explicable only when we consider the shadow cast by that Cold War alliance. The idea of enlargement had been planted by two men who had spent years fighting against communism. In an Oval Office meeting in April 1993, Lech Wałęsa and Václav Havel, the respective presidents of newly postcommunist Poland and the Czech Republic, urged Clinton to complete what his predecessors had started and expand NATO eastward into the Soviet Union's former colonies.[72]

The idea stuck. These two nations, along with Hungary, joined the alliance in 1999. In the interim, Clinton necessarily came to put great

---

[68] Clinton, *My Life*, p. 666; and Christopher, *Chances of a Lifetime*, p. 255.

[69] Clinton, *My Life*, p. 667.

[70] The description of Dayton is offered by Holbrooke, *To End a War* (New York: Random House, 1998), p. 234.

[71] Holbrooke, *To End a War*, p. 234.   [72] See Goldgeier, *Not Whether but When*, p. 20.

store in the credibility of NATO. Its failure to intervene decisively in the Balkans – the first time NATO had ever used military force in its history – would have called into question the rationale for its expansion. Clinton's war against Serbia in 1995 and again in 1999 was a test of NATO's credibility – and, by implication, of Clinton's statesmanship – more than simply a reaction to Serb excess. The alliance could hardly expand into Eastern Europe when southern Europeans were still killing each other. What authority would the enlarged alliance have if it could not force a peace? If Bosnians could not be defended, of what value would a declaration of common defense be for the Czechs, Poles, and Hungarians? The entire credibility of the enlargement strategy rested on intervening effectively.[73] Attacking Christian Serbs in defense of ethnic Muslims, however, won Clinton few points with Islamist militants.

As was soon to be made clear, Clinton's reward for saving Bosnia (and later freeing Kosovo) was not Islamist approbation, but the plotting and planning of 9/11, which, had preparations gone more smoothly, as the terrorists intended, would have occurred before he had left office. Ronald Reagan initiated a similar blowback in Afghanistan in the 1980s, if for different reasons. The sectarian character of those being supported mattered less than the geostrategic aims that that support advanced. For Clinton, supporting the cause of the Bosnian Muslims was not exclusively moral. By attacking Serbia, Clinton showed he was serious about the United States staying engaged in Europe. Despite his opening to Russia, Clinton's interventions reminded Moscow that Cold War security guarantees in Europe did not vanish along with the USSR. Reagan, despite warming to Gorbachev, made the Soviet occupation of Afghanistan as difficult as possible by covertly supporting its chief resisters, the mujahedeen. Indeed, both conflicts – 1980s Afghanistan and 1990s Bosnia – radicalized the side that America supported and determined, perversely, its anti-American trajectory. The mujahedeen became the Taliban. Several Islamists in the struggle against Serbia formed the cadre of al-Qaeda operatives that went onto use Afghanistan as a base for the 9/11 plot. Both Reagan and Clinton realized one national security objective, the negation of Russian power, but in so doing unleashed another: Islamist terrorism.

---

[73] See Ronald D. Asmus, *Opening NATO's Door: How the Alliance Remade Itself for a New Era* (New York: Columbia University Press, 2004).

NORTHERN IRELAND AND THE "WIN-WIN" SCENARIO

As one terrorist threat gathered, another diminished. In some important respects, Clinton was responsible for both developments. The last redoubt of British sovereignty in Ireland was an unlikely focus of his diplomacy. In January 1994, against British government advice, Clinton authorized a 48-hour US entry visa for Gerry Adams. As leader of Sinn Féin, Adams was regarded as a war criminal in some British government circles. It was, said Margaret Thatcher, like the British prime minister inviting Timothy McVeigh, who in April 1995 had killed 166 people in Oklahoma City, to Downing Street for peace talks.[74]

Despite the row at its beginning, however, Clinton's involvement in the Northern Ireland peace process opened more avenues of compromise than it foreclosed. When a power-sharing deal was finally signed in 1998, an American chaired the negotiations. The issue was presented to President Clinton as a "win-win."[75] If he helped lock paramilitaries – the anti-British Irish Republican Army (IRA) most crucially – into a democratic politics, he could claim the mantle of peacemaker. If the IRA violated that faith, Clinton would have exposed them as frauds. Clinton faced few foreign policy issues that had so little downside and risk. Alienating Downing Street over Sinn Féin, for example, was essentially cost-free when compared to the deterioration in US–Russian relations caused by NATO expansion.

Clinton's engagement in the peace process is explained in large part by the Cold War's end rather than by its shadow.[76] The demise of the central imperative of Anglo–American relations in the Cold War – to contain Soviet power – meant that Clinton could risk short-term British disaffection over his Irish intercession without fear that it would harm long-term US–UK cooperation on a grander strategic level. What, after all, given the end of the USSR, compelled that cooperation? And yet we should not ignore an important, if imperfect, analogue to Clinton's diplomacy in Northern Ireland. In 1956, at the height of Cold War tensions, when the London–Washington partnership should have been at its most robust, President Eisenhower abandoned Prime Minister Anthony Eden. Expecting American support in a joint British–French–Israeli military

---

[74] Thatcher speech at Harding University, Arkansas, April 29, 1995.
[75] See Lynch, *Turf War*, p. 37.
[76] See Michael Cox, Bringing in the "International": The IRA Ceasefire and the End of the Cold War, *International Affairs* 73, 4 (October 1997): 671–693.

invasion to reclaim the Suez Canal from Egypt, Eden found that Eisenhower instead chose to chastise his putative allies and committed no aid in their cause. If anything, the Northern Ireland demarche, certainly at its beginning, mimicked that of the Suez Crisis. A US president was prepared to offend his British ally when he determined it was in error.

THE 1996 ELECTION

In November 1996, Bill Clinton was reelected president. His campaign against Bob Dole, a senator from Kansas, the oldest man ever to run for the office, was framed hardly at all by foreign policy. With no Cold War and no obvious crisis to take its place, the rather odd global interregnum continued. Dole attempted to appeal to Americans' nostalgia, affording Clinton the opportunity to present himself as "a bridge to the future." The baby boomer Arkansan won 31 states to the older Kansan's 19 – though, as in 1992, Clinton again failed to secure a majority of the votes cast (49.2%). However, given the GOP gains only two years earlier, winning at all represented a considerable achievement and remains an example of Clinton's innate powers of recovery. In the space of four years he had dispatched three conservative general election opponents: George Bush Sr., Bob Dole, and (twice) Ross Perot. What his enemies could not achieve electorally, they sought legally, expending much political energy and capital trying to impeach Clinton in 1997–1998.

CONCLUSION

As Clinton moved toward his second term, he could do so aware he had improved – even if he had fallen some way short of transforming – his foreign policy fortunes. Haiti had a restored (if nominal) democracy. The Mexican economy had not crashed. Russia was (imperfectly) embracing the free market. Bosnia was en route to stability. NATO's enlargement was on track. Northern Ireland was increasingly locked into a peace process. Clinton had played an important, positive role in each of these developments. Indeed, given how poor Clinton's performance had been for most of his first term, this shift in fortunes is extraordinary. The bar for success in and after 1996, as Michael Mandelbaum observed, was consequently a low one:

The seminal events of the foreign policy of the Clinton administration were three failed military interventions in its first nine months in office: the announced intention, then failure, to lift the arms embargo against Bosnia's Muslims and bomb the Bosnian Serbs in May 1993; the deaths of 18 US Army rangers at the hands of a mob in Mogadishu, Somalia, on October 3; and the turning back of a ship carrying military trainers in response to demonstrations in Port-au-Prince, Haiti, on October 12. Together they set the tone and established much of the agenda of the foreign policy of the United States from 1993 through 1995.[77]

Coming to power in 1993, Clinton had promised an economic focus at home and "new think" abroad. He ended his first term having achieved the basis for domestic renewal (his second term would be remembered as one of America's most prosperous), but a revolution in foreign policy did not obtain. Despite his oft-quoted intention to transform and even downgrade US foreign policy, Bill Clinton reverted more to a Cold War type. As political scientist G. John Ikenberry observed in 1996, the United States was still using the international architecture it had created in the late 1940s; the end of the Cold War had not dismantled these structures but, rather, proved their utility.[78] The Soviet Union had died, but the world order that had choked it off endured. And Bill Clinton was busy using – not transcending – that order to fashion his foreign policy legacy. The United Nations, so tangential to global politics in the Cold War, remained immobilized by the two great autocracies at its core – China and Russia – obliging Clinton to circumvent it. It was not the United Nations, Clinton told the Democratic National Convention in August 1996, but the United States that was the world's indispensable power.

Crucially, internationalism and multilateralism – supposedly unleashed by the end of the Cold War – had not solved two key problems that would bedevil Clinton and his successors for much of the next two decades: terrorism and Iraq. The apparent timidity of American reprisals for Islamist terrorism served to embolden that menace. When al-Qaeda bombed the Khobar Towers military housing complex in Saudi Arabia in 1996, killing nineteen US soldiers, Clinton's response was Reaganesque in its minimalism. In Iraq, the UN solution – and America's deference to it – was making a bad situation worse. Saddam Hussein was content to control the box that US and UN officials believed they had contained him within. His dominion increased in proportion to the plight of his people. His intentions and capacities became opaque. Regime change, Clinton was soon to concede, provided the only reliable means of eliminating the threat he posed.

---

[77] Michael Mandelbaum, Foreign Policy as Social Work, *Foreign Affairs* 75, 1 (January/February 1996): 16–32, 16.

[78] G. John Ikenberry, The Myth of Post–Cold War Chaos, *Foreign Affairs* 75, 3 (May/June 1996): 79–91.

3

Bill Clinton

The Return of Old Think, 1997–2000

> Gone was the Soviet Union forever. We are certain that we shall – with the grace of Allah – prevail over the Americans and over the Jews.
>
> —*Osama bin Laden, May 1998*[1]

While a terrorist storm brewed, Bill Clinton enjoyed in his second term one of the greatest economic upswings in modern American history. He balanced the federal budget, something that seemed impossible during the Reagan profligacy of the 1980s. He took the credit for a dot.com revolution in the information technology (IT) sector; his vice-president half joked that he had invented the Internet. Unemployment fell to negligible levels. In 1996, the most far-reaching reform of the welfare state since the 1960s was enacted, fulfilling Clinton's campaign promise to "end welfare as we have come to know it." As Donald Trump's real estate empire grew exponentially, the bust of the Bush Sr. years gave way to boom under Clinton.

Despite these successes, about which Americans became very nostalgic in the Great Recession of the later Bush and early Obama years, Clinton's second term was to witness the most protracted domestic political battle since Watergate, and the most controversial war since Vietnam. In time, Clinton would be vilified for failing to see a gathering terrorist threat that fully materialized less than nine months after he left office.

---

[1] Osama bin Laden interview with ABC reporter John Miller, May 1998; at https://pbs.org/wgbh/pages/frontline/shows/binladen/who/interview.html.

A NEW FOREIGN POLICY TEAM

The naming of Madeleine Albright as Clinton's new chief diplomat indicated a newfound energy in foreign policy. After four years of the staid, solid, but often enervating Warren Christopher, the first female secretary of state represented a switch to a bolder international posture. From the outset Albright "wanted it known that she was as different from her predecessors as a pink skirt is from a pinstriped suit."[2] Albright was determined to use the impressive military power of the United States. Even with defense spending at its lowest (as a proportion of GDP) since the 1930s, the United States still spent more than the next fifteen highest-spending countries combined. "What's the point of having this superb military, you're always talking about," Albright asked Colin Powell, "if we can' t use it?"[3] She declared, "Freedom is America's purpose."[4] Her frame of reference was explicitly the ideological struggle of the Cold War; the world remained a moral arena in which the righteous must be prepared to make war. Born in 1937, the daughter of a Czechoslovak diplomat, the young Madeleine spent her early years escaping, first, the Nazis and then, after World War II, the communists. This exposure to tyranny colored her assessment of its modern variants. She became a consistent advocate of the use of force against Saddam Hussein and Slobodan Milošević. The former survived her tenure; the latter did not.

Samuel ("Sandy") Berger was, like Albright, much more colorful than the man he replaced as national security advisor. Where Tony Lake had been cautious, Berger was a risk-taker; he was eventually to be convicted of stealing documents from the National Archives.[5] Far more comfortable with the politics of foreign policy, Berger represented an approach more attuned to the domestic setting within which his boss had to work. Not least, Berger was cast in the role of internal peacemaker – to smooth foreign policy disagreements within the second-term team. To effect an external peace, in an apparent effort to build a consensus within

[2] Thomas W. Lippman, *Madeleine Albright and the New American Diplomacy* (Boulder, CO: Westview Press, 2000), p. 2.
[3] See Powell, *My American Journey*, p. 57 and Thomas Blood, *Madam Secretary: A Biography of Madeleine Albright* (New York: St. Martin's Press, 1997), p. 162.
[4] Madeleine Albright, The Testing of American Foreign Policy, *Foreign Affairs* 77, 6 (November–December 1998): 50–64.
[5] Apparently to evade censure by the 9/11 Commission for counterterrorism missteps under his watch. He was given a $50,000 fine and sentenced to a three-year probation and 100 hours community service. Berger died in 2015.

Washington, William Cohen, a Republican senator, was named as the new secretary of defense. The irony of these supposedly bipartisan picks was their participation in what were soon to become highly rancorous foreign policy politics.

Richard Holbrooke, though not commanding one of the key foreign policy portfolios (his perceived ambition meant he was never offered the secretary of state role he coveted), nevertheless became one of the most dynamic diplomats of Clinton's second term (and of Obama's first term, until his death in 2010). Holbrooke became America's chief hawk in the Balkans and Afghanistan. Clinton had restaffed himself with men and women accustomed to a certain limelight who saw the world as their most obvious stage.

Vice-President Al Gore remained a consistent advocate of military force against America's foes, not least Saddam Hussein's Iraq. Gore spent much of the 1990s arguing for regime change in Baghdad. When Gore himself ran for the presidency in 2000, he picked for his running mate the hardest of "hard power" Democrats. Senator Joseph Lieberman would eventually quit the Democratic party because he saw threats where his fellow Democrats did not. Clinton's new foreign policy chiefs were determined to use the full spectrum of American power. The contrast with the introverted and dysfunctional team of 1993 was marked.

A historical comparison is instructive. In 1964, American liberal zeal had at least been checked by a cautious British realism. Harold Wilson, the British Labor prime minister, remained unpersuaded by the case for war in Vietnam.[6] Her Majesty's troops sat out the conflict. The inability to carry along its perennial ally was symptomatic of US failure in Southeast Asia. In May 1997, Tony Blair became the first Labor prime minister in eighteen years. Under him, British checking power was transformed into an enabler of American ambitions. He was to play an important and contentious role in supporting the major wars Clinton and Bush were to fight over the next decade, most controversially in Kosovo and Iraq. For all the talk of a new era in foreign policy, Clinton relied significantly on the reconstitution of the central Anglo-American axis of the Cold War. Like Albright and Holbrooke, Blair believed military power was a key ingredient of a moral foreign policy. He called for "a more subtle blend of mutual self-interest and moral purpose" in Western diplomacy.[7]

---

[6] See Peter Busch, *All the Way with JFK? Britain, the U.S. and the Vietnam War* (Oxford: Oxford University Press, 2003).

[7] Tony Blair, speech at Economic Club, Chicago, April 24, 1999.

Clinton, noted the new prime minister, was "plainly delighted to have a fellow third-way progressive in power."[8]

As in the 1960s, it was not Republicans but Democrats, not the right but the left, that provided the fervor for war abroad. When a Republican administration did fight, as in Afghanistan and Iraq, after 9/11, it did so using too few troops rather than too many. Clinton and Blair, on the other hand, almost fetishized military power, using it on dozens of occasions between 1997 and 2001. If there was a foreign policy ideology in Clinton's second term, it was a liberal interventionist one – a retread of Kennedy and Johnson.

THE COLD WAR WITH IRAQ

"The best and the brightest" liberals of the Kennedy administration fixated on the plight of South Vietnam, but their heirs in the 1990s kept Iraq central to US foreign policy thinking.[9] Bill Clinton used military force against its regime on at least four occasions during his eight-year term. In June 1993, in reprisal for an assassination attempt on George H. W. Bush, he launched twenty-three cruise missiles at the headquarters of Saddam's secret police. Twice in September 1996, as punishment for Saddam sending his troops into the Kurdish enclave in northern Iraq, Clinton fired cruise missiles at targets around Baghdad. In December 1998, with regime change now official US policy, Clinton ordered a three-day air campaign in retaliation for Saddam's expulsion of UN weapons inspectors. Operation Desert Fox was the single largest assault until the full-scale invasion under George W. Bush. Clinton's aggressive containment of Saddam – which had the effect of indirectly punishing his people – cost the United States about $1 billion every year.

In the periods between these attacks, the Clinton administration maintained UN-mandated no-fly zones in northern and southern Iraq, ostensibly to protect Saddam's Kurdish opponents in the north and Shia opponents in the south, which led to recurrent air skirmishes and the downing of several Iraqi aircraft. In 1998, Clinton articulated the central rationale of what would be Bush's later attack on Iraq: "One way or other, we are determined to deny Iraq the capacity to develop weapons of mass destruction and the missiles to deliver them. That is our bottom line."[10] Later that year Clinton signed the Iraqi Liberation Act, which

---

[8] Tony Blair, *A Journey* (London: Hutchinson, 2010), p. 13.
[9] See David Halberstam, *The Best and the Brightest* (New York: Ballantine Books, 1969).
[10] Clinton in Thomas W. Lippman, In U.S., Calls Grow Louder for Saddam Hussein's Removal, *Washington Post*, February 5, 1998.

pledged the United States to do what his successor went on to achieve: "To remove the Saddam Hussein regime from power in Iraq and to replace it with a democratic government."[11] The Washington consensus on changing the Baghdad regime was durable and robust.

The next chapter considers how that consensus led George W. Bush to topple Saddam. Bill Clinton's role was to contain the regime's ambitions but, in the process, bring Iraqi society to the brink of collapse. In the decade before America and its allies invaded, the Clinton administration was complicit in the maintenance of a UN sanctions regime that has been blamed for the death of some 500,000 Iraqi children. Clinton's containment of Iraq had the effect of bankrupting the country and hollowing out what remained of its civil society. If the Bush Jr. occupation of 2003 was a disaster, it was one begun by his predecessors, who did enough to pacify Iraq but not enough to change its government.

President Clinton had four objectives in Iraq – all of which, he hoped, could be fulfilled short of war. He was successful in at least three of them. First, he meant to deter Iraq from attacking its neighbors, particularly Saudi Arabia. Saddam was depicted as a serial aggressor whom the United States must box in. In 1980, he had attacked Iran, ten years later Kuwait. After Desert Storm in 1991, the capacity of the Iraqi army to repeat such action was severely constrained. Saddam's belligerent rhetoric against his neighbors belied his ability to act on it. The UN sanctions regime, through which Clinton waged his cold war on Iraq, though it slowly deteriorated through the 1990s, made the re-equipping of Saddam's military forces a matter of smoke and mirrors.

Second, and related to the first, was the objective that eventually forced George W. Bush into war: the removal of Saddam's weapons of mass destruction (WMD) capacity. After Israeli planes destroyed Iraq's nascent nuclear program in 1981, Saddam's neighbors and their Western allies viewed his nefarious weapons plan with more misgivings than they had intelligence to act against him. The truth is that Saddam was never able to arm his regime commensurate with his ambitions. The dictator became adept at fostering suspicions among both his near and far enemies, but never their certitude. Clinton, despite making the negation of WMD a central objective of his Iraq policy, was never so sure of that capacity that he was willing to invade the country. Instead, he trusted that sanctions and occasional military force would, over time, cause Saddam to fade away.

---

[11] Iraq Liberation Act of 1998, Public Law 105–338, 105th Congress.

Third, while he hoped for Saddam's natural and/or political demise, Clinton made changing the Iraqi regime official US policy. While the momentum behind the Iraq Liberation Act (1998) was assorted legislators and think thanks, Clinton's signing of the bill reflected the hard line toward Iraq that many Democrats urged through the 1990s. His vice-president, Al Gore, was as much a study in how to be uncompromising on Iraq as he had been on the other targets of American aggression during the Clinton years, notably the Balkans. A liberal hawk in the 1990s, until his reincarnation as a green progressive after 2001, Gore symbolized an assertive stance that began under George Bush Sr. and reached a conclusion under his son. Had Gore been confirmed as president in 2000, there is more evidence to suggest he would have waged a war against Saddam after 9/11 than that he would have turned away.

Fourth, Clinton intended to preserve regional stability. Since the discovery of Middle Eastern oil in the early twentieth century, the United States has attempted to keep the region open for business, to maintain the flow of oil from it. When Arab states raised the price of the fossil fuel, by slowing its production, for example, the American economy paid a high price. After the 1973 war between Israel and Egypt, the Organization of the Petroleum Exporting Countries (OPEC) hiked the barrel price and within days Americans were queuing for gas. This "oil shock" convinced a generation of US foreign policymakers that stability was key to securing American economic interests in the region. And stability would preclude the realization of interests – such as those of Tehran and Moscow – that America defined as threats. After 1990, Saddam became the chief agent of instability. His talent for mischief was proportionate to his WMD capacity – or at least to the perception of it in Riyadh, Tel Aviv, and across the Middle East. Remove it – and him – and stability would obtain. Clinton argued in 1998 that Iraq's WMD "constitutes an unusual and extraordinary threat to the national security, foreign policy, and economy of the United States."[12]

These four objectives drove American policy toward Iraq from 1990 to 2003. The tactics chosen to realize them differed, but the strategic objective remained the same: the removal of Saddam and his replacement with something less bad.

---

[12] In Daniel Byman, After the Storm: U.S. Policy toward Iraq since 1991, *Political Science Quarterly* 115, 4 (Winter 2000–2001): 493–516, 497.

NATO MARCHES EAST

Bill Clinton was far more interested in enlarging the post–Cold War bounty in Eastern Europe than in containing post–Cold War problems such as Iraq. He saw the extension of NATO into Russia's backyard as a means to end the Cold War once and for all; its effect was to antagonize Moscow and thus help prepare the path for a far more assertive Russian government in the opening decades of the twenty-first century. NATO, said Kremlin officials, with a "mirthless smile," was a "four-letter word in Russian."[13]

Clinton often traded on being able to "feel the pain" of the disaffected. This intuition was plentiful when it came to Moscow's former colonies, but lacking when it came to the Russian government itself. Clinton basked in the adulation of the peoples of the former Soviet satellites, who overwhelmingly wanted to join the US-led NATO club. In March 1999, the Czech Republic, Poland, and Hungary officially entered the alliance. Membership, they believed, would offer them, finally, a guarantee against the depredations of Germany to their west and Russia to their east. US foreign policy since 1945 had helped solve the German question but, after 1995, had significantly re-posed a Russia one.

Both Clinton and Madeleine Albright saw Czechoslovakia in nostalgic terms. The president could recall its famous saxophonists, Albright her own childhood escape from its Soviet-imposed communism. America's principal foreign policymakers indulged these affections by working with Václav Havel, the new Czech president, to bring his nation, Poland, and Hungary into NATO. Clinton relied on a hopeful assumption that Russia would remain essentially quiescent as its near abroad became a pro-Western camp. Fukuyama's "end of history" predictions (see Chapter 2) suggested that ultimately a democratizing Russia would want to join a US-led economic club. Instead, the Russian government bristled that the cost of capitalism was to be purchased at the price of its security. The persistence of Russian national interests into the post–Cold War era demonstrated how far the logic of the Cold War remained basic to Russian thinking.

The expansion of NATO was a direct fulfillment of a centuries-old Russian fear that the West intended to first encircle and then choke Russia. This geostrategic peril has informed the statecraft of successive

[13] In Talbott, *The Russia Hand*, p. 95.

Russia leaders. No matter how terrible the consequences for the Western invader – from the doomed invasions by Napoléon's France to Hitler's Germany – "the West" would continue to seek the end of Russian power. In Russian eyes, however Bill Clinton disguised it, the NATO expansion was merely the next stage of this Western project. The abandonment of communism had not weakened a Western resolve to contain Russia. Clinton's hopefulness that he could change this deeply rooted thinking was ultimately futile. Indeed, it led him into conflicts with Moscow that he assumed the demise of the USSR had made impossible.

Since 1994, Clinton's Partnership for Peace (PfP) initiative had been softening up Yeltsin for the alliance's expansion. The PfP, a NATO program, was meant to appease traditional Russian fears of encirclement. In March 1997, Clinton had met with Yeltsin and agreed to another stage of nuclear arms reductions (START III). The next month, the US Congress approved the Chemical Weapons Convention (joined by Russia in December 1997). Believing these agreements and his relationship with the Russian leader would smooth the path of NATO expansion, Clinton, in July, supported NATO's formal invitation to Poland, Hungary, and the Czech Republic to join the alliance.

We might suppose that this well-intentioned liberal institutionalism would have assuaged Russian concerns. This was not the case. Indeed, Clinton's attempt to transcend the Cold War merely confirmed to a new generation of Russian leaders that the United States was fighting it by other means. NATO expansion, from the Kremlin's perspective, was less about soft power than the establishment of American hard power in Russia's backyard – something that successive Soviet leaders had precluded not by dialogue and summitry, but by the threat of nuclear retaliation. US presidents from Truman to Reagan acknowledged a Russian sphere of influence in the Baltics and Eastern Europe. Their response to the violent Soviet policing of this sphere – such as the Soviet invasions of Hungary (1956) and Czechoslovakia (1968) – deployed words, not troops. Now, via words and treaties, US troops were violating the Russian sphere. The most obvious manifestation of Russian mistrust was Yeltsin's recommitment to the Serbian cause in former Yugoslavia. While that conflict in Kosovo brewed, Clinton was obliged to turn to a constitutional (and acutely personal) crisis that colored much of his remaining term in office.

IMPEACHMENT AND CONGRESS'S WAR ON CLINTON

Bill Clinton enjoyed great luck as president; the economy roared and the opponents of American power seemed to have dropped, exhausted. His

legacy was tarnished not by foreign wars – he fought these with considerable success – nor by domestic failure – his 1996 Welfare Reform Act was
as significant a piece of legislation as anything since Lyndon Johnson's
Great Society of the late 1960s. What actually compromised his presidency was Clinton's long-standing appetite for sexual intrigue. Clinton
was a serial philanderer before he reached the White House. In it, from
November 1995 to May 1997, in his private study adjoining the Oval
Office, he engaged in a series of bafflingly ill-judged sexual liaisons with a
21-year-old White House intern, Monica Lewinsky.

John F. Kennedy, Clinton's hero, had indulged his considerable sexual
appetites when president. The difference between the early 1960s – with a
press that did not report JFK's behavior and women that stayed silent –
and the late 1990s was profound. Clinton faced a national and international media obsessed with his affair and a woman that would go
on record in explicit detail about it.[14] Nascent under Kennedy, the
politics of gender and their focus on power differentials magnified
Clinton's sexual transgression. As Lewinsky later recalled, "He was
my boss. He was the most powerful man on the planet. He was 27 years
my senior, with enough life experience to know better. He was, at the
time, at the pinnacle of his career, while I was in my first job out of
college."[15] This affair began a chain of events leading to the president's
impeachment by the House of Representatives in December 1998 and
trial in the Senate, resulting in a not-guilty verdict, on almost exclusively partisan lines, in early 1999. What impact did this affair have on
his foreign policy?

Congress was already highly predisposed to frustrate Clinton's agenda
before the president gave them a legal excuse to do so.[16] The mutual
contempt between the executive and legislature in this period became
legendary; according to her testimony, Lewinsky once performed oral
sex on the president while he was on the phone to a congressman.[17]
The Republicans waged a war of attrition against the Arkansan. At home,
both sides were content to see the government shut down (and national

[14] On Kennedy's extramarital affairs see Richard Reeves, *President Kennedy: Profile of
Power* (New York: Touchstone, 1994), pp. 289–292.
[15] Monica Lewinsky, Monica Lewinsky: Emerging from "the House of Gaslight" in the Age
of #metoo, *Vanity Fair* (March 2018) [online].
[16] See Elizabeth Drew, *Showdown: The Struggle between the Gingrich Congress and the
Clinton White House* (New York: Touchstone, 1996).
[17] The Starr Report, 105th Congress, 2d Session, House Document 105-310, p. 30, fn. 162;
at www.gpo.gov/fdsys/pkg/CDOC-105hdoc310/pdf/CDOC-105hdoc310.pdf.

monuments, museums, and Social Security offices padlocked) when budget negotiations failed. Elsewhere, an activist Congress sought to stymie Clinton's treaties and wars.

Clinton clearly had some intimation of the game Republicans were playing. He refused to move a climate change treaty (the Kyoto Protocol, signed in December 1997) to a Senate floor vote he knew he would lose. He later conceded that Kyoto would have been "difficult to pass in the best of circumstances" – and these were far short of that.[18] Clinton's instincts failed him, however, on the Comprehensive Nuclear-Test-Ban Treaty (CTBT). Despite optimistic attempts to establish a politics of liberal internationalism, diplomacy remained stubbornly conditioned by the Cold War. The test ban concept was inspired by both laudable motives – to make the testing of nuclear bombs beyond the pale morally and legally – and geostrategic ones – to retard the proliferation of nuclear weapons to ambitious states whose command and control systems left much to be desired. Liberals and realists found much to like in the terms of the treaty. Clinton assumed most senators would too. That they did not illustrates how far politics infected debate over the CTBT, providing a case study in the fallout that accompanied Clinton's impeachment, but also showing the extent to which Congress can resist treaties it does not like.

The case for CTBT ratification adapted arguments that had been made on behalf of several of the most prominent nuclear arms control treaties of the Cold War. If the testing of nuclear weapons could be stopped, this would improve the prospects of fuller disarmament. This had been the vision of John Kennedy that Bill Clinton wanted to make real. States that sought a nuclear weapon would face not just moral censure but legal consequences – though the treaty was vague on quite what these would be. The argument that a test ban was simply the right thing to do carried significant weight even before the technical arguments for and against were factored in. Clinton thought he had history on his side. Surely even Republicans would see a ban on explosive testing as in the US national interest? Not even politics could infect the moral case for a test ban treaty? Possibly because of his confidence, the president assumed the treaty would pass. What was needed, however, was a coordinated ground campaign to secure the necessary votes. That effort came too late. Needing 66 votes, on October 13, 1999, the Senate rejected the treaty

[18] Clinton, *My Life*, p. 770.

48 to 51. It constituted, according to a scholar of the episode, "the president's worst foreign policy defeat in Congress."[19]

Congressional negation is explained by several factors. The case against passage certainly smelled of politics, but was also grounded in an unease with how the treaty would operate and the types of behavior it would unintentionally motivate. A perverse consequence was the incentive to test before the CTBT came into force. India and Pakistan made their intense rivalry nuclear when each tested a weapon in May 1998, in part to avoid having to do so in violation of the treaty.[20] The penalties such actions would invoke once the treaty was in force were never clear. CTBT is replete with references to "adoption" and "obligations" but not "consequences." Concerns that the treaty would be toothless made US senators skeptical.

This principled objection was amplified by a series of political ones. Politicking for ratification had to take place against the backdrop of impeachment proceedings. Clinton's appeal to morality on behalf of the treaty were undermined by his own sexual conduct, details of which colored popular and political discourse for too much of his second term. The president's lecturing senators on doing the right thing rang hollow. But even without the Lewinsky scandal, the political agendas of the executive and legislature were antithetical. Clinton wanted to institutionalize the new post–Cold War dawn of NATO expansion, nuclear test bans, and climate treaties. Congress wanted to use its power to check such ambitions. It is often argued that the end of the Cold War made Congress much more assertive in its handling of foreign policy. The necessity of maintaining a united front in the face of the USSR had, after all, evaporated along with that opponent. Congressional approval had to be earned by the White House rather than assumed. Suddenly, according to this reading, foreign policy became subject to an especially intense politics held in check for decades by the demands of a Cold War consensus. The test ban treaty, the intervention in Bosnia (and later in Kosovo), were held up as case studies of a new congressional assertiveness.

This version of events is only partly true. The Cold War – as is typical of most wars – placed a premium on national unity. Being sympathetic to the Soviet Union was an impossible position for any budding American

---

[19] Terry L. Deibel, The Death of a Treaty, *Foreign Affairs* 81, 5 (September–October 2002): 142–161.

[20] Despite adoption by the UN in 1996, the treaty cannot come into force until eight nation-states, including the United States and China, pass it.

politician to maintain. However, the politics of foreign policy and national security were not suspended from 1945 to 1989. President Clinton endured the intense scrutiny of opponents on Capitol Hill, but he was not the first president to do so. When a Republican-controlled Congress passed the Twenty-Second Amendment in 1951, Democrat Harry Truman became the first president to have term limits imposed on him. In the two years preceding this constitutional limitation, he was loudly abused for having "lost China" to communism. Dwight Eisenhower, his GOP successor, was in turn accused by Democrats of having "lost space" when the USSR launched the first ever satellite in 1957. Democrats claimed that Sputnik exposed an administration that was so consumed with balancing budgets and cutting taxes it had all but forgotten national security.[21] By the 1970s, a Democratic Congress was so concerned at the growth of the president's power to make war that it passed legislation to rein him in. Richard Nixon was eventually forced to resign the presidency in the face of certain impeachment by Congress over his role in the Watergate scandal. Ronald Reagan narrowly escaped a similar fate over his violation of congressional restrictions on the funding of anticommunist rebels in Nicaragua in the 1980s. The Cold War did not suspend party politics, even if its end seemed to increase their rancor. Indeed, there is a case to be made that Clinton's battle with Congress – fought, according to John Dumbrell, "with a skilled and successful mixture of compromise, evasion, and confrontation" – represents comparative success.[22]

CLINTON AND CHINA

In June 1998, Clinton became the first president to visit China since the Tiananmen Square crackdown, nine years earlier. Within eighteen months, China and the United States agreed on a trade deal, paving the way for China's membership of the World Trade Organization at the end of 2001. In 2000, Congress ratified Clinton's bill to establish permanent trade relations with Beijing. This recognition of China's economic transformation was a potential template for how Clinton's democratic enlargement might work. Its logic was attractive: constrain China within

---

[21] Julian E. Zelizer, *Arsenal of Democracy: The Politics of National Security – From World War II to the War on Terror* (New York: Basic Books, 2010), p. 121.

[22] John Dumbrell, *Clinton's Foreign Policy: Between the Bushes, 1992–2000* (Abingdon: Routledge, 2009), p. 170.

a Western economic architecture and eventually wealth would generate a civil society independent of central control. Facilitate material prosperity, and a Chinese middle class would eventually demand political freedom.

In the months before his 1998 visit, utilizing a similar logic, the Clinton administration had been busily bailing out the flagging economies of several South Asian nations, including $3 billion to Indonesia. In the 1960s, the historian William Appleman Williams saw such largesse as part of an American obsession with maintaining an economic open door, but it was also a means to maintain the democratic stability of states like Indonesia and South Korea. Keep China's economic door open and eventually freedom would walk in.

The logic of the Clinton Doctrine – that economic openness entrenches democracy – remains seductive though is hardly a socio-scientific law. In applying it, Clinton perpetuated a strategic miscalculation begun by Richard Nixon. It consisted of two parts. First, Clinton and Nixon, and each president after them, relied exclusively on economics to do a job that ultimately politics must do. Material prosperity can affirm an autocratic system's right to rule as much as it can challenge it. To challenge it, ideologies rooted in a different conception of state power need to be nurtured. China has no history of representative democracy, of the rule of law, or property rights. US administrations have pretended this can be overcome by helping the Chinese get rich.

Second, Clinton, both by accident and design, continued a Cold War tradition of assuming that Chinese power was a centrally coordinated phenomenon. Some China watchers, on the other hand, attribute much of the state's autocratic character not to Beijing but to its provincial governments. The absence of rights that are taken for granted in the West was deep-seated in the regions of China, and of long standing, rather than a product of the communist central government. Expecting the "end of history" to transform Chinese regionalism was another example of American naivety inherited from the Cold War. The failure to appreciate the complexity of China's political character during that conflict long hampered Sino–US relations. It was a feature with echoes after the Cold War.

THE KOSOVO WAR

Clinton's diplomacy toward China was hardly advanced by bombing its embassy in Belgrade, Serbia, on May 7, 1999. This tragic targeting error – which killed three Chinese reporters – was one of several remarkable features of the Kosovo War. Waged from March to May, it was the most controversial war since Vietnam, fought over a territory about the size of Delaware. It was the first and thus far the only war to take place in the face of an explicit congressional refusal to authorize it. The United Nations was incapable of protecting the civilians it was meant to save or of stopping the action NATO took to save them. Because the US side lost no troops to enemy fire and relied more on technical wizardry than on boots on the ground, it was said to herald a "revolution in military affairs." Kosovo created an illusion that warfare could be cheap in blood and quick in time. The seeds for disaster four years later in Iraq were sown thereby. It was also a war that, rather than transcending the Cold War, relied significantly on its mechanics: NATO and Anglo-American cooperation in pursuit, in part, of Russian containment. We will examine each of these claims in turn.

America's intervention began as an effort to prevent Slobodan Milošević, the leader of Yugoslavia, from denuding Kosovo of its Muslims. His sponsorship of the Bosnian Serbs in their "ethnic cleansing" of Bosnia in the early 1990s was the precedent for his crackdown on "Islamist terrorism" in Kosovo, a province regarded as ancient Serbian land. The 1995 Dayton peace treaty had resolved the war in Bosnia, but left it free to move into Kosovo. The Kosovo Liberation Army (KLA), a hybrid version of the 1940s French Resistance and 1980s Afghan mujahedeen, saw in Bosnia's liberation from the Serbs a template for a free Muslim state in Kosovo. Milošević, leader of a Yugoslavia that now consisted of only Serbia and Montenegro, determined to stop this from happening.

Ironically, what he was quick to characterize as a "war on terror" on the KLA brought Milošević back into US sights. KLA agitation and Serbian counterresponses became more frequent through 1998. Each side accused the other of war crimes. President Clinton, now with a track record of military confrontation with Serbia, allied with Prime Minister Blair and his enthusiastic foreign policy, leaned instinctively toward the Muslims and against Milošević and his Russian sympathizers. Attacks by the KLA were regarded by the White House and 10 Downing Street as, at worst, morally ambiguous and, at best, as self-defense. Reprisals by the Serbs were depicted as the contours of a mini-holocaust. Milošević was the "the butcher of the Balkans." In the public rhetoric of the Clinton and Blair teams, the use of the word "genocide" increased in frequency. War crimes were being committed, Tony Blair told his cabinet on January 21, 1999.[23]

---

[23] In Alastair Campbell, *The Alexander Campbell Diaries, vol. 2: Power and the People, 1997–1999* (London: Hutchinson, 2011), p. 638.

Many Serbs describe the descent into a war with NATO over the next three months as inevitable. Conflict-resolution efforts were merely a pretext, they claim, to demonize Serbia for failing to honor them. If Dayton, Ohio, was chosen as the city where one Balkan war would end, the small French town of Rambouillet was where another one was started. It was here that Secretary of State Madeleine Albright and US Balkan envoy Richard Holbrooke provided the justification Clinton and Blair needed to begin a military campaign. The Rambouillet Agreement imposed terms on Serbia more stringent than those imposed on its fore-bears in July 1914. Austria-Hungary's ultimatum to Serbia was a trigger that initiated hostilities leading to world war. But that assault on Serbian sovereignty was mild compared to what NATO now demanded:

NATO personnel shall enjoy, together with their vehicles, vessels, aircraft, and equipment, free and unrestricted passage and unimpeded access throughout the Former Republic of Yugoslavia including associated airspace and territorial waters. This shall include, but not be limited to, the right of bivouac, maneuver, billet, and utilization of any areas or facilities as required for support, training, and operations.[24]

According to Henry Kissinger:

The Rambouillet text, which called on Serbia to admit NATO troops throughout Yugoslavia, was a provocation, an excuse to start bombing. Rambouillet is not a document that an angelic Serb could have accepted. It was a terrible diplomatic document that should never have been presented in that form.[25]

And Milošević accordingly did not accept it. "I sent Dick Holbrooke back to see him one last time," records Bill Clinton, "but even Dick couldn't budge him."[26]

The bombing started on March 24 and continued for 78 days. NATO targeted Serbian military and then civilian infrastructure. On April 12, twenty train passengers were killed crossing a river. Two days later, 73 Kosovar Albanian refugees – the men and women the war itself was meant to protect – were mistakenly killed when NATO planes bombed their convoy. Over the ensuing weeks, the alliance committed 25,000 ground troops to the conflict, and threatened more. Tony Blair was a forceful advocate of this escalation.[27] A series of peace negotiations – led

---

[24] The Rambouillet text, Appendix B, Status of Multi-National Military Implementation Force, April 28, 1999; at www.theguardian.com/world/1999/apr/28/balkans12.

[25] Henry Kissinger, interview in *Daily Telegraph* [London], June 28, 1999.

[26] Clinton, *My Life*, p. 850.   [27] See Blair, *A Journey*, pp. 238–240.

most visibly by Vice-President Al Gore and Russian foreign minister Viktor Chernomyrdin – in conjunction with the military campaign eventually resulted in Milošević's submission. By June 20, he completed the withdrawal of the Yugoslav military from Kosovo. Fifteen months later Milošević was himself overthrown.

For the third time in less than nine years, the United States waged a war to liberate a Muslim population from the purported depredations of their government. Kuwait, Bosnia, and Kosovo were to be followed by similarly though not identically conceived wars against the oppression of Muslims in Afghanistan, Iraq, and Libya. The Syrian government was threatened with war in 2013 if its regime persisted with chemical weapons attacks on its Muslim population. When it persisted, after a lull, in 2017, President Donald Trump launched strikes against Damascus. The trend is clear though often missed: the United States deployed significant military force abroad at least ten times between 1989 and 2011: Panama (1989); Iraq (1991, 1998, and 2003); Somalia (1992); Haiti (1994); Bosnia (1994–1995); Kosovo (1999); Afghanistan (2001); and Libya (2011). Panama and Haiti excepted, every action was justified, at least in part, as the rescue of Muslims from brutalization.

What was Clinton's motive for advancing this trend? It would be naive to insist that the Muslim liberation thesis is wholly explanatory – though ahistorical too, to insist that the sectarian dimensions of the conflict played no part in Clinton's decision to bomb Serbia. The combination of personal revulsion and geostrategic interests produced an enabling environment for NATO aggression. Clinton and Blair both cast the campaign against Milošević as the direct result of Serbian ethnic cleansing in Kosovo. Clinton's regret at having stood idly by during the Rwandan genocide in 1994, he says, made him determined to not repeat the omission. Blair, for his part, was keen to give teeth to his "doctrine of the international community" and test it against Serbia – a state guilty of "a monstrous and unpardonable outrage."[28] Indeed, for both men, the demands of international morality were such that the premier instrument of international legality, the United Nations, was to be ignored for its refusal to allow the air war.

Woven into this Anglo-American moral fervor was a more ancient enmity toward Russian interests. It could hardly have escaped notice that the Serbs were regarded by Moscow as allies, as Orthodox kin, to be

---

[28] Blair, *A Journey*, p. 237.

defended – a Slavic alliance that helped spark the First World War. For centuries, Russia had perceived itself as the protector of the Slav peoples of the Balkans. Now, the Arkansan was threatening to liberate Kosovo from Russia's cousins, for that would be and was the practical effect of a war on behalf of the KLA. To add insult to Russian injury, Clinton made war on Serbia only weeks after concluding the expansion of NATO into the Czech Republic, Hungary, and Poland. In the weeks after the bombing stopped, Clinton was to narrowly avoid direct confrontation between his troops and Yeltsin's as they both converged on Pristina airport. This episode was later depicted in popular patriotic movie, funded by the Russian government: *The Balkan Line* (2019). Putin has long observed the iniquity of US action toward Serbia.

In London and Washington, however, offending Russia was viewed as a necessary consequence of maintaining NATO credibility in South Central Europe; "What price NATO credibility?" asked Tony Blair.[29] Realists explain the Kosovo intervention, not as the result of a newfound Western moralism or love of Muslims, but as a way to contain Russian power by advancing the cause of its historic opponent: the NATO alliance, the fiftieth birthday of which coincided with the Kosovo War. Clinton's greatest foreign policy achievement, certainly to this point, was the enlargement of NATO. Should it be unable to act east of the old Cold War line, the rationale for that enlargement into Serbia's near neighbors Poland, Hungary, and the Czech Republic would be exposed as a chimera.

At the time, Albright protested that America had all along sought to placate Russian concerns and had even countenanced inviting Moscow to join NATO. US diplomats called this effort the Partnership for Peace (or PfP), but it labored in the Cold War's shadow. Russia, even under the hapless Boris Yeltsin, was skeptical of Western motives; under his more ruthless successor, it became determinedly antithetical. If Clinton wanted to forget the Cold War, Vladimir Putin did not.

The often Americentric history of the post–Cold War decades assumes the new-dawn, new-think approach of the Clinton administration was more widely-shared than the historical record allows. Many Russians were and remain nostalgic for the Cold War. Putin, the longest-serving Russian leader since Joseph Stalin, described the demise of the USSR as the "greatest geopolitical catastrophe" of the twentieth century. Perhaps

[29] Blair, *A Journey*, p. 239.

what is remarkable is less this Russian revanchism than the US delusion that its own interests toward Eastern Europe and Russia were transformed by Soviet collapse. Clinton and Blair's humanitarian war should not obscure the continuity with Cold War strategy that their Kosovo intervention highlights. As George W. Bush was to observe when Russia went to war with Georgia in 2008, the Cold War spheres of influence were not as easy to erase as many in the West assumed. Obama was to say much the same when Russia annexed Crimea in 2014.

The Kosovo War delivered two contradictory messages. First, it demonstrated how military technology had become so advanced on the Western side that wars could be fought with confidence that few of its soldiers would be killed. Second, the supposedly low-cost interventionism that this "revolution in military affairs" presaged actually relied on a very traditional view of American statecraft. This revolution, like that ushered in by the use of nuclear weapons in 1945, did not propel international relations in a wholly new direction. Both revolutions altered military calculations, but neither rendered war obsolete. The advent of computers did not shield the United States from war any more than did splitting the atom. Despite protestations that Kosovo represented a new departure in warfare, its character was rooted in the Cold War.

The Kosovo War was waged by and through the North Atlantic Treaty Organization, the Cold War international institution par excellence. While NATO had done very little fighting in the Cold War, the US-led alliance was the key bulwark against the USSR throughout the conflict. Indeed, liberated from some of the constraints the Soviet Union imposed upon it, NATO was used substantially to continue the containment of Russian power after the collapse of the USSR: first, in its near abroad through the ascension of Eastern European states into it; second, by using NATO to dislodge by force a Russian ally, Serbia, from its spiritual homeland, Kosovo. The Kosovo War, like every campaign of the Cold War, was waged by the United States in order, at least in part, to constrain and contain Russian power. And like every US military action in the Cold War, with the exception of Korea, the war was waged without a United Nations resolution, a pattern that continued into the post-9/11 era. George W. Bush fought the Iraq War four years later for many of the same reasons – to liberate Muslims and to advance US national security – using essentially the same set of tools, the tried and tested efficacy of the Anglo-American special relationship.

The key difference between Kosovo and every US war that preceded it, which explains why the war became a problematic model for Iraq, was the number of US causalities. Not a single solider on the NATO side was killed by enemy fire (two died as a result of a helicopter accident). Unlike any other war in history, Kosovo was held to herald casualty-free war. Technology, controlled by joysticks several thousand miles away, could now deliver victory previously the preserve of massed boots on the ground. Believers in the Kosovo precedent saw this as a revolution in military affairs. The nature of warfare, and thus of US interests, had been transformed. Entrenched regimes could now be removed not by large-scale invasion and long-term occupation, but by lightning strikes, technological dominance, and the swift withdrawal of negligible US combat forces. Iraq's fate, with hindsight, was sealed by the US experience and exuberance in Kosovo. "In bypassing the United Nations, engaging in disingenuous negotiations that precluded diplomatic solutions and manipulating the public case for war," as one observer later argued, "NATO's intervention over Kosovo in 1999 was an important precursor to the invasion of Iraq in 2003."[30]

According to British scholar David Hastings Dunn, the Kosovo campaign "represented an important way-marker in the contorted evolution of America's attitude towards the use of force in the post–Cold War period."[31] The war, warned Philip Gordon, had induced "a profound optimism that we ... can invade a country halfway round the world and bring about a reasonable settlement."[32] Kosovo was the enabling war for those that were to follow 9/11.

CAMP DAVID II

In the final summer of his presidency, Clinton spent twelve days at Camp David, the president's woodland retreat in Maryland, renamed by Eisenhower after his grandson, with Israeli and Palestinian leaders in a failed bid to forge a peace agreement. It was a concerted attempt to recreate Jimmy Carter's success there in 1978, when he brought Egypt and Israel into agreement. It was one of the few instances when events favored Carter rather than Clinton. The former was contending with two well-established leaders, Menachem Begin of Israel and Anwar Sadat of Egypt. The 1978 negotiations were the president's central focus over thirteen

---

[30] Ian Bancroft, Serbia's Anniversary Is a Timely Reminder, *Guardian*, March 25, 2009.
[31] David Hastings Dunn, Innovation and Precedent in the Kosovo War: The Impact of Operation Allied Force on U.S. Foreign Policy, *International Affairs* 85, 3 (May 2009): 531–546.
[32] In Dunn, Innovation and Precedent, p. 539.

days, which Carter spent exclusively at Camp David.[33] In 2000, negotiations had to compete with several other priorities on the Clinton agenda, forcing him to fly in and out of the talks during the twelve days. The dispute in 1978 was between two nation states: Egypt and Israel. In 2000, it was between leaders who did not recognize each other's states: Israel and Palestine.

Clinton's presidency had begun hopefully. In September 1993, he beamed as he presided over a historic, if awkward, handshake between the Israeli Prime Minister Yitzhak Rabin and Palestine Liberation Organization (PLO) Chairman Yasser Arafat. The Oslo Accord that this sealed gave the Gaza Strip and West Bank, two of the most densely populated regions in the world, over to Palestinian control. Clinton followed this up in 1994 by brokering a rapprochement between Jordan and Israel. His finale in 2000, however, as a National Security Council staffer involved in the 1978 Camp David negotiations observed, was consumed by "distractions, hesitation, and frustration".[34]

Part of the problem was the absence of a clear model to follow. Indeed, the idea that the United States could "make peace" as a matter of will ignores the entrenched positions and agency of the competing sides. A mutual antipathy between Arabs and Jews long predates the creation of the United States. There were, of course, enduring enmities in the Irish conflict, but there, as not in the Middle East, America was able to play the role of honest broker. The Good Friday (or Belfast) Agreement (1998), which had been a stunning success for Clinton's diplomacy, offered a poor road map for Israel–Palestine. The Troubles were susceptible to a novel rather than universal peacemaking strategy. Clinton's mini-revolution within that conflict had been the embrace of both extremes at the expense of the middle ground. By the end of Clinton's presidency, Northern Ireland was controlled by the two parties that had flirted most with political violence. Terrorists/political prisoners were released. Democratic parties skeptical of this appeasement went into seemingly irrevocable decline.[35]

---

[33] See Jimmy Carter, *Keeping Faith: Memoirs of a President* (New York: Bantam Books, 1982), pp. 319–403 and *Foreign Relations of the United States, 1977–1980, Volume IX, Arab–Israeli Dispute, August 1978–December 1980*, second revised edition (Washington DC: GPO, 2018).

[34] William B. Quandt, *Peace Process: American Diplomacy and the Arab-Israeli Conflict since 1967*, revised edition (Washington, DC: Brookings Institution Press, 2001), p. 341. Quandt was a member of the US negotiating team in 1978.

[35] See Paul Bew, Northern Ireland Is No Model for Peace Processes, *Sunday Independent* [London], April 1, 2007.

How to adapt this to the Middle East? With great difficulty. Clinton's Irish solution to the Arab–Israeli conflict would have meant empowering Yisrael Beiteinu and Hamas – the opposite ends of the Israel–Palestine political spectrum – and assuming they would see more mutual gain in a compromise with each other than they would lose in ideological authenticity. It also assumes there would be legislative assemblies, as in Belfast, in which members of both might sit. Neither this reciprocity, nor the institutions where it might have been played out, were apparent. Clinton was stuck with trying to persuade skeptical Israeli leaders that they should trust equally skeptical Palestinian ones. A three-way dialogue of mistrust ensued. Israeli leaders changed, but their skepticism did not. Palestinian leaders did not change (Yasser Arafat was chairman of the PLO from 1969 to 2004), and this fact tended to reinforce Israeli doubts of his good faith. Clinton was to leave office with a Second Intifada – a period of intensified Palestinian violence against Israel – under way.

There is a large scholarly industry dedicated to blaming one side or the other (or both) for this recurrent failure. The cycle of violence–diplomacy–violence has been basic to the history of modern Israel since its founding in 1948. Clinton's attempt to solve it was grounded less in the substance of the quarrel – which in its essence is over whether (and where) Israel or Palestine has the right to exist – than in his hope that his own charisma would bring the two sides together. Measuring the impact of a president's personality on any political situation is difficult. But Clinton's uniquely personal approach to the actors in Northern Ireland had a positive effect, which several of them later documented. Israel–Palestine was less susceptible to this style of diplomacy. The "spirit of Camp David," which, Eisenhower said, "must simply mean that it looks like we can talk together without being mutually abusive," eluded Clinton.[36]

Clinton's peacemaking was further hampered by the impeachment imbroglio through 1998 and the Kosovo War in 1999, both of which coincided with a renewed effort to move Yasser Arafat and Benjamin Netanyahu (Israeli prime minister from 1996 to 1999) to an accord. Their signing of the Wye Agreement in October 1998 – after Clinton "pulled an all-nighter" to make it happen – encouraged hope. But his impeachment and then Kosovo robbed Bill Clinton of the necessary political and intellectual space to keep agreement in focus. Wye also had to take root against the backdrop of Israeli elections in May 1999 and Arafat's threat

[36] In Lawrence Wright, *Thirteen Days in September: The Dramatic Story of the Struggle for Peace* (New York: Vintage, 2015), p. 62.

to unilaterally declare a Palestinian state in the same month. Events in the region were conspiring to weaken the prospects of peace, even before Clinton's other agenda items were factored in.

The result was a Herculean but late effort in July 2000 (Camp David II, the sequel to Camp David I in 1978) to clutch a peace from the jaws of stalemate and violence. It was, said Clinton, time for a "Hail Mary Pass." But no touchdown was scored. Clinton blamed Arafat's intransigence and preferred to feel the pain of the Israeli prime minister, Ehud Barak. He had shown a braver willingness to compromise, said Clinton. Both men knew they were on borrowed political time. Clinton would enter his lame-duck period in less than four months. By March 2001, Barak would be replaced. Arafat, whom only death (in 2004) would remove from his leadership of the PLO, chose to dig in and exploit his apparent permanence. The shadow of the first Camp David negotiations was less conducive to peace than Bill Clinton had hoped. Jimmy Carter had presided over a negotiation between Egyptian and Israeli leaders who enjoyed much greater domestic support than Arafat and Barak did a generation later. And the issue in 1978 – over Egypt's willingness to recognize the state of Israel – was not nearly as thorny as in 2000, when the street-by-street status of Jerusalem was part of myriad disagreements. No amount of telephone diplomacy in the remaining months of the Clinton administration was able to rescue what was lost in the Maryland woods that July.

THE 2000 ELECTION

Clinton's popularity, because of and coupled with a booming economy, should have enabled his vice-president to succeed him. Instead, Al Gore lost his home state of Tennessee and was unable to lawyer his way past his Republican opponent, after the closest presidential election in American history was decided in the US Supreme Court. George W. Bush won 271 electoral college votes to Gore's 266, but lost the popular vote 47.9 to 48.4 percent. Unable to guarantee the accuracy of a recount in Florida, the Supreme Court awarded its 25 votes to Bush. This intense politico-legal dispute took over a month to resolve; Bush labored under its legacy for years. Claims that the election had been "stolen" by the Texan meant he had to fight hard for legitimacy from the very beginning.[37]

---

[37] See, for example, Vincent Bugliosi, _The Betrayal of America: How the Supreme Court Undermined the Constitution and Chose Our President_ (New York: Thunder's Mouth Press, 2001).

What foreign policy vision had been validated by Bush's victory? This was a hard question to answer, given the ambiguity of the result. Had the electorate endorsed Bush-style "retrenchment" ("humility," he called it) and rejected Gore's "hawkish internationalism"? Of the two contenders in November, it was Gore who looked the more likely to continue a tradition of military interventionism. Bush, on the other hand, campaigned against the military profligacy of the Clinton years. But a foreign policy clash did not define the 2000 contest, as it would four years later. Opinion polling suggested an electorate that was ambivalent to apathetic about the role of the United States in the world. Gore, we see with hindsight, lost votes among blue-collar Democrats on the issue of the North American Free Trade Agreement (NAFTA), depicted by Republicans as a destroyer of middle-American manufacturing jobs, a phenomenon more fully exploited by Donald Trump sixteen years later. In 2000, however, there was no sapping military occupation abroad that might account for Gore's failure. The rising price of gas, according to Pew, drew the most public attention that year.[38] The world seemed calm to Americans – though a storm was gathering.

CONCLUSION

Bill Clinton's foreign policy more reflected than repudiated the Cold War. This was despite his efforts to transcend the "old think" of Cold War politics. At home, US foreign policy was as prone to party polarization and rancor as it had been in the 1950s. Then, Republicans accused Democrats of "losing China." In the 1990s, no doubt stoked by the passions generated by Clinton's impeachment, Democrats accused Republicans of playing politics with foreign policy. GOP presidential candidates in 2000, in turn, called for humility overseas; America, declared George W. Bush, the Governor of Texas, should do less, not more. Abroad, the world was coming to coalesce not around the blue zone of market democracies – as Clinton, *pace* Fukuyama, had predicted – but into two camps. One held within it the democracies of the world. In the other resided autocracies like Russia and China, determined to match Western wealth without having to embrace Western freedoms.

    Could Bill Clinton have predicted in 1993 that this state of affairs would obtain as he left office? His largely futile investment in Russia's

---

[38] Rising Price of Gas Draws Most Public Interest in 2000, Pew Research Center, December 25, 2000.

transition from penurious communism to gangster capitalism remains an uncomfortable part of his legacy. The engagement of Africa, despite his affection for that continent and its peoples, did not outlast the Somalia episode. Rwanda remains a stain on Clinton's foreign policy for which he was later moved to apologize. It was Clinton's successor who was to earn praise for his war on AIDS on that continent. Clinton left Africa as he found it, largely locked behind regimes whose nostalgia for Soviet subvention and Marxist ideology was too often greater than their desire for political reform and good governance. Communist China began its remarkable penetration of Africa during the Clinton years.

Nevertheless, his foreign policy contained significant achievements. These were both willed and accidental. He willed a peace in Northern Ireland and deployed great diplomatic skill to entrench it. His willingness to depict Serbia as the villain of postcommunist Yugoslavia, and to make war on it, was decisive in the survival of Bosnia and the creation of Kosovo as independent majority Muslim states. His enthusiasm was a key factor in the expansion of NATO into Poland, Hungary, and the Czech Republic. And his grasp of the American domestic economic landscape meant he was able to get NAFTA passed. There was little path-dependency in these achievements. For each, Clinton did something his predecessors did not. He took risks, made wars, and upset friends and foes. He was committed to changing things and, as he often reminded audiences, and as Machiavelli observed, that is the one sure way to make enemies.

But it is also hard to ignore how simple good fortune favored him. He came into office at a moment when democracy seemed an unstoppable, even inevitable, fact of international politics. The playing field was conducive to his game plan. Big shifts were not necessary. Clinton reasoned he could nudge and prod in the direction to which history was already tending. The contrast with Jimmy Carter is telling. Both men came from similar backgrounds. They had run large, poor, southern states. Each was a man of religious faith, articulated for political advantage. Both professed a moral component in their agenda. Both wished to transcend the Cold War. The difference between them is the luck each enjoyed: Carter got little, Clinton got much. The Georgian, we might conclude, was a Bill Clinton, but without the luck.

Carter's ambitious foreign policy was continually negated by events. As the first president elected after Richard Nixon, he promised a fresh start, but was burdened by the distrust of politics the Watergate scandal had generated. Carter's desire to get beyond Cold War binaries and remove the USSR from the center of American foreign policy was undone by Soviet behavior. Its support of African Marxists and invasion of Afghanistan made Carter's efforts to downplay Moscow's importance seem naïve.[39] Perhaps the worst luck Carter suffered was to become president just as Iran was reaching a revolutionary boil. The humiliation heaped on his administration – when students seized the US embassy in Tehran and fifty-four of its diplomats – was to last for its final 444 days. Their release came the day Carter's successor, Ronald Reagan, was sworn in. Carter endured these slings and arrows during a decade of economic crisis and oil shocks.

Clinton's inheritance was benign to positively advantageous in comparison. The Soviet Union had collapsed in 1991 and the Russian Federation that remained represented a geopolitical threat of much less magnitude. Clinton deigned to both fund its democratization and to make war on its ancient cousins, the Serbs. In 1998, he took NATO into Russia's backyard. Russians have not yet forgiven this condescension, but the fact that Clinton enjoyed this room for maneuver suggests how far luck favored him. The demise of the Cold War made old enmities in Ireland susceptible to American intercession. Carter had been chastised for trying to take a line on the Troubles; Clinton was lauded for doing so. And all of this unfolded against a backdrop of economic boom and rising prosperity at home.

But Clinton's luck did not preclude failure. Clearly, his emotional investment in post–Soviet Russia did not entrench democracy there. In the 1940s, George Kennan had urged America to be less an adversary of than an example to the USSR. The mere fact of American politico-economic success would cause Russians to ditch communism. Clinton adapted this prescription in the 1990s. Clinton was adamant that a traditional Russian distrust of Western power could be overcome with economic largesse. However, a revolution in Russian economics, urged and supported by the United States, created disorientation and dislocation for many Russians. This laid the framework for the strongman politics of Vladimir Putin. His nostalgia for the Cold War and his success in defining Russian interests by it was greater than Clinton's faith that the world had moved on. Putin's Cold War fetish was to bedevil – and in Donald Trump's case, seduce – American foreign policy for the next decades.

[39] See *Foreign Relations of the United States, 1977–1980, Vol. XII, Afghanistan* (Washington, DC: GPO, 2019).

In January 2000, at the beginning of Clinton's final year in office, two Arabs met in Malaysia. In May, they slipped quietly into the United States, enrolling in a pilot training school. On September 11, 2001, Nawaf al-Hazmi and Khalid al-Mihdhar would join seventeen other operatives of an Islamic jihadist group called al-Qaeda and carry out the most destructive terrorist attack in history. With dramatic irony, the response to these attacks became the responsibility of a man skeptical of his predecessor's military adventurism and nation-building, who wanted a return to a humbler foreign policy.

4

George W. Bush

A New Cold War, 2001–2004

There are decades where nothing happens, and there are weeks where decades happen.

—*Vladimir Lenin*

In spirit, the Trade Center is a United Nations of Commerce. In concept, the Trade Center is a marketplace for the Free World. In operation, the Trade Center will be a thriving city within a city, the dynamo of the port's trade with the world.

—*Austin J. Tobin, executive director of the New York Port Authority, 1966*[1]

On September 11, 2001, former President Bill Clinton was in Australia and the Australian prime minister John Howard was in Washington, DC. Clinton was raising money for his presidential library. Howard was renewing the Cold War Australia, New Zealand and United States Security Treaty, or ANZUS Treaty – fifty years old that year.[2] Like many Americans on that terrible day, Clinton visibly and publicly wept. He did so for two reasons. The first was that this was the simple human response to so much slaughter. The second, because this day should have been his, the great crisis that might have transformed his presidency instead of transforming that of his successor. The response to the 9/11 attacks would be led not by the man who had liberated Kosovo, enlarged NATO,

---

[1] The quotation is given prominence in the 9/11 Memorial and Museum, New York City.
[2] See John Howard, *Lazarus Rising: A Personal and Political Biography* (New York: HarperCollins, 2010), chap. 31. ANZUS was signed in 1951.

and brought peace to Northern Ireland. Instead, it was to be waged, according to his many detractors, by an untested foreign policy naïf, a man who rose on his father's coattails and whose election was doubtful. Great presidents require great crises. Clinton missed his by a mere eight months.

George W. Bush was the first, but not – it turned out – the last man since 1877 to become president after having received a smaller share of the popular vote than his opponent. His presidency was born with a nagging sense of illegitimacy. Few presidents of the modern era encountered a press and popular culture so keen for him to fail. As a response to his critics, Bush offered humility. At home, he would seek to heal partisanship. Abroad, he would make America less interfering. Clinton had overreached himself in the pursuit of a moral agenda. Bush, instead, called for "a distinctly American internationalism. Idealism, without illusions. Confidence, without conceit. Realism, in the service of American ideals."[3]

This return to normalcy, as Bush painted it, was undone by the terrorist attacks of that September morning. A man previously pledging to do less became the most belligerent Republican president since Abraham Lincoln. The great wars of the twentieth century were joined or initiated by Democratic presidents rather than by Republican ones: both world wars, Korea, Vietnam, Bosnia, and Kosovo. Bush bucked that trend. He left office with the United States in military occupation of two states, one barely pacified, the other seemingly incapable of pacification. The "good war" in Afghanistan was to become the longest in American history. The botched reconstruction of Iraq would linger for decades.

His biography did not cry "war leader." Bush came to politics after decades of waywardness. Psychobiographies paint him as a son with a dad complex. A young man lacking seriousness, he goofed off at elite private schools and at Yale (1965–1968). He later quipped in a commencement address at his alma mater, "To those of you who received honors, awards, and distinctions, I say, well done. And to the C students I say, you, too, can be President of the United States."[4] Bill Clinton's Vietnam War had been fought behind a beard at Oxford University.

---

[3] George W. Bush, "A Distinctly American Internationalism," speech at Ronald Reagan Presidential Library, Simi Valley, California, November 19, 1999.

[4] Commencement address at Yale University, New Haven, Connecticut, May 21, 2001. He also said, "It is great to return to New Haven. My car was followed all the way from the airport by a long line of police cars with slowly rotating lights. It was just like being an undergraduate again."

Bush fought his from the relative security of the Texas Air National Guard. An average businessman in the Texan oil industry thereafter, his early forays into politics were failures. He drank too much. His passion was baseball, not public service. Those who knew the family assumed his steadier younger brother, Jeb, would attain high office. Two events changed his trajectory. He met Laura Welch (he said marrying her in 1977 was "the best decision I ever made") and then underwent a spiritual conversion.

On July 28, 1986, aged 40, George W. Bush awoke with a hangover. He attempted, as usual, to jog it off. "This run was different. I felt worse than usual, and about halfway through, I decided I would drink no more."[5] His new sobriety catalyzed his Christian faith. He became disciplined, if abidingly instinctual, in pursuit of his objectives. It was a trait he would carry into the Oval Office fifteen years later. His detractors would observe in this transformation sanctimony or a con job. Bush believed that it created a path and a signature style that took him to the governorship of the nation's fastest-growing state (he ran Texas from 1995–2000) and ultimately to the presidency of the United States itself.

THE BUSH TEAM

The discipline his conversion afforded him was manifest in how he ran his presidency. From the outset, Bush wanted to present a return to a grown-up White House. He got up early. He ran each morning until his knees eventually told him to switch to cycling. Meetings started on time. He was strict about going to bed. The contrast with his less-disciplined predecessor was deliberately conveyed. Where Clinton had relied on young men and women like George Stephanopoulos and Nancy Soderberg, Bush surrounded himself with political heavyweights. Foreign policy would be run by a triumvirate of seasoned Washington insiders: Dick Cheney, Colin Powell, and Donald Rumsfeld.[6]

If the intention was clear, the effect was mixed. Instead of an administration run by wise men, Bush inadvertently assembled three large egos and expected them not to quarrel. But quarrel they did. As we will see, personal differences were magnified in the tensions produced by a global War on Terror. The battles within that war, most notably over Iraq, suffered from differences among the Bush team more than they were

---

[5] In Stephen Mansfield, *The Faith of George W. Bush* (Lake Mary, FL: Charisma House, 2003), p. 72.
[6] See James Mann, *Rise of the Vulcans: The History of Bush's War Cabinet* (New York: Viking, 2004).

advanced by its synergies. In the post–Bush years, each penned a memoir critical of the others.

At the outset, however, the elevation of Dick Cheney to the vice-presidency signaled a return to a steady realism in US foreign policy. Cheney, 60 in 2001, had been a senior advisor to Richard Nixon and secretary of defense under George H. W. Bush. Despite only a cursory acquaintance with Bush Jr. prior to 2000, Cheney was to earn the title "Bush's brain," which flattered him, undermined his boss, and was eventually to weaken Bush's confidence in him. Cheney's reputation at the time was as the most powerful vice-president in American history. Dan Quayle, vice-president under Bush Sr., had joked with him that all he would do is fundraise and attend funerals on behalf of his boss. "I have a different understanding with the president," replied Cheney.[7]

Colin Powell was the second big beast in Bush's cabinet. The most famous soldier of his era, Powell had served in the Reagan administration (as national security advisor) and under Bush Sr. and Clinton (as chairman of the joint chiefs). Until the advent of Barack Obama, Powell could plausibly claim to be the most powerful African–American in US history. His approach to foreign policy was to eschew military confrontations – if America broke something it would own it, so better not to break it in the first place – and to oppose Donald Rumsfeld.

Rumsfeld was the most colorful and controversial secretary of defense since Robert S. McNamara in the 1960s. He became the youngest and oldest man to hold that post, having first served in the Ford administration in his early forties. The key men who were to lead America into the War on Terror were the products of the Cold War. Bill Clinton recycled Carter officials; George W. Bush recycled Ford, Reagan, and Bush Sr. officials. Even his national security advisor, Condoleezza Rice, had been the protégé of Brent Scowcroft, the last Cold War holder of that office; Rice's PhD thesis was on the Czech army under communism. Her challenge was somehow to bring the large egos of the Bush cabinet into creative tension. She enjoyed more failure than success in this regard.

THE FIRST NINE MONTHS

Bush struck an immediate note of continuity with his predecessor by attacking Iraq. On February 16, he authorized air raids on Iraqi radar

---

[7] In Barton Gellman, *Angler: The Cheney Vice Presidency* (New York: Penguin, 2008), p. 58.

stations for the regime's violation of the no-fly zone. If the substance of US governance had not changed, however, he did alter its style. Compared to the sexual theatrics of the Clinton presidency, Bush presaged a return to steady administration run by adults. And in at least the first nine months, this is what he delivered up. In March, he abandoned Clinton's quixotic quest for ratification of the Kyoto Protocol on climate change; it could never get the numbers in Congress, Bush argued convincingly. He applied a similar realism to China the next month. Whereas Bill Clinton, in striking at Serbia, had accidentally attacked the Chinese embassy in Belgrade, George W. Bush exhibited a far more competent diplomacy toward the People's Republic in the first crisis of his presidency. Bush inherited his father's cautious optimism about China. He would deal with Beijing "without ill will – but without illusions ... unthreatened but not unchecked."[8] In an April standoff with China, eclipsed by the events of September, Bush exhibited a patience rarely attributed to him by his detractors.

On April 1, a US Navy intelligence aircraft was "buzzed" by a People's Liberation Army Navy interceptor fighter. The deliberate contact, with tragic irony, caused the Chinese plane to crash (killing its pilot) and the US crew to crash-land on the Chinese island of Hainan. Beijing demanded the US plane be turned over to them. Bush resisted. China had been the aggressor, he said. This toing and froing continued for 10 days. The impasse was broken when Bush decided that continued obstinacy by his administration would cost more diplomatically than it would secure militarily; the twenty-four US pilots on the stricken craft made sure they destroyed as much sensitive intelligence within the plane as possible before China took possession. The conservative *Weekly Standard* condemned Bush for accepting a "profound national humiliation," but the new president had made clear in his handling of the crisis how realpolitik he was prepared to be.[9]

Pilots had often been chess pieces in the Cold War. Francis Gary Powers had famously been shot down over Soviet air space in May 1960. North Korea killed thirty-one Americans when it shot down a US spy plane in 1969. Reagan made moral hay in his denunciation of the USSR's shooting down of a South Korean passenger airliner in 1983. What was different with Bush in April 2001 was his refusal to depict the standoff as a test of his ideological resolve. Rather, he saw a higher

---

[8] Bush, speech at Reagan Library, November 19, 1999.
[9] Editorial, A National Humiliation, *Weekly Standard*, April 16, 2001.

purpose in appeasing the Chinese government over a situation where geography did not favor American bellicosity. He was to realize some reward for this when, after the September 11 attacks, Sino–American counterterrorism cooperation momentarily bloomed – before a more familiar Cold War–style distrust over military intentions resumed.

9/11

As the spy plane crisis ebbed, a new plane crisis flowed. By April 2001, the plotting of the deadliest terrorist attack in American history was as advanced as it was hidden. The official US government report into those attacks opens with simple clarity:

> Tuesday, September 11, 2001, dawned temperate and nearly cloudless in the eastern United States. Millions of men and women readied themselves for work. Some made their way to the Twin Towers, the signature structures of the World Trade Center complex in New York City. Others went to Arlington, Virginia, to the Pentagon. Across the Potomac River, the United States Congress was back in session. At the other end of Pennsylvania Avenue, people began to line up for a White House tour. In Sarasota, Florida, President George W. Bush went for an early morning run.
>
> For those heading to an airport, weather conditions could not have been better for a safe and pleasant journey. Among the travelers were Mohamed Atta and Abdul Aziz al Omari, who arrived at the airport in Portland, Maine.[10]

Despite much implausible conspiracy theorizing around it, the sequence of events on the day itself is now well documented. Following a few days of Vegas-style debauchery, nineteen young Arabs shaved themselves from neck to toe, in apparent obedience to a Koranic stipulation, and boarded four commercial flights, each heading from the East to the West Coast. The aim, realized almost completely, was to hijack the planes, and then simultaneously fly them into the symbolic centers of America's military, economic, and political power: the Pentagon, the World Trade Center, and the White House or Capitol Hill.

Within minutes of the takeoff of each plane, having defeated all the security layers that America's civil aviation security system then had in place to prevent a hijacking, the terrorists rushed the cockpit, incapacitated or killed the captain, and seized control of the plane. Knowing how

---

[10] *The 9/11 Commission Report: Final Report of the National Commission on Terrorist Attacks upon the United States*, Authorized Edition (New York: W. W. Norton, 2004), p. 1.

to steer, ascend, and descend, but not how to land, the rogue pilots set a course for New York and Washington, DC. The first and second hijacked planes, out of Boston, Massachusetts, flew into the North Tower and South Tower of the World Trade Center in New York. The third plane, out of Newark, New Jersey, hit the Pentagon. The fourth plane, United 93, out of Dulles airport in Washington, DC, was later judged to be heading for the White House or the more visible Congress. It was brought down near Shanksville, Pennsylvania, by desperate passengers whose loved ones, via cell phones, had told them the fate of the first three planes. In total, 2,977 people were killed: 2,753 in New York; 184 in Washington, DC; and 40 in Pennsylvania. Ten percent of the dead were New York firefighters who had rushed into the towers, disbelieving that they could fall. The attacks lasted 102 minutes; their reverberations, for years. According to the *New Scientist*, the carcinogens released from the collapse of the World Trade Center will eventually kill more people over the ensuing decades than the number who died on the day itself.[11]

Its perpetrators were members of al-Qaeda – "the base" in Arabic. Its leader was a Saudi national called Osama bin Laden. The heir to a great construction fortune, he instead chose the path of religious warfare against the Saudi Arabian royal family and its key backer, the US government. Affronted by the occupation of his homeland – the land of the prophet – by US troops following the 1991 Gulf War, bin Laden spent the 1990s in whichever country would afford him residency, plotting the death of Americans. He had been exiled from Saudi Arabia in 1992. His initial efforts seemed significant at the time but were small fry compared to his success on 9/11. In August 1998, al-Qaeda bombed the US embassies in Kenya and Tanzania, killing 224 (including 12 Americans) and wounding thousands. In reprisal, Bill Clinton launched ineffective missile strikes on al-Qaeda bases in Sudan and Afghanistan. Neither killed bin Laden. In October 2000, his operatives drove a small boat packed with explosives into the hull of the USS *Cole* as it was docked in Aden harbor, Yemen. Seventeen US sailors were killed. "We thank God for granting us victory the day we destroyed *Cole* in the sea," declared bin Laden.[12]

These attacks, a long way from the American homeland, were an indication of the more audacious action he had in store. From 1998 to

[11] Andy Coghlan, Deaths from 9/11-related Illness Are Set to Exceed Initial Toll, *New Scientist*, September 12, 2016.
[12] Diana Elias, Video Offers Strong Bin Laden–USS Cole Link, *ABC News*, June 19, 2001.

2001, bin Laden organized the most cost-effective terrorist attack in history. Estimates vary, but for an outlay of not much more than $500,000, nineteen terrorists and their sponsors inflicted damages ranging from $10 billion to $5,900 billion – if $5.9 trillion, the estimated and still rising cost of the ensuing War on Terror, is seen as the substantive response to the 9/11 attacks.[13] The ratio of costs to damages is even larger when we factor in the domestic and foreign counterterrorism measures enacted in the years since.

The psychological damages, of course, were incalculable. The expectation that the attack presaged more and worse to come was widespread. It informs an almost primordial fear in the testimony of the men and women of the Bush administration, who became imbued with an intoxicating sense of resolve. If such simple tools could be turned into weapons, how much more terrible might a better funded and equipped enemy be? If the hatred of the nineteen men and their sponsors was so unquenchable, what might they achieve with better resources? These questions, asked in bewildered fashion in the first hours and days after the attacks, increasingly began to inform the response of the US government. This led to two interconnected objectives: first, to go after states that might provide that capacity and, second, to change the sociopolitical environment that gave rise to the hatred. The first was narrow in focus, immediate, and meant the removal from power of the terrorists' chief backers, the Taliban regime in Afghanistan, and, fifteen months later, the toppling of a regime in Iraq that Bush feared might back terrorists. The second objective was imprecise, lacked immediacy, and called for a reformation of Arab politics. Bush grasped the first on the afternoon of September 11 and came around gradually to the second.

In making this link between terrorism and what caused it, Bush was embracing one of two contrasting interpretations of what 9/11 meant. The first saw al-Qaeda's strike as a murderous fluke by lucky criminals, who should be captured and tried. The second, the one Bush shared, interpreted 9/11 not as bad luck but as a systemic failure. These men were the products of a poor environment. Many, starting with bin Laden himself, were wealthy and educated but lacked social status.[14] Unable to

[13] See Neta C. Crawford, United States Budgetary Costs of the Post–9/11 Wars through FY2019, Watson Institute for International and Public Affairs, November 14, 2018; at https://watson.brown.edu/costsofwar/figures/2018/budgetary-costs-post-911-wars-through-fy2019–59-trillion.
[14] See Daniel Pipes, God and Mammon: Does Poverty Cause Militant Islam? *National Interest* 66 (Winter 2001/2): 14–21.

find it in the repressive political climate of the Arab Middle East, they lashed out against the chief backer of multiple Arab regimes: the United States. Change that environment, bring freedom to Arabs, and the problem of terrorism could be solved. The first interpretation obliged a narrowly judicial response, similar to that obtaining after the first attack on the World Trade Center in 1993. The second invited a series of state-level wars against autocratic regimes deemed to be complicit in the breeding of terrorists, either directly by funding them or indirectly by causing grievances to fester. This was a curious inversion of an established pattern. Liberals usually blame crime on wider social ills and want to resolve their root causes. Conservatives have favored narrow solutions to crime: catching and imprisoning the guilty. After 9/11, these diagnoses switched around. Liberals critical of Bush wanted a narrowly criminal investigation. A loose coalition of conservatives and liberals, derided as "neoconservatives," who had lost faith with the do-nothingism of their respective wings, wanted and got Bush to embrace a larger international solution: remake Arab society. As Condoleezza Rice, the national security advisor, put it:

We had a very rude awakening on September 11th, when I think we realized that our policies to try and promote what we thought was stability in the Middle East had actually allowed, underneath, a very malignant, meaning cancerous, form of extremism to grow up underneath because people didn't have outlets for their political views.[15]

In this effort to provide a democratic outlet, the Bush administration was joined by Tony Blair, the British prime minister. Blair had been the first foreign leader to visit the United States after the attacks, attending the emotionally charged address by the president to a joint session of Congress on September 20. His speed was initially informed by a desire to rein in an American overreaction. (As Blair's chief of staff tells it: Margaret Thatcher had told George Bush Sr. to "not wobble" over Iraq in 1990; Tony Blair wanted Bush Jr. to do just that.)[16] However, fears of overreaction soon gave way to fears of underreaction. In Bush, Blair did not have the democratizing hawk he had wanted. But he did see a president willing to question his prior assumptions. Through the lens of the Kosovo war, two-and-a-half years earlier, Bush's new belligerence

---

[15] In Jackson Diehl, Rice's Rhetoric, in Full Retreat, *Washington Post*, January 22, 2007.
[16] Jonathan Powell in Jean Edward Smith, *Bush* (New York: Simon & Schuster, 2016), p. 248.

seemed an appropriate vehicle to realize the loftier ambitions of Blair's hawkish internationalism. Blair had called it his "Doctrine of the International Community."[17] His critics labeled it "warlike idealism."[18]

Renewing that emphasis after 9/11, Blair defined the attacks as of "epoch-making proportions."[19] He said, "this is a moment to seize. The kaleidoscope has been shaken. The pieces are in flux. Soon they will settle again. Before they do, let us re-order this world around us."[20] The caricature of a British poodle doing its American owner's bidding was misplaced. If there was a tail wagging the US dog after 9/11, it was Tony Blair's. His missionary Catholic liberalism and Bush's Christian conservatism fused to produce an enduringly controversial synthesis of realist means for liberal objectives. Its ultimate laboratory would be Iraq – after the "easy" war in Afghanistan.

THE AFGHANISTAN WAR

In power since 1996, the Afghan Taliban government was almost clownishly vicious in its dominion. Asserting a religious duty to remove females from the public sphere, the Taliban dedicated themselves to removing young women from school and to the flogging of women who transgressed their medieval dress codes. Kite-flying was banned. These injustices and inanities attracted little global attention until the Taliban's limited resources – deriving largely from selling opium on the international drug market – were used to support the al-Qaeda terrorist network. What had been ignored as Islamist idiosyncrasies were, after 9/11, deemed a vital national security threat to the United States. The US-led war in Afghanistan thus began with an unimpeachable motivation: to remove the Taliban regime from the crude power that it exercised over the ancient nation.

Bush and his allies resolved to break the connection between the Taliban and al-Qaeda – a terrorist organization dependent on government-level support to wage effective, 9/11-style war on Americans. The 9/11 attacks had revealed how al-Qaeda's capacity was directly proportionate to the state-level support it received – so America resolved

---

[17] See Blair speech at Chicago Economic Club, April 22, 1999.
[18] See Patrick Porter, *Blunder: Britain's War in Iraq* (Oxford: Oxford University Press, 2018), p. 2.
[19] Blair speech to Parliament, September 14, 2001.
[20] Blair speech at Labor Party Conference, October 2, 2001.

to change that state. Afghanistan was to be the "good war" – at least at its beginning. The necessity of its fighting was widely accepted. Some twenty-five allies joined the campaign. Leaving in power a government that had helped the 9/11 conspirators was never tenable. Even America's opponents, like Russia, offered moral and logistical (albeit limited) support.

In his September 20 address to Congress, George Bush demanded that the Afghan government surrender all al-Qaeda members operating in its jurisdiction. When the request was refused – "We don't control them," said a Taliban official – America and its NATO allies acted. Displacing the Taliban looked deceptively straightforward. In a matter of weeks, beginning in October, the Central Intelligence Agency had joined up with internal anti-Taliban forces and removed the Islamists from power. The "Afghan strategy" relied on the deployment of comparatively few US personnel. The lead role of the CIA suggested America could achieve its ambitions with minimal use of force; the exploitation of divisions within Afghanistan itself would do the job. The Northern Alliance proved the maxim that the enemy of my enemy is my friend. US success was purchased at the price of very few American casualties. Crucially, the strategy relied on having to do little in the aftermath of regime change, instead relying on anti-Taliban sections of Afghan society and international institutions to fill the vacuum. US troops, already late to the conflict to secure gains made by the CIA in October, would stand down as these actors stood up.

A policy of hopeful assumptions plagued Afghanistan from this point until reality finally set in nearly a decade later. The war was to become the longest in American history. The Bush administration was unable to rebuild the state using endogenous opposition to the Taliban and, in the absence of a unifying approach from the institutions of both the American government and its allies, fell back on counterterrorism as its measure of success. An already hollowed-out Afghan state remained so. Nation-building requires huge troop deployments, long-term commitment, and interagency cooperation. Each was in short supply. The first six to twelve months of any occupation are crucial. The logic is counterintuitive, but it is not invasions that require boots on the ground, but the occupation that follows them. In Afghanistan, however, an *intuitive* logic prevailed.[21] Too few troops were committed to the aftermath. Stunning military success was undone by the failure of what came after.

---

[21] See Conor Keane, *U.S. Nation-Building in Afghanistan* (Abingdon: Routledge, 2016), p. 26.

In seventy-eight days, the same time it took to win the Kosovo War in 1999 and with not many more American casualties, the United States had managed to subdue a nation the size and population of Texas using only about 5,000 ground troops. Bush had, as Terry Anderson wryly observed, "dispatched fewer troops to kill bin Laden, al-Qaeda, and the Taliban regime harboring them than the number of police officers assigned to any large American city, such as New York, Los Angeles, Chicago, or Houston."[22] Tragically, this fetish for military minimalism, learned in Kosovo and honed in Afghanistan, would be repeated barely a year later in Iraq. The War on Terror was becoming *insufficiently* militaristic.

THE BUSH DOCTRINE

Confident that the Afghan campaign was winding down, the Bush team set about establishing a set of strategic guideposts to frame what would come next. These were to comprise what became known as the Bush Doctrine. Its central objective was to stop terrorists from acquiring weapons of mass destruction. Consensus around this goal was strong in the aftermath of 9/11 and has remained so in the decades since. Bush and Obama each said it was their number-one national security priority. The arguments were, and remain, over how to achieve it.

The central features of the Bush Doctrine were presented in the president's speech to Congress on September 20, 2001; to cadets at West Point on June 1, 2002; in his second inaugural address, January 20, 2005; and, most fully, in the National Security Strategy, published by the White House in September 2002. Four key arguments were advanced. Critics were free to focus on the one or two they found most objectionable. Some derided the novelty and utility of all of them. Properly understood, however, the tenets were a reworking of approaches basic to US foreign policy for several decades, not least in the Cold War.

The Bush Doctrine, though Bush never called it that, argues that the president has the right to preempt an attack; that he can act outside of formal alliances and without international legal support, if necessary, to do this; that changing threatening regimes into democracies is worth a try; and that White House power will appropriately increase in order to accomplish the foregoing, but then fade when the crisis has passed. "Taken together," noted Robert Jervis, "these elements imply an

<hr/>

[22] Terry H. Anderson, *Bush's Wars* (New York: Oxford University Press, 2011), p. 87.

extraordinarily ambitious foreign policy agenda, involving not only the transformation of international politics, but also the re-making of many states and societies along democratic lines."[23] The Doctrine's defenders thought it Lincolnian. Its detractors warned it was impossible to implement. We will consider each tenet in turn.

Preemption

The first argument Bush made was that he had the obligation to preempt threats before they could be made real. "We will not hesitate to act alone, if necessary, to exercise our right of self-defense by acting preemptively,"[24] he said. "If we wait for threats to fully materialize, we will have waited too long."[25] In making this argument, Bush drew on a long-standing notion that waiting for the absolute certainty of an attack before doing something about it was absurd. According to Franklin Roosevelt, on September 11, 1941, "When you see a rattlesnake poised to strike, you do not wait until he has struck before you crush him."[26] Such reasoning, Bush made clear, was why preemption had been "long maintained" in US national security strategy: "For centuries, international law recognized that nations need not suffer an attack before they can lawfully take action to defend themselves against forces that present an imminent danger of attack."[27]

The problem with preemption was not its novelty – it has been axiomatic in statecraft for centuries – but the prophetic precision on which it relied. The right to preempt was not in dispute; adjudging "imminence" was. Good judgment needs accurate intelligence. The most sophisticated intelligence-gathering organization in the world had singularly failed to uncover, let alone preempt, the 9/11 plot. And yet that same organization, albeit in a revamped form, would have to be relied upon to get it right next time – and every time after that. Its first test, as we will see, was the preemption of Iraq's weapons of mass destruction (WMD) capacity – and it failed it significantly. Intelligence suggested Saddam Hussein had far more and complex weapons than turned out to be the case. This

[23] Robert Jervis, Why the Bush Doctrine Cannot Be Sustained, *Political Science Quarterly* 120, 3 (Fall 2005): 351–377, 352.
[24] White House, The National Security Strategy of the United States of America (September 20, 2002), p. 6; at http://nssarchive.us/.
[25] George W. Bush speech at West Point, New York, June 1, 2002.
[26] FDR, *Fireside Chat*, September 11, 1941.
[27] National Security Strategy (2002), p. 15.

intelligence, the veracity of which could only be tested by acting on it, was a crucial motivation in the US decision to make war upon him. But the intelligence was imperfect, to say the least.

Preemption also widened the potential scope of targets. If 9/11 had brought Iraq into US sights, by the same logic, Iran should have been similarly targeted. Its nuclear weapons development was more advanced than that of its neighbor. Its regime was fiercely anti-American and had a track record of terrorism sponsorship. Unlike Saddam Hussein, the Iranian government was avowedly Islamist. As the British scholar David Hastings Dunn asked, shouldn't "real men want to go to Tehran," which posed a much more compelling test of the Bush Doctrine?[28] The answer Bush proffered was "no, not yet." By making Iraq the subject of preemption, he hoped to persuade other regimes to abandon their WMD ambitions. This arguably worked in the case of Libya, as we will see in the next chapter. It did not work in the cases of Iran and North Korea. These two regimes upped their efforts to develop a deployable nuclear weapon, and neither was militarily preempted for doing so.

Coalitions of the Willing

The second tenet of the Bush Doctrine, closely connected to the first, is the right claimed by the United States to act outside of formal alliances if the situation requires it: "America will implement its strategies by organizing coalitions – as broad as practicable – of states able and willing to promote a balance of power that favors freedom." Bush referred to these as "flexible coalitions" or "coalitions of the willing."[29] Critics derided this as unilateralism, but Bush was not seeking to go it alone. Instead, his doctrine called for any and all allies to join the United States in tackling terrorism. But those alliances did not have to be formalized international institutions like the UN or even NATO. The mission would decide the alliance, not the alliance the mission. This meant that the United Nations could not expect to be the arbiter of what was moral or legal for the United States to undertake. Twice, Bush sought UN approval to remove Saddam Hussein. When it was twice refused, he organized a coalition to undertake it.

---

[28] David Hastings Dunn, "Real Men Want to Go to Tehran": Bush, Pre-emption and the Iranian Nuclear Challenge, *International Affairs* 83, 1 (January 2007): 19–38.

[29] National Security Strategy (2002), pp. 25, 10, 11.

Making war without the UN's say-so was an affront to those governments that saw the institution as a way to check American power. But the unilateralism that China, France, Germany, Russia, and others charged Bush with was not a revolution in American foreign policy. The United Nations had similarly been unable to constrain US behavior – or indeed that of the other permanent members of its Security Council – during the Cold War. With the exception of Korea in 1950, when the USSR failed to veto America's entry into the war, all American wars were waged outside of the United Nations. Its longest, in Vietnam, was fought, as Iraq was soon to be, with a coalition of willing nations (notably Australia and South Korea), not the United Nations. This Cold War precedent offered the Bush Doctrine significant legitimacy, albeit at the price of international legality. Making America safe, as the administration was to argue forcefully in 2002–2003, was more vital than appeasing international lawyers. As one White House official later claimed, international law was not much more "than a debate between academics."[30]

The 1999 Kosovo War fought by Bill Clinton had similarly relied on coalitions of the willing. That war had taken place, as would Iraq four years later, despite securing no "permission slip" from the United Nations. Clinton and now Bush measured the legitimacy of action not by how far they were able to cajole Paris and Moscow into supporting them, but by how likely the coalition they assembled was to succeed – a form of instrumental multilateralism. Russia opposed both wars. In 1999, France supported the United States; in 2003, it did not. The Bush administration argued, with some consistency, that US national security could not be contingent on French approval. Critics of the 2003 coalition mocked its posse-like status – rounded up by "Bush the cowboy" – but it was more similar to than different from that which bombed Serbia in 1999. "Is there a certain, magic number of supporting nations that bestows legitimacy?" asked Robert Kagan. "Or is it the quality of one's allies that matters more than the quantity when defining 'multilateralism'? Is France worth more than Spain?"[31] A member of the Bush administration asked, "How many nations, need to support an action before it is considered sufficiently multilateral and therefore justifiable? Ten? Fifty? One hundred and fifty? And what happens if a nation, perhaps for reasons of

[30] Douglas Feith, Under Secretary of Defense for Policy (2001–2005), comments at Clements Center, University of Texas, Austin, November 1, 2013.
[31] Kagan, *Of Paradise and Power* (2004), p. 146.

corruption or bad motivation, seeks to prevent a particular action from being taken?"[32]

Regime Change and the Freedom Agenda

The third tenet of the Bush Doctrine was the claimed right to overthrow regimes that threatened the United States. As with preemption and unilateralism, this was held as both a violation of Cold War precedent and as illegal if undertaken without UN approval. These criticisms were partly right and partly wrong. It was right insofar as we understand the Cold War as an exercise not in regime change but in the containment of governments opposed to US interests. Washington did not attempt to overthrow Chinese or Russian communism; it did mean to contain their influence. However, the means to this end often meant complicity in the destabilization and/or overthrow of regimes sympathetic to Beijing and Moscow.[33] Latin America was the most obvious testing ground of the theory. Communist Cuba was subject first to a failed invasion and then to a decades-long economic embargo. In Chile in 1973, the CIA supported the overthrow of a new Marxist government. In the 1980s, Ronald Reagan funded (illegally) an insurgency against the communist government of Nicaragua and played a controversial role in propping up right-wing regimes in Argentina and El Salvador.

However, given what was at stake in the Cold War, regime change was accomplished very rarely. Dictators, from Fidel Castro to Mao Zedong, lasted in power far longer than their White House counterparts. After the Cold War, this pattern endured. The leaders of Iran, North Korea, and Venezuela, men who defined themselves by their anti-Americanism, were not removed by the United States. Only after 9/11 did regimes start to fall as per US design and, even then, they were limited to just two: Afghanistan and Iraq. In his first State of the Union Address, January 20, 2002, President Bush described an "axis of evil," made up of Iraq, Iran, and North Korea, "arming to threaten the peace of the world." But by the end of his term, with the toppling of Saddam Hussein, the axis had been reduced by only a third. Obama and Trump went on to cut deals with the other two. The right to change regimes was a narrow one and

---

[32] Peter Wehner, cited by Norman Podhoretz, Is the Bush Doctrine Dead? *Commentary* (September 2006), p. 21.
[33] See Lindsey A. O'Rourke, *Covert Regime Change: America's Secret Cold War* (Ithaca, NY: Cornell University Press, 2018).

was confined to just those in Kabul and Baghdad. Like Bush, Reagan spoke of a "confederation of terrorist states" – comprising Iran, Libya, North Korea, Cuba, and Nicaragua – all of which remained intact by the time he left office.

What came to drive the Bush Doctrine was less the technical task of removing bad governments. Rather, it was the faith Bush himself came to place in freedom as a cure for American insecurity. A man given to spiritual conversion, it was perhaps no surprise that his pre–9/11 realism matured into its opposite. His National Security Strategy put it this way:

> The United States must defend liberty and justice because these principles are right and true for all people everywhere. No nation owns these aspirations, and no nation is exempt from them. Fathers and mothers in all societies want their children to be educated and to live free from poverty and violence. No people on earth yearn to be oppressed, aspire to servitude, or eagerly await the midnight knock of the secret police.[34]

The weakness was the disconnect between the aspiration to build "a balance of power that favors freedom" with the hard yards of nation-building necessary to achieve it. Bush's faith in this simple but compelling creed, rooted in the American political tradition, may well have increased proportionate to the catastrophic realities of post–invasion Iraq. But the idea that democracy was a necessary ingredient of his new approach was present in the buildup to the Iraq invasion. It was not hastily welded on when WMD stockpiles did not materialize. In a classified planning document, in August 2002, the aim was to create in Iraq a society "based on moderation, pluralism, and democracy."[35] When Rice's mentor, Brent Scowcroft, told her, "Condi, it's just not going to happen. You can't build democracy that way," her response was a firm, "Oh yes you can."[36] This newfound optimism in previously pessimistic foreign policymakers was a remarkable feature of the post–9/11 years. In several respects, Bush and Rice were countering an intellectual mood that they had once shared: that American power was of limited use in transforming the lot of the globally oppressed. The author Robert Kaplan codified this realist world view in *The Coming Anarchy* (2000). US efforts to democratize the world would

---

[34] National Security Strategy (2002), p. 3.
[35] In Michael Gordon and Bernard Trainor, *The End Game: The Inside Story of the Struggle for Iraq, from George W. Bush to Barack Obama* (London: Atlantic Books, 2012), p. 8.
[36] In Gordon and Trainor, *End Game*, p. 8.

come to naught, he argued.[37] The Bush administration, after the trauma of that September morning, no longer agreed.

It was not enough that the Bush Doctrine simply remove regimes who might flirt with WMD proliferation; they had to be remade along democratic lines. That was the long-term cure to the sickness of terrorism, according to President Bush.

Presidential Power

To make preemption, flexible alliance-building, and the freedom agenda work, Bush said he needed the powers of a war president. This final tenet of the Bush Doctrine most clearly relied on an American historical precedent: that presidential power increases proportionate to the emergency the nation faces. When the emergency subsides, so does the presidential power, at least in theory.[38] In order to round up Confederate agitators in the Civil War, Abraham Lincoln, without consulting Congress, suspended the constitutionally protected right of *habeas corpus*. To continue the suspension after the war, he claimed, would be like giving "emetics" to a healthy person.[39] The next great expansion of presidential power was in World War II – to meet the emergency presaged by Japanese and German aggression. Harry Truman later used that global conflict to build a national security state with the president at its core. Bush placed himself alongside Lincoln and FDR in claiming powers to meet the 9/11 foe. He set about enhancing the Cold War apparatus Truman had bequeathed him. As Stephen F. Knott argues, "expansive notions of presidential power, particularly in the national security arena, are as old as the nation itself."[40]

Congress eagerly handed Bush all the powers he wanted. Three days after the attacks, it passed Joint Resolution 23. This allowed the president "to use all necessary and appropriate force against those nations, organizations, or persons *he determines* planned, authorized, committed, or aided the terrorist attacks that occurred on September 11, 2001."[41]

---

[37] Robert D. Kaplan, *The Coming Anarchy: Shattering the Dreams of the Post Cold War* (New York: Penguin Random House, 2000).

[38] See Richard A. Posner, *Not a Suicide Pact: The Constitution in a Time of National Emergency* (New York: Oxford University Press, 2006), pp. 44–45.

[39] Abraham Lincoln, letter to Erastus Corning and Others, June 12, 1863.

[40] Stephen F. Knott, *Rush to Judgement: George W. Bush, the War on Terror, and His Critics* (Lawrence: University Press of Kansas, 2012), p. 22.

[41] S. J. Res. 23 – Authorization for Use of Military Force. Emphasis added.

A lone Californian congresswoman, Barbara Lee, voted no. The War on Terror would be waged using presidential power as its primary political instrument. This had several practical effects. As commander in chief, Bush was now able to empower his secretary of defense to plot the military campaigns of his global war. Any judicial response to 9/11, one grounded in a criminal investigation of its plotters, which had been the main emphasis after the first attack on the Twin Towers in 1993, was superseded by a military one. Donald Rumsfeld became an extremely powerful voice in the Bush administration, his Department of Defense first among equals. Colin Powell, ironically the administration's most senior former solider, was marginalized as secretary of state; diplomacy would now not be enough.

A second and controversial effect of the presidentialization of the War on Terror was the powers Bush now claimed to pursue terrorists extrajudicially and to "enhance" their interrogation if necessary. This position was outlined by John Yoo, a deputy assistant in Bush's Office of Legal Counsel and later professor at University of California Berkeley.[42] The constitutional rights of terrorist suspects, like those of Confederate insurgents in 1864, were downgraded in order to realize a greater national security. Those seeking to destroy the US Constitution could not, if they were caught, claim its protections. From April 2002, the US military began placing "enemy combatants" in a US naval holding facility at Cuba's Guantánamo Bay, part of the island rented from Fidel Castro. The USA PATRIOT Act (the acronym is for Uniting and Strengthening America by Providing Appropriate Tools Required to Intercept and Obstruct Terrorism) became law on October 26, 2001. Like Joint Resolution 23, the PATRIOT Act commanded a large consensus on Capitol Hill (357 to 66 in the House, 98 to 1 in the Senate).[43] Senator Barack Obama would go on to vote for its reauthorization in 2006 (and again as president in 2011 and would keep Guantánamo Bay open). The Act's provisions allowed the FBI to wiretap suspects, to search their email and financial records, and to detain immigrants indefinitely. While the Act was subject to numerous, often successful, legal challenges, its net effect was to increase the president's role in the counterterrorism campaign.

---

[42] See John Yoo, *War by Other Means: An Insider's Account of the War on Terror* (New York: Atlantic Monthly Press, 2006).

[43] Russ Feingold (D-WI) was the lone opponent in the Senate.

WHY IRAQ?

The Bush Doctrine was not a Talmudic text. The ordinary processes of decision-making, good and bad, intervened throughout the anxious months after 9/11. The Iraq War was conceived and implemented subject to the politics of American foreign policy and to the fears that the attacks on New York and Washington had induced. Turf wars over the direction of the 9/11 response were intense. The broader political consensus around limiting terrorist capacity only invited arguments over how to achieve this. Those in the Bush administration who wanted war with Iraq decided it was a crucial means of stopping that regime leaking weapons of mass destruction to terrorists willing to use them. Removing Saddam Hussein was the surest way of stopping him proliferating a weapons capacity that the United States, along with Russia and France, had played a part in giving him during his war with Iran in the 1980s. Those against the Iraq War saw this as a distraction from the fight against al-Qaeda. Richard Clarke, a counterterrorism advisor to several presidents, including Bush, was outspoken in his criticisms of elisions in strategy.[44] Egyptian president Hosni Mubarak warned it would produce a "100 bin Ladens."[45]

Much scholarship is dedicated to the illogicality of going after Saddam in the wake of September 11. But in those terrifying days, adding him to the list of possible targets was not irrational. In his fateful July 1990 meeting with US Ambassador April Glaspie, a week before he attempted to expunge Kuwait from the map, Saddam proffered a threat he had some cause to rue as America picked itself up after 9/11. "You can harm us," he said, "but we can harm you ... We cannot come all the way to you in the United States, but individual Arabs may reach you."[46] The American fear it articulated explains, in part, why Saddam's regime was targeted as a consequence of an attack it had nothing to do with. George W. Bush's motivation in going after Saddam as a direct result of al-Qaeda's attack remains the cause of great controversy. There are *at least* three schools of thought on why he chose to do it.[47]

---

[44] See Richard A. Clarke, *Against All Enemies: Inside America's War on Terror* (New York: Free Press, 2004).

[45] Mubarak warns of "100 bin Ladens," CNN.com, March 31, 2003.

[46] Excerpts from Iraqi document on meeting with U.S. envoy, *New York Times*, September 23, 1990.

[47] These, and several other motivations, are sketched by Steve A. Yetiv, *Explaining Foreign Policy: U.S. Decision-Making and the Persian Gulf War* (Baltimore: Johns Hopkins University Press, 2004), pp. 120–144.

The first one is a variation of economic determinism. Bush attacked Iraq, as had his father, to realize oil security in the Middle East.[48] Conquering Iraq, according to this argument, allowed the United States to maintain the most visible military footprint in the region, thus guaranteeing the free flow of oil. The September 11 attacks were merely an excuse to expand the American "military industrial complex." While this interpretation is one predominantly heard on the liberal left, it is not its preserve. Several prominent realists and conservatives were opposed to the war for similar reasons. For them, the attack on Iraq was an unwarranted extension of military force into a theater the United States could only inflame in a futile effort to control. Far better to buy oil without recourse to war, said realists, than to wage war and end up having to buy it anyway, as America found. There is little evidence, however, that economics played much of a part in deciding on war. The *Pentagon Papers* (written in 1967 and leaked in 1971), revealing the secret, real motivations behind the war in Vietnam, made no economic case. The Iraq War was similarly unmoored.

The second school advances an "unfinished-business" hypothesis and relies more heavily on a cognitive level of analysis. According to it, Bush Jr. was completing the work of Bush Sr. Because the father had failed to remove Saddam, the son felt obliged to finish the job.[49] A variety of motives are attributed to the younger Bush in this regard. He was acting on an Oedipal impulse to supersede his dad – Oliver Stone's 2008 bio-pic *W* makes much of this theory – and/or the son wanted to avenge Saddam for plotting his dad's assassination (which failed in 1993). The 9/11 attacks, according to both these schools – oil security and familial grudge – were merely an excuse to act on the basis of long-standing ambitions, geostrategic and personal, held by the president and his senior staff. Both schools lack evidence to sustain their claims.

The third school links the invasion of Iraq with the physical security fears caused by 9/11. Unlike the popular interpretations, it tends to be more forgiving of George W. Bush and accepting of the dilemma Iraq posed for him in the wake of 9/11. The simple human fears that the attacks provoked are hard to exaggerate. The men and women who experienced that day firsthand, and were to lead the response, were

---

[48] Steven Hurst argues this in *The United States and Iraq since 1979: Hegemony, Oil and War* (Edinburgh: Edinburgh University Press, 2009).
[49] Jacob Weisberg argues this in *The Bush Tragedy: The Unmaking of a President* (London: Bloomsbury, 2008), p. 185.

profoundly affected by it.[50] The most impressive military and intelligence-gathering machine in world history had been out-thought by a few dozen "cave-dwelling" terrorists.[51] Old certainties that the US homeland was impregnable vanished in less than two hours that September morning. The physicality of that day served to reinforce the psychological experience. Concerned that a plane was heading for the White House, the vice-president was forcibly carried to a secure bunker by secret service agents. Donald Rumsfeld found himself digging in the rubble of the Pentagon to rescue his comrades. President Bush's 9/11 had been spent in a disorientating cross-country flight on the president's plane, Air Force One, which was low on fuel, it later transpired, with nowhere to land.[52] His finest hour was in the smoldering ruins of the World Trade Center three days later, when he told rescue workers, through a foghorn, that "the people who knocked these buildings down will hear all of us soon!"

Such experiences were profound and lasting. They provoked imaginative thinking, because it was a lack of imagination that had failed to preempt the 9/11 plot. The targets of American reprisal expanded rather than contracted. Iraq, a nation with which the United States had been in an alternating hot and cold war since 1990, was hardly going to escape a reckoning, given the lowered threshold of risk that 9/11 induced among the Bush team. The Iraq War, by this accounting, was a response to the fear that a worse attack was inevitable. Unless the link between states and terrorists was severed, eventually a weapon or weapons of mass destruction would be used by them against the United States. This fear was a key catalyst of Bush's renewed focus on Iraq:

9/11 hit and we had to take a fresh look at every threat in the world. There were state sponsors of terror. There were sworn enemies of America. There were hostile governments that threatened their neighbors. There were nations that violated

[50] See Melvyn P. Leffler, The Foreign Policies of the George W. Bush Administration: Memoirs, History, Legacy, *Diplomatic History* 37, 2 (April 1, 2013): 190–216; and his remarks at Clements Center, University of Texas, Austin, November 1, 2013 and Miegunyah Lecture, University of Melbourne, October 17, 2016.

[51] Al-Qaeda was considerably more sophisticated than this caricature allows for. It was bureaucratically robust, observes Lawrence Wright, and "included committees devoted to military affairs, politics, information, administration, security and surveillance." See Wright, *The Looming Tower*, p. 142.

[52] See George W. Bush, *Decision Points* (New York: Crown Publishing, 2010), pp. 126–151; Dick Cheney, *In My Time: A Personal and Political Memoir* (New York: Threshold Editions, 2011), p. 1; and Donald Rumsfeld, *Known and Unknown: A Memoir* (New York: Penguin, 2011), pp. 336–337.

international demands. There were dictators who repressed their own people. And there were regimes that pursued WMD. Iraq combined all those threats.[53]

"In brief," insisted Condoleezza Rice, "the president and his national security principals believed Saddam was a security threat."[54] They were not alone in believing this. Concerns that Saddam Hussein had or was about to have a WMD capacity were widespread after 9/11 – though not because of 9/11. The Iraqi dictator had played a cat-and-mouse game for over a decade to conceal the nature of his arsenal. His success in this effort is revealed in the consensus that Bush joined.

That consensus included the US Congress (which in October 2002 voted for war 77 to 23 and 296 to 133); the American people (who that November returned large Republican majorities in the congressional midterms); the US and international intelligence communities; and the leaders of Australia, the Czech Republic, Denmark, Great Britain, Hungary, Italy, Poland, Portugal, and Spain.[55] Even Germany, a nation that did not join the eventual war against Saddam Hussein, conceded, in the months before it, that "Iraq has produced weapons of mass destruction and that we have to assume that they continue to have weapons of mass destruction."[56]

On November 27, Hans Blix, the UN official charged with finding the weapons that so many governments believed Iraq still had, ordered his inspectors back into the country. On December 19, he announced that Saddam was still in breach of his UN Security Council obligations (under Resolution 1441, passed on November 8). On January 9, he warned that Iraqi "transparency is increasing – but does not exclude dark corners or caves … Unresolved disarmament issues remain."[57] On January 27, he declared that "Iraq appears not to have come to a genuine acceptance, not even today, of the disarmament which was demanded of it."[58] Five days later, adding to a sense of national crisis, if entirely unrelatedly, the space shuttle *Columbia* exploded upon reentry over Texas, killing all on board.

---

[53] Bush, *Decision Points*, p. 228.
[54] Condoleezza Rice, *Democracy: Stories from the Long Road to Freedom* (New York: Twelve Books, 2017), p. 275.
[55] See Harvey, *Explaining the Iraq War*.
[56] German Ambassador to the United States Wolfgang Ischinger, NBC's *Today*, February 26, 2003.
[57] Hans Blix, UN Security Council Briefing, January 9, 2003: Inspections in Iraq and a Further Assessment of Iraq's Weapons Declaration; www.un.org/Depts/unmovic/bx9jan.htm.
[58] Blix, UN Security Council Briefing, January 27, 2003, An Update on Inspections; www .un.org/Depts/unmovic/Bx27.htm.

On February 5, Colin Powell told the UN that "Today, Iraq still poses a threat."[59] A week later, George Tenet, the CIA director, revealed that North Korea had a nuclear missile capable of hitting the US homeland.

All this might not have mattered but for 9/11. Saddam's fate was sealed on that day. Tolerance for him, limited at best before that attack, vanished after it. A Cold War analogy is appropriate here. Assumptions of the opponents' rationality and caution in that conflict were often misplaced. China, it was argued, would never come to the aid of North Korea in 1950; the risks would be too great for the new communist regime in Beijing. And yet that is what the People's Republic did, causing the loss of hundreds of thousands of lives, some 40,000 of them American. An assumption of rationality on the behalf of the North Vietnamese meant American planners were surprised by its attack on US vessels, seen as a deliberate provocation, in the Gulf of Tonkin in 1964. Two years earlier, few believed that Khrushchev would gamble so recklessly by placing offensive nuclear missiles in Cuba, ninety miles off the coast of Florida. In November 1979, it was widely predicted that the new revolutionary government of the Islamic Republic of Iran would not risk the international ignominy of taking hostage every official at the US embassy in Tehran. And yet when militant students did so, the new regime was complicit in the outrage for a full 444 days. The next month, again to consternation in Washington, the USSR marched into Afghanistan.[60]

In each of these decisive Cold War episodes, the United States found itself exposed by *not* assuming the worst. The psychological trauma induced by this default to optimism helps explain why the US response to each assault was so considerable. American commitments to the defense of South Korea made a full-scale Korean war all but inevitable. US troops have remained on the peninsula ever since. Kennedy walked to the edge of the nuclear precipice in Cuba in 1962. The Gulf of Tonkin Resolution presaged full-scale military escalation and the Vietnam War. The Iranian hostage crisis led to the American sponsorship of Saddam's regime in Iraq and Jimmy Carter's call for it to attack Iran. The Soviet invasion of Afghanistan became the pretext for the massive US defense

[59] US Secretary of State Colin Powell Addresses the U.N. Security Council, February 5, 2003, US Department of State Archive; https://2001-2009.state.gov/secretary/former/powell/remarks/2003/17300.htm.

[60] On "surprises" in US history see John Lewis Gaddis, *Surprise, Security, and the American Experience* (Cambridge, MA: Harvard University Press, 2004).

buildup in the early 1980s. Given this history, ignoring Iraq after 9/11 would have been more astonishing.

Between September 2001 and March 2003, it was widely asserted that Saddam Hussein was rational – and therefore containable and deterrable – and, anyway, had nothing to do with the 9/11 plot. Even without the national security surprises of the Cold War as a guide, Saddam's behavior was at best unpredictable. Assertions of his rationality became less believable for Bush. Fidel Castro, a secular Marxist, said he was prepared to suffer the nuclear annihilation of Cuba in order to negate American power.[61] How far would Saddam Hussein, a tyrant who claimed he was the next Nebuchadnezzar, the first king of Babylon (c. 600 BC), be prepared to go to realize his ambitions? Safety, Bush concluded, lay in removing Saddam's capacity to miscalculate, which meant doing to him what no US president had done to Castro: remove him from power.

Fear of surprise, grounded historically in the Cold War and immediately in 9/11, made for a president receptive to worst-case scenarios. Uncertainty within Western intelligence circles and among their political masters led to credulity over what weapons were hidden in Iraq. An Iraqi informant for British MI6 crafted his reports of WMD having watched a Sean Connery movie, *The Rock*. The Bush team saw the next attack as a near certainty. They processed intelligence, from whatever source, accordingly. Skepticism became a highly rationed commodity. "Because we cannot be sure we should not act" was replaced by, "Because we are not sure, we must." This new thinking, championed by George Tenet, the CIA director, became known as the "one percent doctrine." If there was just a one percent chance of an attack occurring, the United States must regard it as a 100 percent certainty. "Conventional risk assessments no longer applied," declared Tenet, "We could not afford to be surprised."[62]

September 11 represented a tipping point in US tolerance of the Iraqi regime. Before that day, boxing Saddam in and waiting for his physical or political demise was the default position. After 9/11, waiting and hoping was seen as inadequate. If there existed the slimmest chance that his regime was developing a WMD capacity, America must act as if it were an accomplished fact. There were a number of objections to this

---

[61] See James G. Blight and Janet M. Lang, *Armageddon Letters: Kennedy/Khrushchev/ Castro in the Cuban Missile Crisis* (Lanham, MD: Rowman and Littlefield, 2012).
[62] See George Tenet, *At the Center of the Storm: My Years at the CIA* (New York: Harper-Collins, 2007), pp. 264–265, and Ron Suskind, *The One Percent Doctrine: Deep Inside America's Pursuit of Its Enemies since 9/11* (New York: Simon & Schuster, 2006).

heightened threat perception. But their makers were unable to argue that continued tolerance for Saddam was the better policy after 9/11. This is what that day changed. It made the continuing containment of the Iraqi regime politically untenable. Why hope for the best when we can be sure? A robust political consensus in Washington demanded certainty. That is why Saddam Hussein's fate was sealed on September 11, 2001. But the case for war was wider than WMD.

The Bush administration relied on five arguments to make its case for war with Iraq before it settled on one big one. The first concerns Saddam's rationality and whether, after 9/11, he could be trusted to not sponsor a similar or worse attack. Bush said he could not be. The second referenced Saddam's violation of international sanctions. Since 1990, he had transgressed every United Nations resolution and maintained a brutal hold on power in the process. Why, said Bush, should international law be used to protect him from a removal that a series of international laws had meant to make more likely? Third, Saddam was presented, not implausibly, as a serial aggressor (he invaded Iran in 1980 and Kuwait in 1990, fired missiles at Saudi Arabia in 1991, attacking Israel directly and indirectly in between) who would eventually resume this pattern of behavior. Fourth, the nature of his rule made its ending just and moral. He was complicit in the genocide of ethnic populations, of mass torture, and the deaths of hundreds of thousands of Iraqis through the exploitation of a UN oil-for-food program. An Iraqi opposition was waiting in the wings, according to its ambitious and self-proclaimed leader, Ahmed Chalabi, and would quickly establish a more just regime. Lastly, and cumulative of the foregoing, were concerns, magnified by the trauma of 9/11, that Saddam had weapons of mass destruction capable of being proliferated to the sorts of terrorists that had struck on that day. Until 9/11, the other arguments made Saddam a threat, but a tolerable one. After that day, because of that day, that tolerance evaporated.

Saddam Hussein had not become suddenly more deadly or untrustworthy, necessitating war against him. Rather, his record, his form, his rap sheet, was viewed through a different lens. As Donald Rumsfeld explained:

We acted [to remove Saddam] because we saw the existing evidence in a new light, through the prism of our experience on 9/11 ... that experience changed our appreciation of our vulnerability and the risks the US faces from terrorist states and terrorist networks armed with weapons of mass murder.[63]

---

[63] Rumsfeld testimony to the Senate Armed Services Committee, Washington, July 9, 2003.

Tony Blair argued the same:

> After 9/11 ... the calculus of risk changed fundamentally. We believed that we had to change policy on nations developing such weapons in order to eliminate the possibility of a link between WMD and terrorism. Saddam's regime was the place to start, not because he represented the only threat, but because his was the only regime actually to have used such weapons, there were outstanding UN resolutions in respect of him and his record of bloodshed suggested he was capable of aggressive, unpredictable, catastrophic actions.[64]

This desire to sever the link between unpredictable autocrats and WMD terrorism was central to the Bush case for war in Iraq.

One of the most persuasive defenses of this case for war was made by its most powerful skeptic. On February 5, 2003, Secretary of State Colin Powell told the United Nations Security Council:

> I cannot tell you everything that we know. But what I can share with you, when combined with what all of us have learned over the years, is deeply troubling. What you will see is an accumulation of facts and disturbing patterns of behavior. The facts on Iraqis' behavior – Iraq's behavior demonstrate that Saddam Hussein and his regime have made no effort – no effort – to disarm as required by the international community. Indeed, the facts and Iraq's behavior show that Saddam Hussein and his regime are concealing their efforts to produce more weapons of mass destruction.
>
> Leaving Saddam Hussein in possession of weapons of mass destruction for a few more months or years is not an option, not in a post–September 11th world.[65]

He later regretted his certitude, based on exaggerated intelligence, claiming the speech was a blot on his record.[66] But the weight it carried at the time, because Powell was considered "soft on Iraq" and was the only member of the Bush team with actual combat experience, was considerable.[67]

The team that decided on war with Iraq were realists, Powell included, raised on and schooled in Cold War strategy. Much has been made of a cabal of neoconservatives determined to remake the Middle East in an American image.[68] Those who identified as "neocon" were actually very

---

[64] Blair statement on Chilcot Report, July 5, 2016.
[65] Colin Powell, address to the UN Security Council, February 5, 2003.
[66] Steven R. Weisman, Powell Calls His UN Speech a Lasting Blot on His Record, *New York Times*, September 9, 2005.
[67] See Bob Woodward, *Plan of Attack* (New York: Simon & Schuster, 2004), p. 291.
[68] See, for example, Stefan Halper and Jonathan Clarke, *America Alone: The Neo-Conservatives and the Global Order* (Cambridge, UK: Cambridge University Press, 2004).

small. Paul Wolfowitz, *deputy* secretary of defense, has carried a burden of the blame for Iraq, belied by his actual role in the campaign. His strong ideological assessment of the challenges facing America after September 11 were recurrently elided by men senior to him who made security, not ideology, their objective. His boss, Donald Rumsfeld, did not much rely on Wolfowitz for advice. Indeed, the deputy had trouble getting any meaningful face time with the secretary. In the months leading up the war, Wolfowitz found himself increasingly excluded from deliberations. Once in occupation of Iraq, Wolfowitz found himself ignored.[69] As Frank Harvey documents convincingly, neoconservatives in the Bush administration actually lost many of the debates over Iraq.[70]

The Bush team that constructed the case for war and oversaw its implementation were more conservative nationalists than they were neoconservatives, more *natcon* than neocon. Vice-President Cheney construed Saddam Hussein as a national security threat first and as an ideological foe a distant second. Donald Rumsfeld shared this assessment. Both men were instrumental in crafting a military campaign against the Ba'athist dictator that privileged decapitation – to remove the threat – rather than democratization – to advance a higher ideological purpose. What would come after could not be worse, so little energy was expended worrying about the days after. Imperialists plot and plan how to rule over their conquered subjects. The Bush administration did precious little of that. Removing Saddam was valuable for its "demonstration effect" rather than its democratization effect. It would terrify American enemies elsewhere into passivity.[71]

THE IRAQ WAR

The initial war against Saddam's regime was a remarkable success. But the tactics that afforded such a decisive victory were paid for in long-term strategic failure. Rumsfeld carries much of the praise and blame for this. In March 2003, he was able to test his transformation of the US military into a machine of "unprecedented ... speed, precision, surprise, and

[69] See Andrew Cockburn, *Rumsfeld: His Rise, Fall, and Catastrophic Legacy* (London: Scribner, 2011) and Thomas E. Ricks, *Fiasco: The American Military in Iraq* (New York: Penguin, 2006), p. 179.
[70] Harvey, *Explaining the Iraq War*, p. 5.
[71] See Daniel Deudney and G. John Ikenberry, Realism, Liberalism and the Iraq War, *Survival* 59, 4 (August–September 2017): 7–26, 15.

flexibility."[72] The rapier-like quality of the US thrust into Iraq, beginning at 9.00 PM Iraqi time on March 19, 2003, was a marvel to behold. Instead of the anticipated air campaign, which had begun hostilities in 1991, General Tommy Franks swept across the country in tanks. Within a few days the situation George H. W. Bush had always feared obtained: US coalition troops were policing the streets of Baghdad.

"Policing" should be used advisedly. The military flexibility Rumsfeld had touted as key to victory soon became the occupation's greatest weakness. "Flexibility" and the "light footprint" liberated the Iraqi capital, but left it a looter's paradise. US Central Command had recommended at least 500,000 troops be deployed. Rumsfeld said 160,000 was enough. He was warned that this would produce Vietnam II. "Of course it won't be another Vietnam!" retorted the secretary of defense. "We are going to go in, overthrow Saddam, and get out. That's it."[73] As a consequence, the pacification of Baghdad, a newly liberated city of 5.7 million people, relied on only 25,000 coalition troops. Freed from decades of Baathist control, the citizens vented their fury and acted on their opportunities. The already hollowed-out departments of the Iraqi government were systemically stripped of every vestige of material value – down to the copper wire in the electrical cables. US troops stood idly by. This sin of omission cast a pall over the entire venture.

Everything in the years since has in some way been tied to correcting the problems caused by this initial inability to impose order. Without order, assertions of liberty are meaningless. Order depended on a force of some half a million troops – ironically the number mobilized in 1991 but not used to topple Saddam and occupy his country – primed for the long haul. What the people of Iraq got was a quarter of that, most conditioned to expect a swift return home. The result was what Thomas Ricks, in one of the most compelling narratives of US failure, called a "fiasco."[74]

In May 2003, Paul "Jerry" Bremer flew into Baghdad to replace General Jay Garner, the overburdened and already semi-retired head of the Coalition Provisional Authority. Unlike Garner, who was meant to monitor a rapid US withdrawal, Bremer was granted full plenipotentiary

---

[72] Congressional testimony, July 9, 2003.

[73] In Walter A. McDougall, *The Tragedy of U.S. Foreign Policy: How America's Civil Religion Betrayed the National Interest* (New Haven, CT: Yale University Press, 2016), p. 11.

[74] Thomas E. Ricks, *Fiasco: The American Military in Iraq* (New York: Penguin, 2006). For a review of major studies of failures in Iraq see Andrew Preston, The Iraq War as Contemporary History, *International History Review* 30, 4 (December 2008): 796–808.

132   *In the Shadow of the Cold War*

powers, becoming the de facto Iraqi head of state, until his removal in June 2004, a period in which every advantage of victory was essentially squandered. Where Garner had endeavored to deliver an agreed plan – the Iraqi Interim Authority, or IIA – Bremer arrived skeptical that it would work. Garner had stuck to process; Bremer abandoned it. According to one observer:

What was missing was not a plan, but the implementation of it. The differing approaches of Garner and Bremer are at the heart of the matter. Garner stayed in close touch with Washington, supported the IIA concept, and moved smartly to implement it. Bremer relied on ambiguous verbal guidance received in a lunch meeting with the President more than [on] the written work on the IIA, a concept about which he harbored serious reservations. He kept Washington at arm's length, and did what he thought best on the basis of his personal judgment.[75]

Bremer's role model was Douglas MacArthur, the US general who engineered both Japanese defeat and reconstruction. Japan in 1945, said MacArthur, "had become the world's great laboratory for an experiment in the liberation of a people from totalitarian military rule and for the liberalization of government from within."[76]

[America must] destroy the military power. Punish war criminals. Build the structure of representative government. Modernize the constitution. Hold free elections. Enfranchise the women. Release the political prisoners. Liberate the farmers. Establish a free labor movement. Encourage a free economy. Abolish police oppression. Develop a free and responsible press. Liberalize education. Decentralize the political power.[77]

If the model was superficially a good one, Bremer's use of it led him to commit two fundamental mistakes. First, he disbanded the Iraqi army. This had the immediate effect of rendering some 400,000 soldiers unemployed, and yet still armed. "Abruptly terminating the livelihoods of these men," said one Iraqi expert, "created a vast pool of humiliated, antagonized, and politicized men."[78]

Second, Bremer banned the Ba'ath Party from any role in the government and bureaucracy of post–Saddam Iraq. As the official US report into postinvasion Iraq observed, "Most of Iraq's technocratic class was

---

[75] Stephen Benedict Dyson, What Really Happened in Planning for Postwar Iraq? *Political Science Quarterly* 128, 3 (Fall 2013): 455–488.
[76] MacArthur, *Reminiscences* (New York: McGraw Hill, 1964), p. 282.
[77] MacArthur, *Reminiscences*, pp. 282–283.   [78] Faleh Jabar in Ricks, *Fiasco*, p. 162.

pushed out of the government as part of de-Ba'athification,"[79] a process Sunnis viewed as the "de-Sunnification" of Iraq. Nearly every school-teacher had been a Sunni and a member of the party. At a stroke, the United States made them all unemployed, thus destroying what was left, after a decade of UN sanctions, of the Iraqi state education system. Few things enrage the middle class of any nation more than tinkering with the schooling of its children. Jerry Bremer did so, oblivious to the discontent that would follow. The now-displaced Sunni *ancien régime* focused its antipathy in two directions: toward the American occupiers and toward the Shia. Long "brutalized by Ba'th Party goons," Shia men filled the vacuum left by the US invasion and took revenge on them.[80] Al-Qaeda, Osama bin Laden's Sunni terrorist group responsible for 9/11, could not believe its luck. Bremer had gifted them an environment where they could kill both Americans and Shia and earn new recruits by doing so. The recipe for the sectarian bloodbath that was to follow was drawn up on Bremer's desktop. It would only be halted after a fundamental reappraisal in Bush's second term.[81]

The eventual capture of Saddam Hussein on December 13, 2003 – pulled from a hole in the ground near his boyhood town of Tikrit – could not salve Bremer's failure. He had proudly announced the capture with a "We got him!" press conference in Baghdad. The stunning image of the fallen dictator, looking like a bedraggled Karl Marx, was met with applause in the United States. For many Sunnis in Iraq, however, the capture, humiliation, and eventual hanging (in 2006) of their former leader confirmed a Shia conspiracy against them. US troops were not in their country to liberate them, but to empower their sectarian opponents. The appalling treatment of inmates by rogue US personnel at one of Saddam's old prisons, Abu Ghraib, was similarly seen by Sunnis as evidence of a malign American intent. The episode, first reported in April 2004, was a public relations disaster for American efforts to mend fences with Muslims.

In reality, coalition forces were ecumenical in their targeting of Iraq's various ethno-religious groups. US troops had fought ferociously against

---

[79] James A. Baker III and Lee H. Hamilton, co-chairs, The Iraq Study Group Report (December 2006), p. 20; at www.bakerinstitute.org/research/the-iraq-study-group-report/.

[80] In Lisa Blaydes, *State of Repression Iraq under Saddam Hussein* (Princeton, NJ: Princeton University Press, 2018), p. 319.

[81] Bremer's side of the story is told by him in L. Paul Bremer III, *My Year in Iraq: The Struggle to Build a Future of Hope* (New York: Simon & Schuster, 2006).

Sunni insurgents in the Battle of Fallujah in April 2004. The next month the fight was taken to Shia militias in Karbala, Najaf, and Baghdad's Sadr City. The Pentagon could claim at one juncture that al-Qaeda was the greatest threat to Iraqi security, killing its leader in Iraq in June 2006, and then announce, months later, that the Shia Mahdi Army now had that status. The issue remained not any nefarious, sectarian intent on behalf of the US-led occupation, but the paucity of allied personnel available to stabilize Iraq.

Who was responsible for this nearly catastrophic lightness of touch? This question can be answered in two ways. First, and only partly absolving Bush, is the fact that he inherited an army that was downsizing. The number of active-duty soldiers fell from 700,000 in 1991 to 400,000 a decade later. Failures in Iraq were thus a product of a long-term downward trend in military spending. Bush attempted later to redress this, but only toward the end of his term. Second, the blame, many have argued, should be laid at the feet of the men and women who planned the reconstruction of Iraq. Former members of Bush's team have written voluminously about the decisions surrounding Iraq:

[Douglas] Feith blamed Colin Powell and the CIA. Former CIA chief George Tenet wrote a memoir blaming Vice President Dick Cheney and Rice. Bremer's memoir blames Rumsfeld. Former White House press secretary Scott McClellan's book blamed Karl Rove. Rove's memoir blamed McClellan. Bush revealed that he considered replacing Cheney ... Rumsfeld, for his part, fingers Bremer ... and blames the State Department for just about everything ... "There were far too many hands on the steering wheel, which, in my view, was a formula for running the truck into a ditch."[82]

Somehow the president himself managed to avoid the burden of blame – or at least he paid no electoral price for the gross mismanagement of Iraq.

THE 2004 ELECTION

In 2004, amid a War on Terror and a US-inspired civil war in Iraq, George W. Bush campaigned against his rival on the basis that he had lied about his military service in the Vietnam War. Of dubious foundation, this charge "threw the Kerry–Edwards campaign off stride."[83]

[82] Dana Milbank, Don Rumsfeld, Playing a Dead-End Game in His Memoir, *Washington Post*, February 6, 2011.
[83] Donald T. Critchlow, *The Conservative Ascendancy: How the GOP Right Made Political History* (Cambridge, MA: Harvard University Press, 2007), p. 273.

How could John Kerry be trusted to wage a war against Osama bin Laden when he had improperly waged one against Ho Chi Minh? Legitimacy in the current war was made to depend on fidelity to the previous one. Despite a strong case that Bush himself had avoided appropriate military service in Vietnam, the charge stuck to Kerry. Bush was able to portray himself as the leader of a war cabinet that had taken the fight to the enemy, deposing two anti-American regimes in his first term in office.

Foreign policy became central to the election. Most campaigns are framed by domestic issues and economics. The 9/11 attacks changed this pattern. Terrorism was a key issue. Osama bin Laden even recorded a video, released the week before polling, to remind American voters that he was still at large and intended to attack them again. America's wars abroad were central to the debates in 2004. Kerry, despite his opening salute to the Democratic Convention that nominated him, was not able to counter a relentless focus on his supposed effeteness, his propensity for flip-flopping on issues, and his unjustly maligned service in Vietnam. Americans had a war leader in George W. Bush, and they returned him to the White House, and his party to Congress, that November. Bush won 51 percent of the popular vote to Kerry's 49 percent and 274 electoral college votes to Kerry's 252, and slightly increased the GOP majorities on Capitol Hill.

CONCLUSION

The years 2001 to 2004 were the most tumultuous of the post–Cold War era. The Bush administration had gone from a professed humility in its foreign policy to the waging of a civilizational war for universal freedom in the heart of the Middle East. It had replaced suspicions about nation-building with an exaggerated confidence in military minimalism and the light footprint to avoid the hard work of long-term occupation and reconstruction. The war on Iraq was undertaken in defense of United Nation resolutions, but was unable to secure from that body any resolution allowing war. Bush's diplomacy opened fissures with and within Europe that continue to obtain. Great Britain, Italy, Poland, and Spain joined the coalition of the willing. France and Germany, let alone Russia, did not. China watched somewhat bemused at the path Bush embarked upon. Those remarkable four years saw the launching of a global War on Terrorism that lead to the swift (but temporary) defeat of the Taliban regime in Afghanistan and the extension of US government powers to surveil its own citizens. Constitutional rights were reinterpreted to meet the demands of the post–9/11 emergency. Congressional obstructionism, the hallmark of relations between the White House and Capitol Hill during the Clinton years, had become congressional facilitation as lawmakers looked to their commander in chief to wage a counterterrorist war. President Bush had been transformed from a humble candidate, keen on international retrenchment, to an imperial president determined to achieve American security by exporting democracy to peoples with no experience of it.

However, while the 9/11 attacks looked revolutionary in design and effects, they generated a continuity of response. The war in Iraq, like Kosovo four years earlier, was to be fought without the need for the mobilization of huge US armies. Such means replicated their shared objective: the liberation of Muslim populations from bad government. The international diplomacy leading up to war in 2003 was more similar to than different from that leading up to April 1999: Clinton and Bush decided on war despite having no authority from the United Nations to wage it. Great Britain, under the same prime minister, Tony Blair, cheer-led for each campaign. Russia and China opposed them. The structure of international politics was not reset after 9/11. Intimations that it might be, including a brief rapprochement with Russia, which saw in al-Qaeda a common foe, did not prosper. Rather, after 2001, US–Russian relations moved back toward a Cold War setting.

5

George W. Bush

Truman Redux, 2005–2008

Out of this nettle, danger, we pluck this flower, safety.
—*William Shakespeare*[1]

Bush will go down as the worst and by far the dumbest president in history.
—*Donald Trump, 2006*[2]

Despite a reputation for being intellectually challenged, George W. Bush was an avid reader. One of his favorite books was David McCullough's biography of Harry S. Truman, a president who "knew how to make a hard decision and stick by it." The book, said Bush, "reminded me how Truman's decisions in the late 1940s and early 1950s laid the foundation for victory in the Cold War and helped shape the world I inherited as president."[3] Like his predecessor, Bush found himself fighting "an unpopular war," that he hoped would "enable . . . the rise of a democratic ally."[4] For Truman, this had been South Korea; for Bush, it was Iraq.

The analogy is a good one. The Korean War, 1950–1953, was widely regarded as a failure. The northern half of that nation was lost to a bizarre communist experiment, which Donald Trump made controversial strides trying to engage seven decades later. The southern half lived a precarious life, fitfully authoritarian and dependent on US economic and military

---

[1] *Henry IV*, Act 2, Scene 3.
[2] In Maureen Dowd, Trump Fired Up, *New York Times*, December 23, 2006.
[3] George W. Bush, *Decision Points* (New York: Crown Publishing, 2010), p. 174.
[4] Bush, *Decision Points*, p. 175.

protection. Nearly 40,000 Americans lost their lives in the Korean War. Hundreds of thousands of Koreans lost theirs. The long-term prospects for South Korea, however, turned out to be remarkably good. As North Korea lurched from famine to nuclear testing, living on welfare from China and imported heating oil from the United States, its southern neighbor became one of the most dynamic economies and creative societies in Asia.

Bush wanted Iraq to follow a South Korean path. Such thinking had not greatly influenced his original invasion in 2003. By 2005, however, Bush was preparing his own version of the Korean War: the Iraqi Surge. As in 1950, the military intervention was designed to provide enough stability to make democratic government not perfect but possible, enough stability to protect the nation from the depredations of nefarious neighbors. "As in Truman's era," noted Bush, "we were in the early years of a long struggle."[5]

Also, like Truman, Bush won an election many had predicted he would not. John Kerry was to play Thomas Dewey to Bush's Truman. Despite an unfolding disaster in Iraq, George W. Bush secured reelection in 2004 with nearly the same number of votes as Barack Obama was to get four years later. Bush's staunchest allies in the War on Terror, Australia's John Howard and Britain's Tony Blair, both won their respective general elections in 2004 and 2005. Like the Cold War, the War on Terror rested on a political consensus abroad – formed around, but not exclusive to, this English-speaking alliance, and at home, where Republican and Democrats agreed on the necessity of countering the perceived threat. Korea and then Vietnam and Iraq each exposed splits in this consensus, but they were over the appropriate battles to fight within the wider war. In each case, one administration handed over command to another, which in turned escalated so as to begin withdrawal. US foreign policy at the beginning of Bush's second term had historical precedents.

THE SECOND-TERM FOREIGN POLICY TEAM

In July 2004, George Tenet, carrying part of the blame for 9/11 intelligence failures, had resigned as CIA director. Thereafter, President Bush avoided a wholesale clearout of his cabinet. He did, however, realize some changes were necessary. Some officials went up, others down. Condoleezza ("Condi") Rice cemented her place in Bush's circle of trust with her elevation to secretary of state, replacing an increasingly

[5] Bush, *Decision Points*, p. 175.

semidetached Colin Powell. Stephen Hadley stepped into her previous role as national security adviser. Perhaps the two most important personnel developments were the replacement of Donald Rumsfeld at Defense and the gradual downgrading of Vice-President Cheney.

Rumsfeld's departure in early 2006 meant Robert Gates took charge of a remarkable shift in Iraq strategy. Cheney, caricatured as the evil genius behind the throne in the first term, was to slip in his boss's estimation to a complaining advocate of personal causes, in the second.[6] References to Cheney become noticeably less warm, when they appear at all, in Bush's memoir. He was especially "stung" by the vice-president's accusation that in not pardoning Lewis "Scooter" Libby, Bush was leaving "a soldier on the battlefield."[7] The surge of 20,000 soldiers into the Iraq battlefield was to become the defining issue of Bush's second term.

THE SECOND INAUGURAL

The build-up to the surge, and the boldness it required, was telegraphed in Bush's second inaugural address. Gone were the references to humility that had framed his campaign in 2000. Instead, Bush declared:

There is only one force of history that can break the reign of hatred and resentment, and expose the pretensions of tyrants, and reward the hopes of the decent and tolerant, and that is the force of human freedom.

We are led, by events and common sense, to one conclusion: The survival of liberty in our land increasingly depends on the success of liberty in other lands. The best hope for peace in our world is the expansion of freedom in all the world.[8]

In his first inaugural in 2001, Bush had used the word "freedom" five times. In his second, he used it twenty-seven times. The sapping war in Iraq that had interposed between both speeches, rather than making him more circumspect, had made Bush bolder. The war had been only partially couched in these terms in 2003. Some have argued that the "freedom agenda" did not propel the Bush administration into the Middle East. Richard Perle, a chief advocate of the war, said the "idea that we went into Iraq to impose democracy on the Iraqis or on the region is just nonsense."[9] But Bush now seemingly wanted to construct a new

---

[6] This caricature is taken to absurd lengths in the 2018 movie *Vice*, directed by Adam McKay.

[7] Bush, *Decision Points*, p. 105.

[8] George W. Bush, *Second Inaugural Address*, Washington, DC, January 20, 2005.

[9] In Maria Ryan, "Exporting Democracy"? Neoconservatism and the Limits of Military Intervention, 1989–2008, *Diplomacy & Statecraft* 21, 3 (September 2010): 491–515, 491.

rationale for military force. This had been present in his thinking in the aftermath of 9/11. The democratic universalism of the Bush Doctrine had, however, taken a back seat to wars in Afghanistan and Iraq. These had been conceived of and sold as wars to destroy the link between terrorists and rogue states. They were narrow in their initial objectives: topple the suspect regime and then leave. The difficulty of leaving, however, led to secondary objectives: let's create the conditions for something other than repressive government. According to his press secretary, Bush was "intoxicated by the influence and power of America ... [and] believed that a successful transformation of Iraq could be the linchpin for realizing his dream of a free Middle East."[10]

THE SURGE

To invade is to govern. This critical maxim was slow to dawn on the Bush administration. The unwillingness to more fully occupy Iraq left American troops and the Iraqis they had liberated vulnerable to an ensuing chaos. There were enough troops to humiliate an Arab people by their presence, but not enough to create a stability that might have lessened the humiliation. Ironically, deploying with numbers too small for the task entailed having to stay longer. There was, then, an underlying logic to increasing the US military presence in order to speed up its ultimate withdrawal. Bush called it "the surge." The more troops that went in, the sooner more troops could come home. It was a political gamble from the beginning. By early 2006, the US occupation was a disaster. That summer "was the worst period of my presidency," Bush wrote. "I thought about the war constantly."[11] A simpler policy would have been to draw down swiftly and leave Iraq to its civil war. His friend Mitch McConnell, fearful Iraq would lose their party votes in that year's midterms, encouraged him to do this. But it entailed a risk as well. It was not tenable for the world's global power to desert a weak, postauthoritarian state on the brink of collapse. The president calculated there was less ignominy in recommitting to the reconstruction and its failing than in turning tail and guaranteeing failure.[12]

---

[10] Scott McClellan, *What Happened* (New York: PublicAffairs, 2008), p. 131.
[11] Bush, *Decision Points*, p. 367.
[12] See Timothy Andrews Sayle, Jeffrey A. Engel, Hal Brands, and William Inboden, eds., *The Last Card: Inside George W. Bush's Decision to Surge in Iraq* (Ithaca, NY: Cornell University Press, 2019).

From March to December 2006, the Iraq Study Group (ISG) worked to
avoid this conclusion. The ISG, a bipartisan panel consisting of five
Democrats and five Republicans, headed by two former congressmen,
looking for a consensus way forward, concluded that no "go-big"
approach was capable of rescuing the situation. Citing the testimony of
a general appearing before it, the group concluded that "all the troops in
the world will not provide security."[13] President Bush chose to ignore its
findings:

Rather than pull troops out, [in December 2006, when the ISG presented its
findings] I was on the verge of making the toughest and most unpopular decision
of my presidency: deploying tens of thousands more troops into Iraq with a new
strategy, a new commander, and a mission to protect the Iraqi people and help
enable the rise of democracy in the heart of the Middle East.[14]

His determination in this regard had been decisively framed by another
report. The American Enterprise Institute's "Choosing Victory: A Plan
for Success in Iraq" argued that "victory is still an option." But it
depended on "a surge of seven Army brigades and Marine regiments to
support clear-and-hold operations that begin in the spring of 2007."[15]
While it sounded narrowly technical, the surge was to become, as Condi
Rice warned her boss, "one of the most consequential decisions of all
time."[16]

   The American Enterprise Institute's Frederick Kagan was to the surge
what George Kennan had been to Cold War containment – the strategist
without which US foreign policy would have lacked a rationale in a global
war. Unlike Kennan, however, the 36-year-old Kagan eschewed balance
and compromise. Napoléon was successful, he argued, for the same
reason: while others debated, he acted. And now so should Bush. After
several tours of Iraq with his partner, Kimberly Kagan (both were military
historians), and using General H. R. McMaster's study of the stabilization
of Tal Afar, Iraq, in 2005 as a model, Kagan arrived at a plan that,
according to Bob Woodward, "carefully and systematically answered

[13] James A. Baker III and Lee H. Hamilton, co-chairs, The Iraq Study Group Report
(December 2006), p. 30.
[14] Bush, *Decision Points*, p. 355.
[15] Frederick W. Kagan, Choosing Victory: A Plan for Success in Iraq Phase I Report, a
Report of the Iraq Planning Group at the American Enterprise Institute (Washington, DC,
2006).
[16] Rice in Bob Woodward, *The War Within: A Secret White House History 2006–2008*
(New York: Simon & Schuster, 2008), p. 304.

the question of how additional US troops could be used to protect the Iraqi population."[17]

Bush explained the new strategy in a TV address on January 10, 2007:

The situation in Iraq is unacceptable to the American people, and it is unacceptable to me. Our troops in Iraq have fought bravely. They have done everything we have asked them to do. Where mistakes have been made, the responsibility rests with me.... This will require increasing American force levels. So I have committed more than 20,000 additional American troops to Iraq. The vast majority of them – five brigades – will be deployed to Baghdad. These troops will work alongside Iraqi units and be embedded in their formations.[18]

Bush was rebelling against a trend of long duration. There were over 700,000 active-duty soldiers in the US military in 1991. By 2001, facing the prospect of protracted warfare in two lands with a combined population of over 60 million people, the United States could call on only just over 400,000 soldiers. A "peace dividend" cut of over 30 percent between the end of the Cold War and 9/11 severely compromised the wars in Afghanistan and Iraq. America simply had too few men and women to fight. Even an increase to 566,000 from 2001 to 2011 could not mask the deficit. Deploying too few troops did not save lives; it cost them. A lesson of the Cold War had been lost and was only slowly relearned: to achieve stability and democracy, US forces needed to stick around. The military "occupation" of South Korea was technically still in force. That state, despite setbacks, is a free, liberal regime – a paradise compared to its northern neighbor. Japan suffered enormous destruction at the hands of the US military and yet that same military, in the early decades of the Cold War, was key to the political and economic transformation of Japan. Boots on the grounded counted for much. It is difficult to envisage how a light footprint, as per the terms of US strategy in 2003, could have achieved similar results. And yet in Iraq the assumption was that it could. By 2006 a new assumption was needed.

The surge combined a number of lessons that the occupation of Iraq had made clear. The US Army could not expect to cow an angry population into stability and cooperation, let alone into Jeffersonian democracy. Its early emphasis on pure security – the raiding of a suspect's home and the accompanying humiliation of his family – was replaced by a greater social awareness. Under the command of David Petraeus, US forces learned a more humane and constructive method of engagement. Petraeus

[17] Woodward, *The War Within*, p. 278.
[18] Bush speech on Iraq, Washington, DC, January 10, 2007.

outlined this new approach in his *Counterinsurgency Field Manual* (2006). It was the first time in 20 years that the US military had seriously revised how it fought a COIN (COunterINsurency) campaign. It did not turn Private Billy Bob from Texas into a social worker, but it did oblige his commanders to consider how violent body-count counterterrorism merely begat more violent terrorism. It was like playing a game of whack-a-mole. The Petraeus Doctrine meant the occupying forces had to listen to the occupied more and corral them less. As commanding general of all coalition troops in Iraq from February 2007 to September 2008, Petraeus encouraged his commanders to negotiate with local leaders to fix routine problems – like the water supply – in the expectation that this would secure cooperation for larger projects – like democratic control and deradicalization.

The surge was not just about an increase in numbers, but a change in mind-set of both the occupied and the occupiers. And it largely succeeded, despite predictions that it could not. It did not transform Iraq into a functioning democracy – but that was never the goal. The surge did contribute to an understanding in Washington and Baghdad that, by boxing clever, enough stability could be realized to make national governance possible. The so-called Anbar Awakening is cited in defense of this claim. Fed up with the violent resistance to the US-led occupation, the leaders of three traditionally rivalrous families in the Anbar Province of Iraq decided to cooperate with coalition troops, and among themselves, to resist the resistors. The collaboration began the demise of al-Qaeda in Iraq. The surge created conditions, rather than dictating them colonial-style, whereby the ordinary pulling and hauling that is politics could take place.[19] The tribes did not need to love each other, or the Americans, for this to happen. They did need to realize that greater political and economic advantage could be achieved in allowing routine disagreements than by sectarian bloodshed.

Iraq remained a highly contested political space. Bush remained optimistic: this was a good thing, he told himself, the foundation for a lasting peace, rather than the basis for renewed conflict. But replicating the Anbar Awakening across Iraq, generally, and in Baghdad, particularly, assumed a template where there was none. Bush invested much faith in Nouri al-Maliki, prime minster of Iraq from 2006 to 2011. Just as President Kennedy wrestled with his faith in the leader of South Vietnam,

---

[19] See Carter Malkasian, *Illusions of Victory: The Anbar Awakening and the Rise of the Islamic State* (New York: Oxford University Press, 2017).

Ngo Dinh Diem, Bush hoped power would turn al-Maliki into a states-man capable of bringing post–Saddam Iraq together. Instead, what he got was an insecure and awkward politician obsessed with his relative position. Diem had hated Buddhists; al-Maliki, a Shia, loathed Sunnis. The sectarianism of both men perplexed their respective US sponsors. South Vietnam could never, as a consequence, achieve the internal cohesion necessary to resist the depredations of North Vietnam. al-Maliki was similarly unable to keep sectarian rivals inside his tent. He did not trust them, or they, him.[20]

The surge was designed less to make Iraq's path to democracy smoother than to create a road map for full American withdrawal. The United States could not quit with Iraq in chaos. The surge had done much to lessen such a possibility, but hardly indefinitely. Possibly a deteriorating faith in al-Maliki's leadership was a catalyst but, by 2008, Bush had decided to end the US presence in the country. Under the terms of a Status of Forces Agreement (SOFA), negotiated in 2008, the US and Iraqi governments agreed that coalition troops would quit Iraqi cities in June 2009. By the end of 2011, all troops were to be removed. President Obama first tried to speed this up before arguing that a residual troop presence was required. The Iraq government responded with a resounding "no." The SOFA terms were fulfilled two weeks ahead of schedule, on December 16, 2011.

IRAQ AND VIETNAM

The similarities between the US experience in Iraq from 2003 to 2011 and in Vietnam from 1965 to 1975 are profound. As in Southeast Asia, official reasons for fighting the war were rejected almost as soon as they were posited. As Iraq went wrong, that popular and scholarly dismissal grew. The domestic American context of the Vietnam War was one marked by protest and dissensus. The Watergate scandal of 1973–1974, forcing the resignation of President Richard Nixon, served to illustrate the rottenness of the system. Wars fought by it, especially ones without decisive and swift conclusions, were unlikely to prosper. Media that were overwhelmingly against the war very quickly made spinning its reversals almost impossible. Armed with the purported truth behind the initial

---

[20] See Edward Miller, *Misalliance: Ngo Dinh Diem, the United States, and the Fate of South Vietnam* (Cambridge, MA: Harvard University Press, 2013); and Toby Dodge, *Iraq – From War to a New Authoritarianism* (Abingdon, Oxon: Routledge, 2012).

intervention – in the secret Pentagon Papers – the media and the universities became the moral arbiters of the war. As John Lewis Gaddis observed, "Revisionism did not just precede orthodoxy with respect to Vietnam: for historians, it has always been the orthodox view of the war."[21]

The parallels with Iraq are telling. The weapons of mass destruction (WMD) rationale earned the necessary consensus to make the war possible. The Iraq reconstruction, because no WMD were found, soon fractured that consensus. The war had been waged on the basis of lies and deception. "Bush lied, people died!" and "Bliar" (Blair) became leitmotifs of the anti–Iraq War movement, on the streets and in university lecture halls. Vietnam had the Pentagon Papers; Iraq had the Dodgy Dossier, a British government–inspired exaggeration of the threat Saddam Hussein posed.[22] The resistance to US troops, as in Vietnam, was by an oppressed, occupied, and colonialized people whose first ambition was not to spread an ideology but to get their nation back. American imperialism and hegemonic ambition compelled both wars. Poor military planning doomed each venture. In the increasingly frayed political and cultural discourse of the Bush years, Iraq became a direct echo of Vietnam.[23]

The shadow cast by the 1960s on the 2000s was a long and dark one. In one important respect, however, the comparison helps us understand the initial motivations behind each war. As we move away in historical time from both, we are better able to judge the official *casus belli*. Both administrations, JFK–LBJ and Bush, went to war for the reasons they publicly espoused at the time: to defend South Vietnam from communism and to denude Iraq of a suspected WMD capacity. That both efforts were nearly catastrophic does not mean they were founded on a deception. Indeed, the honesty – one could argue naïvety – of Presidents Kennedy, Johnson, and Bush was the common feature across both wars. Being wrong about the necessity of the wars does not absolve the instigators – but error is not fraud.

---

[21] John Lewis Gaddis, Were the Hawks Right about the Vietnam War? *Atlantic Monthly* (April 2000), p. 4.
[22] See Porter, *Blunder: Britain's War in Iraq.*
[23] For further parallels see James H. Lebovic, *Planning to Fail: The U.S. Wars in Vietnam, Iraq, and Afghanistan* (New York: Oxford University Press, 2019); Timothy J. Lynch and Robert S. Singh, *After Bush: The Case for Continuity in American Foreign Policy* (New York: Cambridge University Press, 2008), pp. 147–188; and David Ryan and John Dumbrell, eds., *Vietnam in Iraq: Tactics, Lessons, Legacies and Ghosts* (New York: Routledge, 2006).

AN IRAQ EFFECT?

Proponents of America's resistance to communism in Vietnam sometimes claim that such resistance meant that Malaysia, Singapore, South Korea, Thailand, and even Australia were thus also protected from communism. A tactical battle in Vietnam was lost, but a wider strategic war advanced.[24] The claim is controversial. It is similarly so when applied to the Middle East. But the impact of Saddam's demise is difficult to write out of the history of the period. This was to become evident after Bush left office and the region entered a period of political turmoil known as the Arab Spring, considered in the next chapter. But even before those convulsions, the fate of Iraq seemed part of a wider reformation of governance. Saddam's demise was a revelation for other dictators and the people over whom they ruled. After Saddam was pulled from his "spider hole" in December 2003, Muamar Gaddafi, the Libyan leader, apparently told Silvio Berlusconi, the Italian prime minister, that he would "do whatever the Americans want, because I saw what happened in Iraq, and I was afraid."[25] Iraqi elections, held in January 2005, were a hugely symbolic achievement. The peoples of the Middle East, they suggested, were not destined to live in dynastic autocracies.

That same month, Saudi Arabia held its first municipal elections since the 1960s and in Egypt, President Hosni Mubarak announced he would run for reelection later that year. In February 2005, Lebanon had its Cedar Revolution, deposing its pro-Syrian Ba'athist regime. Walid Jumblatt, the otherwise fiercely anti-American leader of the Lebanese Druze, said the Iraqi elections were "the start of a new Arab world."[26] According to the realist-leaning *National Interest*:

Dreams of democratic openings, competitive elections, the rule of law and wider political freedoms have captured the imagination of clear majorities in the Arab world. The dominance of the idea of democracy in the public space has even forced authoritarian ruling establishments to cast about for new pro-reform language in order to communicate their policies to the populace. Even Islamist and leftist opposition movements have, at least rhetorically, dropped most of their

---

[24] See Michael Lind, *Vietnam: The Necessary War: A Reinterpretation of America's Most Disastrous Military Conflict* (New York: Free Press, 2000); and Mark Moyar, *Triumph Forsaken: The Vietnam War, 1954–1965* (New York: Cambridge University Press, 2006).

[25] In Robert S. Litwak, *Regime Change: U.S. Strategy through the Prism of 9/11* (Washington, DC: Woodrow Wilson Press, 2007), p. 193.

[26] In David Ignatius, Beirut's Berlin Wall, *Washington Post*, February 23, 2005, A19.

skepticism about political rights, freedoms and pluralist mechanisms, developing a strategic commitment to gradual democratic reform.[27]

Nine months after Saddam's fall, Georgia, a former colony of the USSR and birthplace of its greatest dictator, Joseph Stalin, had its Rose Revolution. Eduard Shevardnadze, a former Soviet foreign minister, was replaced as president by the pro-American Mikheil Saakashvili. In the month of Bush's second inauguration, Ukraine underwent an Orange Revolution. The pro-Moscow Victor Yanukovych was replaced by the Western-leaning Viktor Yushchenko, a violation of Russian security Vladimir Putin would not forgive. Scholars will, of course, debate the cause and effect of the Iraq War in the political reformations that followed. For the Bush administration, they were evidence that they had pushed over an autocratic domino.

RUSSIA'S WAR WITH GEORGIA

Vladimir Putin did not like dominos. He watched the revolutions in Iraq, Lebanon, Georgia, and Ukraine with growing unease. The use of American power to remove dictators concerned him. When, in April 2008, NATO announced that Georgia and Ukraine would become new members of the alliance, his response was to invade both countries: Georgia in August 2008 and then Ukraine six years later. Urged to abandon Cold War thinking, Putin demurred. Throughout his tenure, the former KGB colonel persisted with a profound mistrust of Western motives. Putin's actions in his near abroad reflected a traditional Russian fear of encirclement and invasion. Napoléon Bonaparte (in 1812), Kaiser Wilhelm (in 1914), and Adolf Hitler (in 1941) had each sought to conquer Russia. Putin saw NATO as their natural successor. In 2006, he had launched a cyber war on Estonia, a former Soviet satellite, in revenge for it joining the alliance. The Baltic states, however, did not suffer invasion. Georgia and Ukraine were a different matter.

Although Estonia, Latvia, and Lithuania border Russia, they have had a semidetached status with their larger neighbor. Forced into the USSR in 1939, when Stalin cut a deal with Hitler, those countries were liberated in 1991. This was resented by Putin, but he was unwilling to fight a conventional war when they subsequently joined NATO in 2004.

---

[27] Amr Hamzawy and Nathan Brown, Arab Spring Fever, *National Interest* [online], August 29, 2007.

The status of Georgia and Ukraine, however, was felt much more keenly in Moscow. Their location was more fundamental to traditional Russian concepts of security. Allowing them to join a Western alliance would, feared the Kremlin, reduce Russia's strategic depth. Georgian and Ukrainian warm-water ports are crucial to Russia's access to the Black Sea and hence to the Mediterranean. Having them fall into NATO hands was unthinkable for Putin. The alliance's expansion beyond the Dnieper River would, warned Putin, "be taken in Russia as a direct threat to the security of our country."[28]

In January 2008, 77 percent of Georgian voters goaded him by endorsing further integration into NATO. In April, NATO affirmed this decision. George W. Bush encouraged it. A tense standoff between Moscow and Tbilisi, the Georgian capital, ensued. In May, Putin handed the Russian presidency (but not its power) to Dmitry Medvedev. By August 1, Putin had had enough. On the pretext that Russian "citizens" were being persecuted in the disputed territories of Abkhazia and South Ossetia (the latter the birthplace of Joseph Stalin), within Georgia, he invaded the country. Scores of Georgians were to die in Russian air attacks on its major cities. A truce brokered by the French, with American support, ended the fighting almost three weeks later. While its terms dictated Russian withdrawal, the deal could not prevent Moscow recognizing the independence of Abkhazia and South Ossetia from Georgia, a violation of Georgian sovereignty that the United States protested but could not prevent.

As in the Cold War, when the USSR enjoyed largely unchecked freedom of action in its own backyard, President Bush found himself unable to do much about what became known as the Medvedev Doctrine: "Protecting the lives and dignity of our citizens, wherever they may be, is an unquestionable priority for our country... there are regions in which Russia has privileged interests."[29] Barack Obama was to find himself similarly denuded of options when the doctrine was applied to Ukraine under his watch. As Robert Kagan observed:

The Russo-Georgian war established a modus operandi that Putin would employ against Ukraine almost exactly six years later. In both cases, the Russian attack was preceded and accompanied by extensive cyber warfare and "fake news."

---

[28] In Steven Erlanger, Putin at NATO Meeting, Curbs Combative Rhetoric, *New York Times*, April 5, 2008.

[29] In Jeffrey Mankoff, *Russian Foreign Policy: The Return of Great Power Politics* (Lanham, MD: Rowman & Littlefield, 2011), p. 39.

In both cases, Russian forces moved in surreptitiously before the main attack. Both invasions were cloaked in ambiguity and confusion, leading many in the West to blame the victims. In both cases, Moscow claimed to be defending pro-Russian populations from alleged mistreatment. But the real purpose was to restore Russian hegemony over former Soviet republics seeking to integrate into the liberal world order.[30]

As we shall see, Obama, like Bush, wanted to accommodate Putin rather than face him down. In August 2008, Bush complained about, but could not check, Russian aggression – a pattern Obama continued after 2009. The same Russian leader elicited the same responses from these two different American presidents.

AN AMBIVALENT CHINA POLICY

The Chinese Communist Party was similarly concerned at Bush's targeting of autocratic regimes. His military focus on the Middle East, however, kept him away from East Asia – and that suited Beijing. Bush was a study in pragmatic ambivalence when it came to China. He certainly never made it part of his freedom agenda. Expectations of renewed tension were high during the April 2001 spy plane episode (see Chapter 4). Its resolution and the ensuing intervention of the September 11 attacks calmed Washington–Beijing relations. Indeed, the War on Terror presented Bush with an opportunity to "Nixononify" his foreign policy. In 1972, President Nixon had used a shared Sino–American fear of Soviet power to begin his opening to China. After 2001, Bush was content to allow a common fear of Islamism to further warm relations with Beijing. The Chinese government painted the threat it faced from internal Islamist terrorism as the flip side to the external threat it posed to the United States.

Just as the strategic imperatives of the Cold War had brought China and America closer together, so too did the War on Terror. The realist maxim that "the enemy of my enemy is my friend" explains more about the Sino–American relationship of the last half-century than explanations grounded in assertions of liberal progress. Bush politely welcomed China's commitment to a common counterterrorist response – though only in the most elastic definition could ethnic Uighurs in Xinjiang be considered on al-Qaeda's side – and otherwise continued the policy begun

[30] Robert Kagan, Believe It or Not, Trump's Following a Familiar Script on Russia, *Washington Post*, August 7, 2018.

by Nixon, Bush Sr., and Bill Clinton: trusting that trade would lead to political liberalization. For both the Chinese leaders whom Bush dealt with, the priority was not terrorism but Taiwan, a hangover of the Cold War. Jiang Zemin (president from 1989 to 2002) said the island was "the most sensitive part of our relations" with the United States.[31] Hu Jintao (2002 to 2012) saw Chinese foreign policy through a domestic lens, which kept Taiwan similarly central. He prioritized internal harmony and development. Peaceful coexistence with the United States, rather than great-power competition, framed his outlook. He had less of the internationalist zeal of Mao and more the introspection of Confucius. The ancient philosopher of harmony and balance made something of a comeback under Hu, featuring in the opening ceremony of the 2008 Beijing Olympics and in the name of China's soft-power project launched under him: the Confucius Institutes.

Bush spoke of his freedom agenda, even on his visits to China, but never made the Chinese oligarchy its target. As a consequence, observed Henry Kissinger, "In Bush's presidency, U.S.–China relations were the matter-of-fact dealings of two major powers ... they found their interests intersecting in enough areas to confirm the emerging sense of partnership."[32] This partnership was to be tested in the trade wars and Taiwan politicking of the later Trump presidency.

In important respects, both Hu and Bush were leaders framed by their respective Cold War experiences, particularly of the 1960s. The future Chinese leader was chastened by the upheaval of the Cultural Revolution. Soon after university, he had been sent into the countryside, to a remote and rebellious province (Gansu), to learn the purity of peasant life. This dislocation taught him the virtues of patience. Advantage came from the steady application of effort over the long-haul. It was a life lesson he applied to his leadership of China. Victories were to be piecemeal and incremental rather than spectacular. Hu imbibed the "virtues of dullness."[33] The 43rd American president, conversely, saw in the 1960s Vietnam War the problems of American retreat and introspection. After 9/11, he eschewed both. His confidence in war was in marked contrast to Hu's – and yet the leadership styles of both men were the products of a similar historical Cold War moment.

[31] In Henry Kissinger, *On China* (London: Penguin, 2011), p. 484.
[32] Kissinger, *On China*, p. 492
[33] Sulmaan Wasif Khan, *Haunted by Chaos: China's Grand Strategy from Mao Zedong to Xi Jinping* (Cambridge, MA: Harvard University Press, 2018), chap. 4.

INDIA AND THE END OF THE COLD WAR SHADOW?

Bush was less ambivalent when it came to China's great geostrategic rival, India. His diplomacy toward the world's largest democracy returned significant gains. "The alignment between India and the United States," argued Robert Blackwill, Bush's first ambassador to India, "is now an enduring part of the international landscape of the 21st century."[34] New Delhi became one of the few foreign capitals where Bush was lauded. "The people of India deeply love you," Manmohan Singh, the Indian prime minister, reassured Bush on his final visit to Washington.[35] On what was this affection based? At a simple but important level, the Indian government shared his preference for democracy over its alternatives. According to Ashutosh Varshney, a scholar of the relationship, "Bush is driven by ideology and instincts … Bush's ideology convinced him that, of the two rising stars on the world stage, India was preferable."[36] More controversial is the claim that parts of the Indian polity empathized with the War on Terror because of its anti-Islamist emphasis. Indian politics since independence in 1947 have been continually roiled by Hindu–Muslim rivalry.

The irony in such a claim is that Pakistan, the only state created in the name of Islam, has been far closer to Washington for far longer than has India. Bush determined to change this Cold War legacy without fully escaping it. During the Cold War, India attempted a middle path between the two superpowers. Its leaders, from Jawaharlal Nehru, in the 1950s and 1960s, to his daughter, Indira Gandhi, in the 1970s and 1980s, sought a "nonaligned" status. In reality, this meant an economy that mimicked the Soviet Union – condemning India to decades of slow economic growth – and distrust of Washington, which sought to use Pakistan, irrespective of its Islamic character, to balance an India too closely aligned, despite its professed neutrality, to a Soviet world view. Nixon and Kissinger controversially backed Pakistan's unsuccessful efforts to prevent Eastern Pakistan (now Bangladesh) from separating from it in 1971. In secret tapes, Nixon said India deserved "a massive famine" for aiding the breakup of Pakistan.[37]

---

[34] Robert D. Blackwill, A Friend Indeed, *National Interest* 89 (May/June 2007), pp. 16–19, 16.

[35] In Anand Giridharadas, India Has a Soft Spot for Bush, *New York Times*, January 10, 2009.

[36] In Giridharadas, India Has a Soft Spot for Bush.

[37] In Gary J. Bass, Nixon and Kissinger's Forgotten Shame, *New York Times*, September 29, 2013.

After the Cold War, Pakistan was to become a key country of contestation for both the United States and China, both of whom wanted to use it to balance against India. But successive American presidents, from Clinton to Trump, never quite trusted Pakistan in this endeavor. Islamabad was either too close to Beijing or too welcoming of Islamists for the Americans to embrace it unreservedly. When Barack Obama ordered Navy Seals to capture and ultimately kill Osama bin Laden on May 2, 2011, he violated Pakistani sovereignty to do it; the terrorist kingpin had been living in a secret compound near a Pakistan military base for several years. Especially concerning after 9/11 was the Pakistan bomb; the state had acquired nuclear weapons, and tested them, in 1998. A former Pakistani nuclear scientist, A. Q. Khan, had, over decades, sold some of its blueprints to the highest bidders – including Iran, Libya, and North Korea.[38]

The repository of this long-standing American tension with Pakistan (and with China) was India. President Bush visited New Delhi in March 2006. The visit sealed a nuclear deal negotiated between both governments over the preceding three years. The US–India Civil Nuclear Agreement applied International Atomic Energy Agency safeguards to India's nuclear energy program (its military nuclear program was separated from its civil program). In return, the United States committed to full, civil nuclear cooperation. What he was unable to achieve with the more concerning Pakistani nuclear program, Bush did achieve with the Indian. It was not quite his Nixon in China moment – the United States and India remain large democracies, skeptical in varying degrees about China, and greater convergence seems likely – but the partnership with New Delhi advanced the interests of both and established a framework for future cooperation. France went onto negotiate a similar agreement with India in 2008.

LATIN AMERICA'S LEFT TURN

Despite the novelty of a president who spoke Spanish, Latin American political development did not favor the Bush Doctrine. The 9/11 attacks did not bring about a moment of hemispheric unity. Only one Latin American leader, Álvaro Uribe of Colombia, supported the Iraq War. Instead, Bolivia (in 2005) and Ecuador (in 2006) joined Venezuela

---

[38] See Catherine Collins and Douglas Frantz, The Long Shadow of A. Q. Khan, *Foreign Affairs*, January 31, 2018.

(from 1999) in taking a left-wing turn against US influence in their region. Part of this was a move toward Iran, one-third of Bush's axis of evil. Cooperation between Tehran and the three Latin American regimes increased significantly during Bush's second term. In September 2006, Venezuela's Hugo Chavez waved a copy of Noam Chomsky's *Hegemony or Survival: America's Quest for Global Dominance*, an anti-Bush screed, at the UN General Assembly.[39] Álvaro Vargas Llosa, a Peruvian–Spanish commentator on international affairs, condemned this vogueish anti-American radicalism as "The return of the idiot."[40]

How far did this antipathy carry over from the Cold War? From the perspective of some in the Bush administration, the answer was "considerably." The coming to power of left-wing governments in Bolivia, Ecuador, and Venezuela was interpreted as a return to the Marxist experiments of Cuba, Guatemala, and Nicaragua during the Cold War. One Bush supporter went further in claiming that Islamism had replaced communism as the revolutionary catalyst: "The southern front in the War on Terror, which runs through Latin America's institutions of state, is cracking under a combined assault of political revolution, Islamist terrorism, and the world's most heavily armed drug cartels."[41]

The warming toward Iran by some Latin American leaders did not help counter this assessment. Iran was a key and certainly unintended beneficiary of the Iraq War. Within days, George W. Bush had removed a regime that Tehran had failed to get rid of in eight years of bloody war in the 1980s. The vacuum left behind was filled less with US troops imposing the early stages of a democratic reformation than with Iranian agents keen to stoke Shia grievances and establish an Iran-friendly government in Baghdad. For certain Latin American nations to join Tehran in this and wider efforts to bolster its international credentials stuck in the craw of many in the Bush administration. But the dynamic had important Cold War parallels and sources – even though conditions, despite Bush's concerns, favored American interests much more after that conflict than during it.

Successive US administrations saw Latin America as an easy target for ideological subversion by the Soviet Union. Iran after the Cold War was

---

[39] Noam Chomsky, *Hegemony or Survival: America's Quest for Global Dominance* (London: Penguin, 2003).
[40] Álvaro Vargas Llosa, The Return of the Idiot, *Foreign Policy*, October 13, 2009.
[41] Mario Loyola, All along the Watchtower: The War on Terror Has Arrived in Latin America, and Is Headed Our Way, *National Review*, March 18, 2009.

hardly a replacement for that lost sponsor. In Washington, however, a Cold War mentality persisted toward the region. Dick Cheney, a congressman during the Iran–Contra scandal of the late 1980s, continued to see Iran as a conspirator making trouble for the United States wherever it could. Indeed, ever since World War I, Latin America had been viewed by Washington as the soft underbelly of the US homeland, ripe for penetration by Germans, then Russians, then Iranians. Eisenhower, Kennedy, Nixon, and Reagan had all engaged in often controversial efforts – sometimes violating "both self-interest and common human decency," according to Odd Arne Westad – to negate Soviet influence.[42] This did not stop in 1989. The first invasion of the post–Cold War era was in Panama. George W. Bush's first foreign trip as president was to Mexico. Just as Vladimir Putin continued to see the former satellites of the USSR as his backyard, George Bush continued to see Latin America as his.

This meant a policy toward the region that sought to both curtail radicalism and to advance democratic gains – a direct echo of Kennedy's 1961 plan for the continent. Bush continued with the economic embargo of Cuba (then in its fifth decade) and, when Hugo Chavez decided to use Venezuela's oil revenues to keep Castro's regime alive, Bush extended the embargo to Venezuela in 2006. According to a former US diplomat based in Havana, the alliance between the two Bolivarian states "drove the Bush people crazy."[43] To further isolate them, Bush increased US military cooperation with Paraguay and Colombia.[44] Like Kennedy before him, Bush never quite got the balance right. Throughout his term, he faced the charge that he did not take Latin America seriously. This is, in part, explained by the much greater focus on Iraq. There is also the legacy of the Cold War to factor in. Chile, which should have provided fertile soil for Bush's freedom agenda (it remains the only country on earth to have moved from "developing" to "developed world" status), often seemed to prefer the politics of historical grievance toward the United States. CIA complicity in the toppling of the Marxist president Salvador Allende in 1973 inhibited the Chilean political class that remembered those events from having a fuller partnership with Washington. The long shadow of the Cold War was hemispheric rather than narrowly US-centric.

---

[42] See Odd Arne Westad, *The Cold War: A World History* (New York: Penguin, 2018), p. 363.

[43] Wayne Smith in Juan Forero, Cuba Perks Up as Venezuela Foils Embargo, *New York Times*, August 4, 2006.

[44] See Gary Prevost and Carlos Oliva Campos, eds., *The Bush Doctrine and Latin America* (Basingstoke: Palgrave Macmillan, 2007).

AFRICA AND AIDS PREVENTION

In a rare nod to his predecessor, President Barack Obama laid out Bush's success in Africa:

I believe that history will record the President's Emergency Plan for AIDS Relief as one of his greatest legacies. And that program – more ambitious than even the leading advocates thought was possible at the time – has saved thousands and thousands and thousands of lives, and spurred international action, and laid the foundation for a comprehensive global plan that will impact the lives of millions. And we are proud that we have the opportunity to carry that work forward.[45]

George Bush Sr. had closed his presidency with an invasion of an African country, Somalia. "No one should have to die at Christmas," he told the American people in December 1992. His son's legacy was deeper and saved more lives on that continent. Its inspiration was humanitarian before it was anything else. But no foreign policy is exclusively one thing and not another. Bush made his case for a revolution in the treatment of AIDS – the President's Emergency Plan for AIDS Relief or PEPFAR – on the basis that it was simply the right thing to do:

My administration launched PEPFAR in 2003 to address the HIV/AIDS pandemic that threatened to wipe out an entire generation on the continent of Africa. Nearly 15 years later, the program has achieved remarkable results in the fight against disease. Today, because of the commitment of many foreign governments, investments by partners, the resilience of the African people and the generosity of the American people, nearly 12 million lives have been saved. And nearly 2 million babies have been born HIV-free to infected mothers.[46]

Bush's summary is an accurate one. Ideological opponents claimed it was yet another manifestation of a condescending neocolonialism. Others said it was a displacement activity to obfuscate the collapsing neocolonial situation in Mesopotamia. Bush said it was to save lives that would otherwise be lost. He increased U.S. spending on HIV/AIDS programs from $1.6 billion in 2004 to over $5.5 billion in 2009. Total PEPFAR spending tripled across his second term.[47] In eleven African nation-states, through his Millennium Challenge Corporation, Bush attempted to tie economic aid to meaningful political reform – again a policy continued by his successor ("tough love," Obama called it).

[45] Obama, speech on World AIDS Day, December 1, 2011.
[46] George W. Bush, PEPFAR Saves Millions of Lives in Africa. Keep It Fully Funded, *Washington Post*, April 7, 2017.
[47] See www.pepfar.gov/documents/organization/252516.pdf.

The relief effort was not without a wider strategic context, though this finds little expression in the Bush team's justification of PEPFAR. The penetration of Chinese capital and consequently of Chinese power into Africa continued across the post–Cold War years, essentially unchecked by the West. More goods are imported into sub-Saharan Africa from China than from any other nation. European colonial guilt afforded Beijing a largely free hand. US policy was consistently compromised by larger concerns elsewhere. Bush's initiative was a means to correct that imbalance. It also provided leverage over African governments in their faltering struggle against Islamism. PEPFAR was an undiluted public-relations victory for the United States in a continent that sometimes flirted with anti-Western Islamism.

THE GREAT RECESSION AND THE 2008 ELECTION

Bush's second term endured two crises at home. One came from God, the other from mammon. The president's response after Hurricane Katrina, which devasted New Orleans on August 29, 2005, alongside the then disastrous Iraqi occupation, reinforced concerns that he was incapable of coordinated leadership. While the troop surge in Iraq allayed some of those concerns, Bush did not escape the legacy of Katrina. As in Iraq, Bush was too slow to react to the peril into which New Orleans had fallen. Federal resources were made available too slowly; federal troops deployed inadequately. Looting, a deeply uncomfortable reminder of the aftermath of the Iraq invasion, negated what little social cohesion the storm had left intact. This did not bode well for the global financial crisis that overtook Bush's administration in its final months.

On October 9, 2007 the Dow Jones Industrial Average (DJIA) hit an all-time high of 14,164. Then the decline began. Within a year, it fell to 10,365. In March 2009, it reached a new low of 6,443. In the final two years of the Bush administration, the stock market lost over half its value. The depth of the crisis was captured on September 15, 2008, with the unthinkable collapse of Lehman Brothers. A global economic panic ensued. Its reverberations would not just condition the final months of the Bush administration, but the opening years of Barack Obama's, and ultimately would be a primary catalyst for the election of Donald Trump in 2016. Economists continue to debate the recession's central cause. Rather than a crisis of federal spending on wars abroad or welfare at home, the emergency began when the markets lost faith in the ability of "subprime" – risky, poor – borrowers to repay their debts. "The kindling for the fire that consumed Wall Street and nearly the entire economy was mortgages that should never have been taken out in the first place."[48] Housing markets in the United States, Britain, and Europe, collapsed. Home foreclosures became an everyday experience across much of America; from January 2007 to December 2011 more than four million Americans had their homes repossessed, with another eight million awaiting the same fate. Unemployment rose sharply – almost doubling for those without a college degree (from 8 percent in 2008 to 16 percent two years later). An administration that had found its first enemy in Islamist terrorism found its final one in loose credit.

Against this backdrop, the presidential election campaign played itself out. Although terrorism had been the central issue in 2004, four years later it was the economy – a reversion to the normal pattern. The Afghanistan, Iraq, and wider terror wars had been huge and controversial undertakings by the Bush administration. However, a case can be made that Bush's decision to bail out America's two largest mortgage lenders – Freddie Mac and Fannie Mae – in September 2008 and, a month later, to approve the largest federal banking bailout in US history, had longer-term consequences for the global economy and for American politics. Together, the Great Recession and the Bush wars made a future foreign policy of retrenchment more likely. Interventionism at home seemed to oblige withdrawal abroad. Candidate Obama indicted the costs of the "dumb" war in Iraq and vowed to stop such adventurism. This campaign strategy was not without precedent. In 1952, Dwight Eisenhower campaigned on a more frugal foreign policy – as an antidote to the costs, in blood and treasure, of the Korean War. In 1976, Jimmy Carter's pitch was to escape the expensive legacy of Vietnam and wage moral campaigns abroad, not physical, military ones. In 1992, during the Bush Sr. recession, Bill Clinton promised a domestic economic focus and an end to "old-think" militarism.

In all these cases, however, the retrenchment was short-lived. The 1950s frugality gave way to the belligerence of 1960s interventionist liberalism in Southeast Asia. The 1970s Carter "malaise" became the revitalized new Cold War of Ronald Reagan in the 1980s. Bill Clinton telescoped this process. Within his own first term, he was to become a profligate user of American military power abroad, which he deepened in his second. In 2008, history now asked if the pattern would continue with

---

[48] Nelson D. Schwartz, The Recovery Threw the Middle-Class Dream under a Benz, *New York Times*, September 12, 2018.

President Obama. Or had his economic inheritance been such that retrenchment was not a choice but a necessity?

CONCLUSION

In assessing the foreign policy of George W. Bush, we are really interrogating two things: his case for war in Iraq and his handling of the occupation that followed. Successes and failures elsewhere, supposing they could be disassociated from Iraq, which they cannot, reside at the historical margins. Even Afghanistan, now the longest war in American history, is secondary to Bush's Iraq legacy. The charge sheet is a long one. The Bush team were insufficiently skeptical about Saddam's WMD program. They relied on every source that claimed Iraq was a real and present danger to the United States and its allies and dismissed sources that argued the opposite. If they did not actually fabricate evidence – this remains a charge too far – the Bush White House privileged that which reinforced its threat narrative. Once regime change was accomplished, Bush, and especially Donald Rumsfeld, were negligent in not appreciating the unfolding catastrophe. This negligence seemed almost willful on the defense secretary's part. The original sin of the Iraq War was its deployment of too few troops to make stability possible. Rumsfeld's revolution in military affairs was the root cause of a debacle. When those troops finally appeared, as part of a surge, they were four years too late. Thousands of Iraqi men, women, and children had died by then. More Americans were killed in those four years, 2003–2007, than had died on 9/11.

The geostrategic consequences were not what George Bush and his evangelizing ally Tony Blair had planned for. The British prime minister had expected what followed his Kosovo War in 1999: that he would be lauded as a national liberator and that Anglo-American opponents, like Russia, would be chastened, pliable even. Instead, Bush and Blair created a void in Iraq, filled first by unemployed Iraqi soldiers and bureaucrats, then by al-Qaeda, then by Iran, and then, eventually, by ISIS (the Islamic State of Iraq and Syria). The wars in Afghanistan and Iraq, as Odd Arne Westad argues, "had no meaning in a strategic sense, in effect creating two twenty-first century colonies under the rule of a Great Power with no appetite for or interest in colonial rule."[49]

---

[49] Westad, *The Cold War*, p. 618.

The emboldenment of Tehran remains an especially problematic legacy of the Iraq War. In a matter of weeks, Bush had removed from the region a regime that Iran had been unable to shift in eight bloody years of fighting two decades earlier. The mullahs of the Islamic Republic could hardly believe their good fortune. Their influence upon the liberated Shia of Iraq was powerful and enduring. Vladimir Putin saw this overextension of US power in the Middle East and determined to exploit it closer to home. With Washington consumed with the intricacies of a colonial occupation and nation-building in Iraq, Russia set about asserting its dominion in its near abroad, eventually, as we shall see, extending Russian military power into Syria, at just the moment when the United States was doing its best to quit the region. China watched this American act of self-sabotage and reasoned its hand in Asia would be strengthened and US resistance to its claims weakened. Beijing's penetration of Africa, despite the remarkable humanitarian work Bush had done there, continued apace. John Bolton, Bush's former UN ambassador, the man who was to become Donald Trump's third national security advisor, captured the mood of many Americans in June 2008: "Nothing can erase the ineffable sadness of an American presidency, like this one, in total intellectual collapse."[50]

While the foregoing charges are not easily answered, they should be placed within a larger context. The first is the defining episode of the post–Cold War era: the attacks of September 11, 2001. With hindsight, we know 9/11 would not be the first in a series of escalating terrorist strikes. Al-Qaeda revealed on that day not a poverty of ambition or imagination – they had plenty of both – but one of capacity. They did not have the means to launch anything but the crudest of assaults, using everyday technology. But Americans did not know this at the time. In the immediate aftermath of 9/11, the next attack, possibly more severe, seemed inevitable. The Bush team, when handed this emergency, had two options: assume the worst and plan for it or assume this was the best Osama bin Laden could do and simply track him and his associates down. Because of the impact of 9/11 itself, that second option was neither politically nor psychologically tenable. Instead, large and comprehensive solutions were pursued. At the time, these seemed logical and rested on a strong domestic consensus. That they were poorly and inadequately executed does not impugn their inspiration. 9/11 demanded a bolder

[50] John R. Bolton, The Tragic End of Bush's North Korea Policy, *Wall Street Journal*, June 30, 2008.

and bigger response than is now judged appropriate. But this is the wisdom of detached, academic hindsight. In the devastation and fear of September 2001, going after root causes seemed the right thing to do. This is what the "prism of 9/11" changed.

The second context to place Bush foreign policy within is a wider historical one. The argument here is a version of "it's too early to tell." Zhou Enlai, the longtime Chinese premier, was reputed to have made this answer in 1968 when asked what he thought of the French Revolution of 1789.[51] Are we too close to the Bush administration to fully comprehend what it wrought? We will examine this question next when we consider the Arab Spring. Making definitive conclusions about what Bush's "freedom agenda" accomplished will be the work of future historians.

Harry Truman offers some guidance now. His political career seemed to have ended in failure in 1953. Eastern Europe and China had gone red. He bequeathed a stalemated Korean War to his successor. He was vilified at home for losing the Cold War. Bush, in 2009, was in an analogous situation. He had lost Iraq to Iran. In Afghanistan, the Taliban were resurgent. The global economy was collapsing. Bush left office the most unpopular president in American history.

Yet much historiography now credits Truman with putting in place a plan – both strategic and ideological – for America's ultimate victory over the Soviet Union forty years later. What was indistinct and fantastical in the early 1950s became a reality after 1989. The opponent did collapse. American power stood preeminent. Foundations laid by President Truman endured. If Bush's reputation is following a similar path, what will his legacy be in 2051, a half-century after 9/11? Possibly, it will include recognition of his role in questioning the nature of Arab governance. Bush was the first president to ask whether the peoples of the Middle East were culturally preordained to live under autocrats. His war in Iraq was a test of a then-nascent proposition, perhaps validated in the decades to come, that these men and women were capable of and deserving of democratic government. The Bush Doctrine, rather than a series of exaggerations, might stand muster with Truman's: as the basis for a world order in which democratic rights expand where many experts have said, then and since, that they cannot. Michael Kelly, the first journalist killed in the Iraq War, asked the question this way:

---

[51] Disappointingly, it now seems he was actually referring to French student protests in 1968.

I understand why some dislike the idea, and fear the ramifications of, America as a liberator. But I do not understand why they do not see that anything is better than life with your face under the boot. And that any rescue of a people under the boot (be they Afghan, Kuwaiti, or Iraqi) is something to be desired. Even if the rescue is less than perfectly realized. Even if the rescuer is a great, over-muscled, bossy, selfish oaf. Or would you, for yourself, choose the boot?[52]

Finally, Bush foreign policy was implemented within the long shadow of the Cold War. The Bush White House was staffed by the men and women who knew that conflict better than any other. They had fought its battles – like Vietnam – and had studied its contours. They were survivors of American bureaucracies forged in that setting. The effect of this was an understanding of the 9/11 foes as ideological opponents against whom a global campaign must be waged. Islamist terrorism, like communism, was not a discrete, parochial, monolithic force. It was pervasive and had multiple centers of power that could be opposed. Like communism, its appeal was theological before it was economic. The disciples of both could not be easily reasoned out of their faith. So the Cold War and the War on Terror both became wars on their material capacities. Truman and Bush did not think they could end evil in the world. They did set about severing the link between their opponent's ambitions and the weapons they needed to realize them. For Cold War presidents this meant a sustained arms race. For Bush, it meant denying the enemy the wherewithal to develop weapons of mass destruction.

A measure of Bush's success, as we will examine next, is how far his successor stuck to the fundamentals of his national security strategy. Despite promising change, Barack Obama delivered a surprisingly Bush-like approach to American security. This was telegraphed by him in 2008, but missed by a world seemingly desperate to consign George W. Bush to history.

---

[52] In Jeffrey Goldberg, Remembering Michael Kelly, *Atlantic*, April 3, 2013. Kelly was editor of the *Atlantic* when he was killed.

6

Barack Obama's Flexible Response, 2009–2012

Why is this whole thing being framed around whether I have any balls?
—*President Obama on claims he was dithering on Afghanistan, 2009*[1]

Governor Romney, I'm glad that you recognize that al-Qaida's a threat because a few months ago when you were asked, what's the biggest geopolitical threat facing America, you said Russia — not al-Qaida, you said Russia. And the 1980s are now calling to ask for their foreign policy back because, you know, the Cold War's been over for 20 years.
—*President Obama to Mitt Romney, 2012*[2]

Barack Obama often disparaged his domestic opponents for being stuck in the Cold War. However, from the very inception of his presidential run, it was a conflict that shaped his approach to foreign policy. Rather than transcend the legacy of the Cold War, Obama attempted to both embrace and disdain it. He sought an awkward accommodation between old and new. He was a "change" president who saw great value in continuity. He would attempt to "bend history" toward a liberal future but relied on realist lessons from the past. His presidency extended the Cold War shadow. And as with so many Cold War leaders before him, it started in Berlin.

---

[1] In Ben Rhodes, *The World as It Is: Inside the Obama White House* (New York: Random House, 2018), p. 76.
[2] Presidential debate, Lynn University, Boca Raton, Florida, October 22, 2012; transcript at https://nyti.ms/2rGDi5A.

On July 24, 2008, Obama reminded an ecstatic German audience that their freedom was won not by goodwill but by American power. Even as he disparaged a Cold War mind-set, he reiterated how crucial NATO had been and remained to European freedom. His key allusions were to Ronald Reagan, the president who did more than any other to question the legitimacy of Soviet power. In a calculated attempt to connect himself to Reagan's famous "Tear down this wall!" admonition of 1987, Obama's address was filled with wall references.[3] The Cold War had brought out the best in America, Obama made clear, from the Berlin airlift (1947–1948), to the creation of an Atlantic alliance (in 1949), the utility of which endured after the Cold War in places like the Balkans – and was soon to be used by Obama in Libya. In Berlin that summer, Obama was offering an odd form of transcendence: the problems of the world might be new, from climate change to global terrorism, but their remedy would be found in old partnerships, forged in the Cold War.

Despite a geographically varied upbringing – taking in Hawaii, Indonesia, and Kansas – and a proud assertion of his "world citizenship" – he traveled to Africa, India, Pakistan, and Europe after graduating – Obama came to the presidency with surprisingly little experience in international affairs. As a student and community organizer in his twenties, he had specialized in civil rights law. As a state lawmaker in his thirties, he rose by his navigation of local Illinois politics. His stands on foreign affairs were left-leaning and rather humdrum, "the utterly predictable liberalism of a backbench senator," said one commentator.[4] In the 1980s, he opposed apartheid in South Africa and wanted a nuclear weapons freeze, but otherwise did not betray a particular zeal for causes beyond his own political ambitions. He visited Kenya for familial, not geostrategic, reasons – his father was a Kenyan.[5]

In the 1990s, he had little to contribute in post–Cold War foreign policy debates. He was ambivalent, as far as can be gleaned, about the liberal interventionism of Bill Clinton. Indeed, his grasp of the issues that were sown thereby came retrospectively. During his rise to national political power in the early 2000s, Obama consulted with key foreign-policy makers and scholars of the Clinton era, but seems not to have

---

[3] See Ben Rhodes, *The World as It Is*. Rhodes wrote the Berlin speech.
[4] Michael Gerson, The Obama Era Has Damaged Liberalism, *Washington Post*, January 13, 2016.
[5] See Barack Obama, *Dreams from My Father: A Story of Race and Inheritance* (New York: Times Books, 1995).

inherited their interventionist passions. As a freshman US senator, 2005–2007, his foreign policy positions were not easily labeled.[6] The liberal historian Sean Wilentz claimed that Obama "resembles Jimmy Carter more than he does any other Democratic president in living memory."[7]

His Carterish tendencies were arguably apparent even before he became president. By the time he announced his run in 2007, Obama had, on domestic matters, one of the most liberal voting records in the Senate. But, in contrast to Carter in 1976, his intended foreign policy was a study in ambiguity. He made much political hay indicting the failures of George W. Bush's Iraq War, while at the same time claiming the mantle of George H. W. Bush, who had attacked Baghdad in 1991. Like the elder Bush, Obama embraced a cautious realism, eschewing the younger's "dumb" (Obama's adjective) 2003 war. Simultaneously, he sought the counsel of humanitarian hawks, enticing Samantha Power, the young author of an influential book on genocide, to advise him on foreign policy; ultimately she became his ambassador to the UN. He wanted a troop drawdown in Iraq, but reluctantly agreed to a surge in Afghanistan. He made initial overtures to Arab Muslims – promising to curtail American colonial meddling – before joining Britain, France, and Italy in a protracted attack on Libya, resulting in the extrajudicial killing of its leader. It seemed Obama was determined to avoid the charge of consistency in his foreign policy. Rather, flexibility and pragmatism – not doctrine – became the hallmarks of his approach.[8] Both liberals and realists wanted to claim him as one of their own – and, depending on the issue at hand, each group could. Obama was content to straddle several traditions. During the 2008 campaign he said, "The truth is that my foreign policy is actually a return to the traditional bipartisan realistic policy of George Bush's father, of John F. Kennedy, of, in some ways, Ronald Reagan."[9]

From Berlin to Chicago, the wave of euphoria that greeted the election of Barack Obama in November 2008 masked some uncomfortable realities. "Hope" was easy to posit in a campaign, harder to turn into a governing agenda. The change mantra he adopted as a candidate was

[6] See Ryan Lizza, The Consequentialist, *New Yorker*, May 2, 2011.
[7] Sean Wilentz, Sean Wilentz on Obama and Substance, *Newsweek*, August 22, 2008.
[8] See David Milne, *Worldmaking: The Art and Science of American Diplomacy* (New York: Farrar, Strauss and Giroux, 2015), p. 459.
[9] In Milne, *Worldmaking*, p. 467.

especially problematic when it came to America's engagement with the world. What Obama had campaigned on was not a revolution or counter-revolution in US foreign policy, but continuity. He wanted to adopt many of Bush's strategies – and improve them. He wanted to be like John F. Kennedy *and* like Ronald Reagan. He wanted to reject simple binaries *and* embrace his predecessors that had traded in them. His doctrine thus became reactive rather than strategic, which is to argue it was not meaningfully doctrinaire at all. Obama wanted to deal with the world "as it is," rather than force upon it a preconceived template. This meant a recurrent undercommitment abroad, lest entanglement ensue. Obama was JFK-lite. As Robert Singh notes wryly, parodying Kennedy's inaugural address, the new president was willing to "pay part of the price, bear a bit of a modest burden, meet an occasional hardship, support the odd friend, oppose the odd foe."[10]

AN OBAMA DOCTRINE?

The clarity of the Bush Doctrine, whether or not one adjudges it to have worked, came from its central organizing principle: to limit terrorist capacity. Obama shared this one – as his prosecution of "overseas contingency operations," his new name for the War on Terror, was to demonstrate – but sought key departures from Bush. There were at least three key claims made on behalf of the new president's approach. Each took a buffeting in the international politics of his two terms.

Personality and Identity

Obama made his personal characteristics central to his recalibration of American foreign policy. "The day I'm inaugurated, the country looks at itself differently," he insisted in 2007. "And don't underestimate that power. Don't underestimate that transformation."[11] Obama's elevation to the presidency was, indeed, a remarkable phenomenon. The election of a mixed-race candidate, the son of a Kenyan goatherd, with an African–Arab name, to the world's most powerful office, is testament to the capacity for transformation that the United States

---

[10] Robert Singh, *Barack Obama's Post-American Foreign Policy: The Limits of Engagement* (London: Bloomsbury, 2012), p. 6.
[11] Interview on New Hampshire Public Radio, November 23, 2007; in Robert G. Kaufman, *Dangerous Doctrine: How Obama's Grand Strategy Weakened America* (Lexington: University Press of Kentucky, 2016).

retains.[12] His executive inexperience makes his elevation even more remarkable. He had run not much more than a student newspaper – the *Harvard Law Review* – before he entered the Oval Office. Most of his predecessors had governed large southern or western states – Georgia, California, Arkansas, Texas – and all had been white.

Obama believed his personal story would alter how the rest of the world related to American power. This turned out largely to be mistaken. But in 2009, it was an operating assumption of his administration. As the son of a Kenyan, Obama could claim with some legitimacy to have an experience of colonialism – his father had fought against the British presence in his country. In his first speech to an Arab audience, in Cairo in June 2009, he insisted he begin with a history of Western imperialism. As an African–American, Obama was able to elicit sympathies (but rarely concessions) from foreigners, who often saw American history through the lens of race relations. These narratives were belied by Obama's smooth ascent through life, from a highly supportive homelife in Kansas (he was mostly raised by his white grandparents), to elite schools, to Congress, and then to the White House. But the politics of identity and of personality mattered to how he presented his foreign policy and, to an extent, how it was received abroad. Few presidents have been so lauded overseas as Barack Obama. The political scientist James Ceaser derided this as "a foreign policy based on promoting an indecent pandering to an evanescent infatuation with a single personality."[13] But it remained Obama's contention that this popularity could unlock ancient enmities and recast America's image.

Managed Decline

If Francis Fukuyama's *The End of History* (1992) had been the defining text of the Clinton years, encouraging boldness because the West had won, Fareed Zakaria's *The Post-American World* (2008) framed the discourse in Obama's – and demanded circumspection because others were catching up.[14] Zakaria's thesis was less that the United States was declining but that "the rest" were rising. A US-based Indian–American

---

[12] Obama's biographer claims that the notion that his father was a "goat herder" was "a form of romantic overreach." Everyone in rural Kenya herded goats at some stage. See David Remnick, *The Bridge: The Life and Rise of Barack Obama* (New York: Vintage, 2011), pp. 34, 109.

[13] James W. Ceaser, The Unpresidential President, *Weekly Standard*, August 2, 2010.

[14] Fareed Zakaria, *The Post-American World* (New York: W. W. Norton, 2008).

commentator, Zakaria popularized the "rise of the rest" as the defining challenge for twenty-first century American statecraft, starting with Obama's presidency. Just as the West rose after the fifteenth century, and the United States after the nineteenth, the current century would see a third transition, to the BRICs – Brazil, Russia, India, and China – though global power would spread beyond this bloc. "For the first time ever," claimed Zakaria, "we are witnessing genuinely global growth. This is creating an international system in which countries in all parts of the world are no longer objects or observers but players in their own right. It is the birth of a truly global order."[15]

Obama read Zakaria's book. He made several mentions of it in his first term. Much of his foreign policy rhetoric can be read as an effort to render practical what Zakaria had posited conceptually. This meant an approach that relied on these rising others being part of the solution to global disorder. America could step back, reasoned Obama, because it was the rest's turn to step forward. Critics, even on his own side, derided this as an attempt to make the United States "The Dispensable Nation."[16] But realism underpinned the intellectual framing of the challenge. Famous realists like John Mearsheimer and Stephen Walt spent the post-9/11 years bemoaning the overreach of US foreign policy.[17] The recession that began in 2008, which had little to do with this purported overreach, was an opportunity to scale back US commitments. Zakaria, by the same token, had suggested other powers would fill the gaps American left behind.

Engagement

In his first inaugural address, Obama offered an invitation: "To those who cling to power through corruption and deceit and the silencing of dissent, know that you are on the wrong side of history, but that we will extend a hand if you are willing to unclench your fist."[18] His supporters called this "engagement;" his critics called it "appeasement." Rather than

---

[15] Zakaria, *Post-American World*, p. 3.
[16] See Vali Nasr, *The Dispensable Nation: American Foreign Policy in Retreat* (New York: Random House, 2013).
[17] John J. Mearsheimer, *The Great Delusion: Liberal Dreams and International Realities* (New Haven, CT: Yale University Press, 2018); and Stephen M. Walt, *The Hell of Good Intentions: America's Foreign Policy Elite and the Decline of U.S. Primacy* (New York: Farrar, Straus and Giroux, 2018).
[18] January 20, 2009.

define axes of evil, as Bush had done, Obama wanted to pursue a dialogue with America's opponents. Like Bush, however, this moral agility was grounded in the assumption that history favored the American experiment. Around Obama's Oval Office carpet was embroidered Martin Luther King Jr.'s optimistic claim: "The Arc of the Moral Universe Is Long, But It Bends Towards Justice."[19] The role of American diplomacy was to persuade foreign constituencies that history was indeed bending toward an inevitable progressive future. This was Obama at his most liberal. History was on his side. By engaging with hostile regimes, rather than threatening them, this proposition could be universalized.

"Don't Do Stupid Stuff"

Obama's realism was recurrently captured in this admonition – sometimes a cruder synonym than "stuff" was used. Rather than the bending arc of the moral universe, it captures a conception of American foreign policy as the husbanding of resources. Obama's progressive liberalism, built on the notion that we are all in this together, was balanced by an assessment of international politics as an expensive business that the United States was not obliged to fund. Donald Trump was to turn this into his diplomatic ideology after 2017. Obama and Trump each indicted the stupidity of American overextension in Iraq. The liberation of 30 million people from Saddam's tyranny was not worth the cost to US blood and treasure. This aspect of his doctrine explains much about Obama's subsequent reticence to surge troops into Afghanistan, his highly circumspect military action in Libya, his refusal to intervene in Syria, and his ambivalence toward Russian adventurism.

The Obama Doctrine thus looked eclectic and agile or contradictory and hypocritical, depending on the case studies used to assess it. As Colin Dueck observes, scholarly disagreement over what was truly fundamental to it "points to the shifting, ambiguous quality of American foreign

---

[19] Also embroidered were: "The Only Thing We Have to Fear Is Fear Itself" (Franklin D. Roosevelt); "Government of the People, By the People, For the People" (Abraham Lincoln); "No Problem of Human Destiny Is Beyond Human Beings" (John F. Kennedy); and "The Welfare of Each of Us Is Dependent Fundamentally upon the Welfare of All of Us" (Theodore Roosevelt). See Dan Amira, President Obama Installs Appropriately Less-Optimistic Rug in the Oval Office, *New York Magazine* [Daily Intelligencer], August 31, 2010.

policy under Obama."[20] Critics claimed "shifting" meant "shifty." But the Obama team preferred the flexibility of not ever claiming a doctrine. "The world was too complicated to sum up in a doctrine," said Ben Rhodes, Obama's foreign policy guru. "We were going to be damned if we did declare a doctrine and damned if we didn't; looking at the risks of overpromising or oversimplifying, we decided to avoid the question."[21] Leslie Gelb was less kind: "there is a paucity of genuine strategic thinking," he wrote.[22] Without strategy there can be no doctrine.

OBAMA'S TEAM OF RIVALS

The ambiguity of his foreign policy was captured in the team assembled to deliver it. Obama's preparatory reading for the presidency, alongside Fareed Zakaria, included Doris Kearns Goodwin's *A Team of Rivals*.[23] While this was not evidence of the long shadow of the Civil War, it did suggest some historical guideposts. Goodwin argued that Abraham Lincoln's political genius lay in the creative tension of his cabinet. Autocrats often fail because they surround themselves with yes-men. Democratic leaders needed a diversity of voices. Obama's skill lay in appointing a couple of no-women: Hillary Clinton, his rival for the nomination in 2008, and Samantha Power, whose instincts for an expansive humanitarian foreign policy agenda were to repeatedly clash with his preference for retrenchment.

Hillary Clinton, whom Obama so brilliantly outstrategized to win the Democratic nomination, was offered and accepted the position of secretary of state, but could hardly be regarded as a friend and intimate. Observers can only speculate as to Obama's motives here.[24] Certainly, tying her political fortunes to his own while simultaneously removing her from the locus of power – she would be in an airplane or abroad for much of her tenure – made good strategic sense. It also meant Clinton's hawkish dispositions were given less airing in the president's inner circle. Instead,

[20] Colin Dueck, *The Obama Doctrine: American Grand Strategy Today* (New York: Oxford University Press, 2015), p. 1.
[21] Rhodes, *The World as It Is*, p. 122.
[22] Leslie Gelb, The Elusive Obama Doctrine, *National Interest* (September–October 2012).
[23] Doris Kearns Goodwin, *A Team of Rivals* (New York: Simon & Schuster, 2006).
[24] See Mark Landler, *Alter Egos: Hillary Clinton, Barack Obama, and the Twilight Struggle over American Power* (New York: Random House, 2016), and James Mann, *The Obamians: The Struggle Inside the White House to Redefine American Power* (Viking: New York, 2012).

Samantha Power was the preferred hawk-in-residence. If Clinton's military interventionism was tempered by her air travel, Power's was enhanced by Obama's making her UN ambassador in 2013. The two women's personal antipathy – Power had described Hillary Clinton as "a monster" in 2008 – also made it hard for a hawkish wing in the Obama administration to cohere.[25] Obama, determined to avoid the misadventures of his predecessor, organized his team so as to weaken voices advocating war, while at the same time giving them a place at the table.

Some within the early Obama foreign policy team disparaged the Lincoln analogy. Instead, they claimed, the Bush Sr. administration (1989–1993) was their model. Eschewing the free-for-all decision-making of Clinton and the closed shop of Bush–Cheney, Obama attempted to reconstruct the close-knit team of George H. W. Bush. Success in this regard was not immediately apparent. His first national security advisor turned out to be no Brent Scowcroft. James L. Jones endured an unhappy tenure at the National Security Council, failing to win the new president's confidence – and vice versa. In November 2010, Thomas Donilon replaced him. The connection to the outgoing Bush Jr. administration was affirmed by leaving Robert Gates as secretary of defense. Gates was to challenge the president over several issues, not least his boss's reticence over escalating the war in Afghanistan. Gates contributed to a factionalism – rather than a creative tension – that marked the initial team. He was replaced in April 2011 by Leon Panetta. Panetta's directorship of the CIA was then assumed by David Petraeus, the general that had saved George W. Bush's war in Iraq. After an affair with the director's biographer came to light, Petraeus resigned the post in 2012. "Change" became the hallmark of Obama's foreign policy team – though, with hindsight, it was to look remarkably stable compared to the later Trump administration.

Reinforcing the Cold War anchor was Obama's selection of elder statesmen. Henry Kissinger has become perhaps the most ubiquitous presidential advisor of the modern era, again belying claims that after the Cold War US foreign policy changed decisively. Clinton, Bush Jr., and Obama all sought his counsel. Obama continued this raid on 1970s know-how by consulting with Zbigniew Brzezinski. By 2011, Carter's national security advisor (1977–1981) was being described as "the reigning realist of the Democratic foreign-policy establishment."[26]

---

[25] Ewen MacAskill and Suzanne Goldenberg, Obama Aide Resigns after Calling Clinton a "Monster," *Guardian*, March 8, 2008.
[26] Ryan Lizza, The Consequentialist, *New Yorker*, May 2, 2011.

The foreign policy team revealed not schizophrenia but a calculated attempt to transcend the simple binaries of liberal vs. realist and new vs. old. President Obama contended he could be all of these. In the months before and after his election, he presented two visions of what his foreign policy would become. One was purportedly new and liberal; the other was tested and realistic. The foreign policy of his first term was a less a struggle between these two than an attempt to convince adherents of one that it was not the other. Obama's achievement was to have his foreign policy claimed by both sides while fully delivering for neither. His first executive order, on the second full day of his presidency, promised to close the detention facility at Guantánamo Bay within 12 months; this was Obama the liberal. After his eight years in office, the facility remained open; this was Obama the realist.

RECESSION DIPLOMACY

Obama faced two immediate problems. First, at home, he had to lead the American economy out of its deepest crisis since 1929. This was arguably the greater inheritance from his predecessor than were the wars in Afghanistan and Iraq. Second, abroad, he had to help restore a damaged confidence in the West as the wise arbiter of the global economy. He enjoyed considerable success on the first; the economy slowly turned during his time in office; his successor inherited something of a boom. The second, however, proved beyond him. As the West endured a crisis of faith, China used the market turmoil to demonstrate the utility of its approach to economics.

The new president's first overseas trip was to Europe, in an effort to find a consensus on how to prevent a global financial collapse. An Obama aide noted, "[The] awkward fact for us is that we were asking other countries to spend money to stimulate the global economy in order to fix a crisis that the United States had started."[27] The reserves of goodwill Obama enjoyed, certainly at the beginning of his presidency, gave him leverage in London – where the British government pledged nearly $1 trillion in stimulus spending – but less in Europe. To appease them, Obama offered an analysis that his domestic detractors seized on: "I believe in American exceptionalism, just as I suspect that the Brits

---

[27] Rhodes, *The World as It Is*, p. 41.

believe in British exceptionalism and the Greeks believe in Greek exceptionalism." James Kirchick was outraged:

Viewed within the context of the first 100 days of his presidency, Obama's nonsensical statement is part of a disturbing pattern. Since swearing the oath of office, our president has traveled the world criticizing his predecessor, confessing America's supposed sins and otherwise flagellating the nation he leads on the altar of international "public opinion."[28]

His initial attempts at global outreach were derided as the "apology tour." In 2009, he traveled to nearly every continent. Obama's working assumption on this busy itinerary was that a more self-reflective diplomacy would bring advantages that American hubris could not. He made his own story central to this new presentation of American power. According to his speechwriter, "Obama was unique in that the mere fact of his own identity was going to leave an imprint on people abroad."[29] This meant both implicit and explicit referencing of his own racial heritage against the history of race in the United States. His supporters said this would improve perceptions of the United States in the developing world. His detractors said such perceptions were largely immaterial to US interests. Projecting contrition won few concessions with foreign governments.

However, his economic diplomacy through 2009 belies much of the criticism he received. He addressed the Great Recession with reserves of realism rather than modish liberalism. At home, this meant the passage of a $787 billion stimulus bill. Abroad, it meant cajoling partners into a coordinated response to the global crisis. There is no evidence that Obama ever apologized for the American property market being the cause of the crash. He did not question the legitimacy of capitalism. He took aim at corporatism, but he was joining a strong consensus in doing this. The United States and global economies were slow ships to turn around. By July 2009, however, gross domestic product (GDP) growth turned positive. Rather than a blip, this turned out to be the beginning of the second-longest economic expansion since modern records began in 1854. The recession created a context for his first term, and empowered China, as we will see in the next chapter, but it did not become the decisive issue of his foreign policy.

---

[28] James Kirchick, Squanderer in Chief, *Los Angeles Times*, April 28, 2009.
[29] Rhodes, *The World as It Is*, p. 46.

THE AFGHANISTAN SURGE

In December 2010, the deaths of two men, worlds apart, were to have a crucial impact on American foreign policy for years to come. On the December 13th, Richard Holbrooke, special representative to Afghanistan and Pakistan, died of a heart attack. The United States lost thereby one of the most able, if abrasive, diplomats of his generation. Four days later, Mohamed Bouazizi, a young Tunisian street vendor, set himself on fire and, in turn, lit a protest movement across the Middle East. Holbrooke's loss was felt immediately. That of Bouazizi took longer to become apparent.

Richard Holbrooke was a man who inspired as much loyalty among his team as he did distrust among his superiors. This dynamic was to make Obama's efforts to withdraw from Afghanistan harder. Holbrooke was considered too ambitious to be given the secretary of state role that he coveted. Obama had kept Hillary Clinton, his defeated 2008 primary opponent, inside the tent by giving her the job in 2009. Holbrooke was instead charged with ending the Afghanistan War. Having brought the warring parties of the former Yugoslavia to the table in 1995, great peacemaking was now expected of him. However, Holbrooke was never able to build a personal connection with Obama. When they first met, Holbrooke had annoyed the president-elect by insisting he call him "Richard." Obama had greeted him as "Dick."[30] Ronan Farrow, who worked on Holbrooke's team, bluntly acknowledged that "to many Obama loyalists, Richard Holbrooke was the enemy: part of the old guard of foreign policy elites that had accreted around the Clintons and dismissed Obama and his inner circle as upstarts ... he remained exactly what Obama had run against."[31]

This personal antipathy colored much of the Obama administration's handling of Afghanistan. In 2009, the conflict entered its ninth year. Parallels to Vietnam were ubiquitous – even before the ongoing occupation of Iraq was factored in. The president's instincts were to withdraw as soon as possible. His military advisors, including generals David Petraeus (hero of the Iraq surge) and Stanley McChrystal (the new commander in Afghanistan), and his secretaries of state and of defense, wanted a longer timetable. The latter, Robert Gates, had been appointed by George

---

[30] Ronan Farrow, *War on Peace: The End of Diplomacy and the Decline of American Influence* (London: William Collins, 2018), p. 51.
[31] Farrow, *War on Peace*, p. 50.

W. Bush. Obama had retained him at Defense for the purpose of continuity. An annoyed Ben Rhodes recalled the "exorable demand" from this faction "to pour more troops in."[32] The perception that Bush's 2007 surge in Iraq was the obvious template for Obama's in Afghanistan rankled with the new president. He had opposed the Iraq surge when in Congress. Applying it to Afghanistan, now that he was president, meant accepting that Iraq was a tactical error, rather than the strategic catastrophe Obama had campaigned against.

Those that wanted to increase the US military commitment to Afghanistan drew explicitly on a Cold War lesson: taking the country off the US's radar in the wake of the Soviet withdrawal in 1989 had been a disaster for US national security. American refusal to engage in nation-building created the conditions that brought the Taliban to power and al-Qaeda under its protection. The 9/11 attacks were the projection of Islamist power from Afghanistan. Robert Gates had been part of the Bush Sr. administration that had beat a hasty retreat in 1989. He was unwilling to repeat the mistake twenty years later. In May 2009, at a dinner hosted by Hillary Clinton that did not include President Obama, he assured Hamid Karzai, the beleaguered president of Afghanistan, that America was "not leaving" his country "prematurely . . . In fact, we're not ever leaving at all." On hearing this, "at least one stunned participant," records Bob Woodward, "put down his fork."[33]

The debate was over both the number of troops and their role. McChrystal and Gates wanted a surge of between 40,000 and 80,000, easily doubling the numbers of troops already there. This position was leaked to the press before it was presented to the president. "They were boxing Obama into sending troops into Afghanistan and setting him up to take the blame for any bad outcomes that followed if he didn't," claimed Rhodes.[34] Obama was acutely aware of the death toll. In 2008, there were more US causalities in Afghanistan than in Iraq. The next year, 312 US troops were killed in the war. The president often performed the solemn task of meeting the returning caskets at Dover Air Force Base. He also thought a significant escalation was wrong strategically. The Taliban was not a foreign force that could be expelled; they were indigenous to Afghanistan. More troops might scatter al-Qaeda, but the Taliban would endure. This assessment was advanced by John Brennan, the president's

---

[32] Rhodes, *The World as It Is*, p. 62.
[33] Bob Woodward, *Obama's Wars* (New York: Simon & Schuster, 2010), p. 354.
[34] Rhodes, *The World as It Is*, p. 66.

counterterrorism advisor. It computed with Obama's ranking of al-Qaeda as his priority. Brennan assured Obama that beating bin Laden's terrorists did not require the complete destruction of the Afghan Taliban. But if he could deploy the surge to push back the Taliban, this would enable US forces to go after al-Qaeda.

After months of internal reflection and testy meetings (an exasperated Obama claimed the debate was over whether he had "the balls" to see it through), the president ultimately went with a compromise surge of 30,000 troops – more than his vice-president wanted, but less than McChrystal, and the strong faction he represented, hoped. In a speech to West Point cadets on December 2, 2009, Obama made clear the surge was the logical end game of a war against al-Qaeda begun on 9/11. His authority to act, he said, was pursuant to Congress's Joint Resolution 23 (in 2001), which had given George Bush the right "to use all necessary and appropriate force" against the 9/11 plotters. Controversially, then and still, was the 18-month timetable for withdrawal he imposed on the escalation (to the end of 2011).[35] Wouldn't the Taliban just wait for NATO troops to leave? Obama's Afghanistan surge illustrated the flexibility with which he wished to pursue national security. The decision to escalate reflected a hard-nosed realism. The insistence that troops must withdraw because they faced an unbeatable indigenous opponent illustrated his liberalism. The former allowed him to take the war direct to al-Qaeda in Afghanistan and Pakistan – a nuclear-armed state. The latter allowed him, immediately after his West Point speech, to fly Oslo to accept the Nobel Peace Prize.

OBAMA'S WAR ON TERROR, PART I

Prioritizing the fight against al-Qaeda in Afghanistan and Pakistan highlights the nature of Barack Obama's counterterrorism. According to Daniel Klaidman, Obama was "a coolly efficient terrorist killer."[36] If Bush had been the hapless responder to 9/11, Obama was the ruthless dispatcher of its architect. In ordering the capture, which became the killing, of the al-Qaeda leader, Obama offered a snapshot of his wider War on Terror. In his first year in office, he was responsible for the deaths

---

[35] See the retrospective offered by Paul D. Miller, Critics Should Stop Declaring Defeat in Afghanistan, *Foreign Policy*, April 12, 2019.
[36] Daniel Klaidman, *Kill or Capture: The War on Terror and the Soul of the Obama Presidency* (New York: Houghton Mifflin, 2012), dust jacket.

of more alleged terrorists – usually by drone strikes – than his predecessor had been in eight. "By his third year in office," records Klaidman, "Obama had approved the killings of twice as many suspected terrorists as had ever been imprisoned at Guantánamo Bay."[37] President Bush, to much liberal chagrin, had wanted bin Laden "dead or alive" in 2001. Obama delivered him dead ten years later. He authorized the violation of Pakistan air space to do this. He acted entirely unilaterally, informing no allies, to preserve secrecy. He applauded bin Laden's fate and was widely applauded in the United States for engineering it.

The raid that killed the al-Qaeda leader has entered American political folklore, its drama captured by a photograph of the White House principals watching it unfold on a live link from Pakistan. Obama had spent the previous evening publicly ridiculing Donald Trump. At the White House Correspondents Association Dinner, he had spent several minutes making jokes at Trump's expense as he sat immobile at his table. It has been speculated that this was the moment Trump decided to run for president in 2016.[38] The jokes, however, belied the gravity of the raid Obama had just authorized. His great fear was that he had set in motion a replay of the disaster-by-helicopter scenario that had undone Jimmy Carter's presidency in April 1980. Like Carter, Obama had given the go-ahead for a high-risk incursion into foreign air space in pitch darkness by Navy helicopters. A collision in the desert, killing eight servicemen, en route to the besieged US embassy in Tehran had ended the already fading hopes that Carter could be reelected. Operation Eagle Claw was the Obama team's fearful point of reference as US Navy Seals approached bin Laden's secret compound in Abbottabad, Pakistan. One helicopter did crash, but no US personnel were killed. At about 2 AM Pakistan time, bin Laden was declared "EKIA" – Enemy Killed in Action. "We got him!" said Obama.

Barack Obama's War on Terror represented a recalibration of Bush's, rather than its repudiation. Its greatest – or certainly its most symbolic – success was the killing of Osama bin Laden. A wish that George W. Bush was never able to fulfill, the removal of the al-Qaeda leader demonstrated the understanding of the war that Bush and Obama shared. The caricature of both men as polar opposites has obscured a profound continuity. Despite his soft-left approach on so many domestic issues, Obama was an

---

[37] Klaidman, *Kill or Capture*, pp. 117–18.
[38] See Adam Gopnik, Trump and Obama: A Night to Remember, *New Yorker*, September 12, 2015.

advocate of the global War on Terror. He wanted it waged more effectively. Americans did not elect a pacifist to the White House in 2008, but a man who had accepted the logic of George Bush's counterterrorism. Indeed, it had been Obama's willingness to buy into the dominant national security consensus of the post-9/11 decades that meant his thin experience of these matters was never interrogated. He quickly, as a candidate in 2007, defined the number-one national security issue confronting the United States as the nexus between terrorism and technology, the prevention of which had been the basis of Bush's war in Iraq. According to Obama:

We must confront *the most urgent threat* to the security of America and the world – the spread of nuclear weapons, material, and technology and the risk that a nuclear device will fall into the hands of terrorists. The explosion of one such device would bring catastrophe, dwarfing the devastation of 9/11 and shaking every corner of the globe.[39]

He, of course, did not support the Iraq War in 2003. His skepticism was born not of a moral aversion to war, but to this war in particular. Iraq did not advance the counterterrorism objectives that both he and Bush were agreed on: limiting terrorist capacity. It had instead bred terrorists and given them an incentive to be better armed. He and Bush had a tactical difference over a common strategy.

The Cold War was replete with such disagreements. Democratic and Republican presidents all saw the USSR as a threat but differed over how to meet it. Truman's version of containment was insufficient, argued his successor. Vietnam was a front in a global war (Johnson) versus "no it was not" (Nixon). The politics of national security in the Cold War had been substantially about means, not ends. And this character captured much about the debates over the War on Terror. Questioning the Cold War consensus on the nature of threat was electorally problematic. Doing the same after 9/11 was similarly so. As both candidate and president, Obama studiously avoided being cast as a national security outlier. His direct targeting of terrorist suspects is evidence of this, his kill-rate prodigious ("five to ten times the rate of the Bush administration").[40] This record jars with his cosmopolitan-in-chief caricature. Oslo's Nobel Prize

[39] Barack Obama, Renewing American Leadership, *Foreign Affairs* 86, 4 (July–August 2007): 2–16. Emphasis added.
[40] Martin S. Indyk, Kenneth G. Lieberthal, and Michael E. O'Hanlon, *Bending History: Barack Obama's Foreign Policy* (Washington, DC: Brookings Institution Press, 2012), p. 265.

committee hoped that Obama would at least lead a move away from Bush. In 2009, it awarded the new president its peace prize. Obama stood before them that December and made clear he was no Mahatma Gandhi or Martin Luther King Jr.:

> As a head of state sworn to protect and defend my nation, I cannot be guided by their examples alone. I face the world as it is, and cannot stand idle in the face of threats to the American people. For make no mistake: Evil does exist in the world. A non-violent movement could not have halted Hitler's armies. Negotiations cannot convince al-Qaeda's leaders to lay down their arms. To say that force may sometimes be necessary is not a call to cynicism – it is a recognition of history; the imperfections of man and the limits of reason.[41]

The speech could plausibly have been offered by George W. Bush or any number of his Cold War predecessors. The designation of the enemy as "evil" echoed Ronald Reagan's assessment of the Soviet Union. George Bush had somewhat awkwardly after 9/11 grasped for a way to describe its perpetrators as "evil doers." Even Donald Trump was to throw the term around in justifying his first attack on Syria in 2017.

Obama's War on Terror was not painted in morally relativistic shades of gray:

> We must always reserve the right to strike unilaterally at terrorists wherever they may exist. (November 20, 2006)
> * * *
> Today, the dangers extend beyond states alone to transnational security threats that respect no borders. These are threats that arise from any part of the globe and spread anywhere, including to our own shores – dangers like … terrorism. (July 16, 2008)
> * * *
> … the challenges of a new and dangerous world. Today's dangers are different, though no less grave. The power to destroy life on a catastrophic scale now risks falling into the hands of terrorists. (July 15, 2008)
> * * *
> Let me repeat: I am not going to release individuals who endanger the American people. Al Qaeda terrorists and their affiliates are at war with the United States, and those that we capture – like other prisoners of war – must be prevented from attacking us again … we must hold individuals to keep them from carrying out an act of war. (May 21, 2009)[42]

---

[41] Obama, Nobel Peace Prize speech, Oslo, December 11, 2009.
[42] These quotes are helpfully tabulated by Richard Jackson, Culture, Identity and Hegemony: Continuity and (the Lack of) Change in US Counterterrorism Policy from Bush to Obama, *International Politics* 48, 2–3 (March 2011), pp. 390–411, 403–404.

There was not a perfect continuity from Bush to Obama. Certainly, during his first term, Obama attempted to step away from some aspects of Bush's War on Terror – not least the fact that he dropped its title. He disavowed "enhanced interrogation techniques." He ordered CIA probes into Bush's use of torture – resulting in a damning 2014 report. These adjustments tended, however, to be piecemeal rather than fundamental, "a change of emphasis more than a change of direction," noted David Sanger.[43] The central objective endured: preventing the nexus between terrorists and WMD. Indeed, the means expanded under Obama to include the Afghan surge, kill lists, drone strikes, and an acceptance that Guantánamo Bay could not easily be closed. As David Frum observed wryly, Obama had established a "continuity you can believe in."[44]

EGYPT AND THE ARAB SPRING

As the Obama administration upped its killing of terrorists, Muslims in several nations demanded greater freedoms. It would be convenient for both Bush and Obama to find a cause-and-effect here. Known as the Arab Spring, a play on the European "springs" of 1848, 1968, and 1989, protests beginning in early 2011 removed the leaders of Egypt, Libya, and Tunisia. The collapse of communist regimes in 1989, ending the Cold War, seemed the clear analogue. As then, the protests had multiple causes, but a frustration with bad government was a common theme. Mohamed Bouazizi's self-immolation in Tunis was in protest against the arbitrary restriction by municipal bureaucrats of his trade as a street vendor. He had reportedly been slapped by one such official, and his stall had been confiscated. He died of his burns eighteen days later. Ten days after that, on January 14, 2011, following widespread unrest, Tunisian President Zine El Abidine Ben Ali resigned after twenty-three years in power. The removal of Arab dictators suddenly seemed possible.

As had happened in 1989, the speed of events caught the White House by surprise. President Obama had made his first term about mending fences with Muslims. The scandals of the Iraq War, Guantánamo Bay, Abu Ghraib, and torture seemed to dictate that Obama stress a principle of noninterference. US foreign policy under him would meddle less and

[43] David E. Sanger, *Confront and Conceal: Obama's Secret Wars and Surprising Use of American Power* (New York: Crown, 2012), p. 421.
[44] In Stephen F. Knott, *Rush to Judgement: George W. Bush, the War on Terror, and His Critics* (Lawrence: University Press of Kansas, 2012), p. 84.

step back more. In a speech in Cairo, in June 2009, he pointedly did not connect democracy with Muslim development – interpreted as a rebuff to the Freedom Agenda of his predecessor. "No system of government," he assured his audience, "can or should be imposed upon one nation by any other ... America does not presume to know what is best for everyone." Again, pointedly, he declined to travel just a few miles to Israel, the region's only democracy. The next week, Iranians took to the streets of Tehran, to protest what they saw as a rigged election. Obama chose not to foment their discontent. The so-called Green Revolution stalled. Obama, it was observed, did not want a revolution in Iran; he wanted a nuclear deal.[45]

By 2011, however, the demands for change appeared much more widespread than the Obama administration had imagined. By the end of that year, Obama had been complicit in the removal of the leader of Egypt and had joined an invasion of Libya. Egypt's Hosni Mubarak was confined to a cage. Libya's Muammar Gaddafi was pulled from a drainage pipe in the desert, sodomized with a bayonet, and then shot dead. Obama's role in these events, albeit a reluctant one, reasserted a pattern he had tried to escape: since the end of the Cold War, the majority of military interventions undertaken by the United States have aimed to liberate Muslims from bad government.

Regime change in Egypt was a product of American soft power, in Libya of hard – both deployed reluctantly, but deployed all the same. In January 2011, an enormous protest movement occupied Tahrir Square, in the center of Cairo. Protestors wanted many things. They were united, however, in calling for an end to the Mubarak regime, then entering its fourth decade. As in Eastern Europe in 1989, the White House was concerned that this would lead not to peaceful change, but to a bloody conflict. Bob Gates, secretary of defense, wanted Obama to be cautious and pledge support to Hosni Mubarak, America's long-term ally. Hillary Clinton, secretary of state, was friends with the Egyptian leader, as was her husband, going back years. She saw little benefit in regime change. Egypt had been a Cold War ally; its 1978 peace accord with Israel was crucial to US interests in the region. The US intelligence community was worried that removing Mubarak would allow extremists to take over. The Gulf monarchies lobbied Obama similarly. Each called for "restraint" from all sides.

[45] See Jay Solomon, *The Iran Wars: Spy Games, Bank Battles, and the Secret Deals That Reshaped the Middle East* (New York: Random House, 2016).

Having assured Egyptians, eighteen months earlier, of his belief in noninterference, Obama initially attempted to placate cautious voices in his administration and the concerns of pro- and anti-Mubarak forces in the region. This soon became untenable. The protests were too large and angry. Mubarak's offer to quit at the end of his term was greeted with incredulity in both the Oval Office and Tahrir Square. Obama called to tell him to resign. Thomas Donilon, the national security advisor, noted the parallels with the Philippines in 1986. Then, as now, a US president, Ronald Reagan found himself telling a pro-American ally, Ferdinand Marcos of the Philippines, to renounce his power in the face of popular protest. David Cameron, the British prime minister, echoing Margaret Thatcher's admonition to George Bush Sr. to not go "wobbly" on Iraq in 1990, urged Obama to be more aggressive toward the now-tottering Egyptian regime. The president seemed trapped by this conflicting advice. His foreign policy principals wanted Mubarak to leave slowly, if at all. His closest foreign ally wanted this to happen quickly. Because Obama could not resolve this tension, events on the ground did it for him. Mubarak resigned and fled on February 11th.

Obama offered muted applause for the people power that had removed a seemingly entrenched regime. Within months, as many members of his administration had warned, "extremists" – the Islamist Muslim Brotherhood – were elected to power. Their political incompetence was to result in a return to military rule in 2013. Whether it was indecision or ambivalence on Obama's part is a matter of interpretation. However, positions he could avoid in Egypt proved impossible to avoid in Libya, when Libyans acted to remove their "Brother Leader," days after Mubarak fell.

LIBYA AND POST–COLD WAR INTERVENTIONISM

The civil war in Libya (a nation slightly larger than Alaska with the population of Arizona), initiated on February 17, 2011, would oblige Obama to continue a pattern of post–Cold War interventionism that he had always said he would not pursue: the changing of regimes injurious to Muslims by the application of American military force. Such actions in Afghanistan and Iraq had been disasters, said Obama. He had moved to end them as soon as possible. In 2011, however, he found himself reluctantly waging his own war of Muslim liberation.

Hosni Mubarak's autocracy had been enduringly brutal but not bizarre. Muammar Gaddafi's despotism in Libya had been both.

President Reagan referred to him as mad-dog Gaddafi. In 1986, a joint Anglo–American air strike, in reprisal for the Libyan leader's coordination of terror attacks on US military personnel, came close to killing him. Gaddafi's revenge was to bring down a Pan Am passenger jet over Lockerbie, Scotland, in 1988.[46] Convinced his people loved him, Gaddafi tested their loyalty by routinely raping school girls after their in-classroom selection by his secret police.[47] His geostrategic aspirations were large. He began a Libyan nuclear weapons program, which only fizzled out when Saddam's fate for doing the same, and Western blandishments to stop, were made clear to him after 2003. These "new realities," said Gaddafi, changed his approach.[48] Thereafter, Tony Blair sought to rehabilitate him as a poster child for how Arab autocrats could reform and enjoy Western largesse thereby. Instead, his hold on power became more tenuous, the myth of his invincibility harder to sustain. Antigovernment protests began in 2009. The fall of the Tunisian and Egyptian leaders in early 2011 catalyzed those protests. The brutality of his response brought Gaddafi back into Western cross hairs.

The how and why of Obama's Libyan action were strikingly similar to Bill Clinton's in Kosovo (1999) and George W. Bush's in Iraq (2003). All three men helped topple a dictator without any United Nations resolution in place supporting such an outcome. Each claimed to be waging a war of Muslim liberation – or at least they aimed to end the violation of the human rights of Muslim populations. The means chosen to realize this objective was the limited deployment of US military power. Clinton relied on airpower to weaken Serbian resolve. Bush disastrously attempted a light footprint in Iraq, which left the nation free of Saddam but also free of any hope of sociopolitical order. Obama "led from behind" in Libya, offering enough support to make a British and French military campaign work, but not enough to provide postwar stability.[49] The fate of both Iraq and Libya, because of this minimalism, was years of civil war and bloodshed. Bush did, at least, like his father, make war on Baghdad armed with congressional authorization to do so. Neither Clinton nor Obama was supported by Congress in their wars on Milošević and Gaddafi.

---

[46] See Robert S. Litwak, *Regime Change: U.S. Strategy through the Prism of 9/11* (Washington, DC: Woodrow Wilson Press, 2007), p. 171–176.
[47] See "Storyville: Mad Dog – Gaddafi's Secret World," BBC Four documentary (2014).
[48] In Litwak, *Regime Change*, p. 191.
[49] The phrase "leading from behind" has a disputed origin. Ben Rhodes claims Obama would never have used it. See Rhodes, *The World as It Is*, p. 122.

This was both cause and effect of the fraught relationship both men endured with Capitol Hill.

The Libya action, however, also fits a longer tradition in American foreign policy. Throughout the Cold War, as well as after, there had been a bias within US administrations toward Arab and/or Muslim interests.[50] This has not been dogmatic or doctrinaire, and has sometimes been contradictory and hypocritical, but the pattern is marked. In conflicts both large and small, America has tended to support the Arab/Muslim side. In 1948, the Truman administration supported majority-Muslim Pakistan in its war of separation from majority-Hindu India. This proved an enduring Cold War and post–Cold War alliance. When Britain, France, and Israel invaded Egypt in 1956 to overthrow its Arab leader, Gamal Abdel Nasser, Eisenhower refused to help. An era of pan-Arab nationalism, on which Saddam Hussein was to thrive, began thereby. Beginning in the 1970s, successive US administrations supported Turkey in its conflict with Greece. Nixon and Kissinger acted to preserve the Egyptian army by imposing a peace deal on Israel, after a disastrous Arab war on the Jewish state in 1973, becoming Cairo's chief sponsor thereafter. In the Iran–Iraq War, 1980–1988, Reagan backed the Arab side. At the same time, he supported and helped arm the Afghan mujahedeen in their war against Soviet occupation. Their Islamist fighters toured the United States in the 1980s, where, notes Lawrence Wright, "they were lauded for their spiritual courage in the common fight against Marxism and godlessness."[51]

Post–Cold War administrations continued this bias. In 1991, George H. W. Bush made war on Ba'athist (and thus nominally secular) Iraq to liberate Muslim Kuwait. After that war, US troops continued to protect Saudi Arabia, the birthplace of the prophet Muhammad, from Saddam Hussein. Twice in the 1990s, Clinton bombed Christian Serbia to save the lives of Muslims in Bosnia and Kosovo. After Islamist terrorists attacked America on 9/11, George W. Bush liberated, if imperfectly, millions of Muslims from regimes in Kabul and Baghdad. And in 2011, Obama renewed this tradition by supporting an action that led to regime change in Libya. His significant defiance of the trend was Syria – with huge consequences for the depth and duration of its civil war after 2011. Indeed, when Donald Trump launched missile strikes on Syrian

[50] See Barry Rubin, The Real Roots of Arab Anti-Americanism, *Foreign Affairs* 81, 6 (November/December 2002).
[51] Wright, *The Looming Tower*, p. 171.

government facilities (in 2017 and 2018) he was renewing a trend that his predecessor had resisted.

Certainly, Obama viewed intervention in Libya with considerable caution. Hillary Clinton, his secretary of state, was much keener on a shock-and-awe strategy of the kind that had decapitated the Iraqi regime in 2003 – a war she had voted for as a US senator. She was also the heir to the hawkish interventionism of her husband. The result was an approach to Libya that tried to reconcile two competing tendencies. Obama wanted highly circumscribed objectives to obtain; he had ruled out regime change as a goal. Hillary Clinton had more expansive aims; in April 2011 she had helped NATO leaders craft a communiqué that made Gaddafi's ousting a formal political objective of the military action. Derek Chollet, part of the US team that negotiated that agreement, described this as being "caught in a strategic tautology."[52] Obama wanted humanitarian protection to be the exclusive war aim, but this was most effectively achieved by removing the Libyan leader, Clinton's position. The mission creep that Obama had wanted to avoid became, as a matter of military logic, inevitable. As it turned out, the NATO action did not directly kill Gaddafi. Rebels, aided by NATO air cover, achieved this on October 20, 2011.

The parallels with Bush's Iraq war are striking. Both were justified as wars of civilian protection and were condemned by their detractors as wars for foreign oil. Both removed an Arab leader without a UN resolution authorizing such an outcome. Each action enjoyed significant European participation – with British belligerence common to both. The wars in Iraq and Libya were designed to avoid the need for postwar nation-building. The planners of each campaign were highly averse to a boots-on-the-ground strategy. Bush and Obama wanted to go in and get out on the cheapest terms possible. An operating and largely faulty assumption behind both wars was that the international community would fill the vacuum left by the withdrawal of US military power. Instead, it was filled by assorted Islamists and terrorists. This consequence would significantly compromise the electoral prospects of Hillary Clinton. Her Republican opponents made much of her purported failure, as secretary of state, to protect the US ambassador to Libya, killed when his Benghazi compound was attacked by terrorists on September 11, 2012. Iraq after 2003 and Libya after 2011 entered periods of sustained and disastrous internal strife. A key difference, of course, is that Bush

---

[52] Derek Chollet in Mark Landler, *Alter Egos*, p. 189.

recognized this deterioration and attempted to arrest it. Obama was content to leave a liberated but collapsing Libya well alone.

The United States had a well-founded reputation in this regard. The decision of George H. W. Bush to walk away from Afghanistan in 1989 set off a chain reaction that led directly to 9/11, eleven years later. Ronald Reagan's canny and covert arming of the mujahedeen, "holy warriors," in their jihad against Soviet occupation was a significant Cold War success. Moscow's decision to quit Afghanistan was one more nail in the coffin of the USSR. However, the void this left in Afghanistan was not filled by Islamic democrats, but by Islamist radicals; American funding was replaced by Saudi funding. Riyadh-sponsored Wahhabism thus became the dominant version of Islam. The necessity of imposing order, in the absence of any significant Western support, gave the Taliban, a residue of the mujahedeen, enough legitimacy to impose their theocratic vision on the country. That vision ultimately led them to embrace bin Laden and al-Qaeda. "These things happened," affirmed the congressman who secured funds for the anti-Soviet resistance. "They were glorious and they changed the world ... and then we fucked up the endgame."[53] George H. W. Bush's unwillingness to countenance even a token role in post–Soviet Afghanistan handed his son a very large and enduring problem. There is, then, a certain tragic irony in Barack Obama claiming the mantle of Bush Sr.'s realism. Both he and Bush Jr. found themselves dealing with the elder Bush's sin of omission in Afghanistan. Obama, like the Bush Sr. he revered, decided to leave Libya, and soon Syria, to a successor. As a frustrated member of the Obama administration put it: "His modus operandi has been disengagement."[54]

Barack Obama joined his Cold War and post–Cold War predecessors in making war on Libya without Congress's say-so. Jimmy Carter, reflecting on how the 1973 War Powers Resolution (WPR) compromised his foreign policy, supported its attempted repeal in 1995. Ronald Reagan invaded Grenada in 1983 without Congress knowing of the action until it was over. Bill Clinton kept troops in Somalia through 1993 – including those that participated in the Black Hawk Down incident – without congressional approval. He made war in Kosovo in 1999, this time in the face of an explicit refusal by Congress to authorize the campaign. Somewhat ironically, given his reputation as a cowboy, George W. Bush only fought wars approved by legislators – in Afghanistan and Iraq and in

[53] The closing epigraph of the movie *Charlie Wilson's War*, dir. Mike Nichols (2007).
[54] Vali Nasr, *Dispensable Nation*, p. 160.

the wider War on Terror. Obama, in contrast, waged his war against Gaddafi beyond the sixty days demanded by law and without even seeking congressional approval. Since 1973, US presidents have been required by the WPR to seek congressional approval within sixty days of any military deployment – or to bring those forces home within ninety days if no approval is given. Ronald Reagan was at least mindful of taking military action that set the WPR clock ticking, but which ended before Congress became an issue. Presidents Clinton and Obama were much bolder in making prolonged war, irrespective of what Congress thought.[55] Donald Trump continued this tradition in Yemen, ignoring congressional efforts to end US military involvement in that terrible conflict. In so doing, he was drawing on a precedent entrenched by his Democratic predecessors.[56]

SYRIA AND THE ARAB WINTER

The Libyan crisis had persuaded enough members of the Obama administration, Hillary Clinton especially, that intervention was unavoidable. The president had at least joined a military action that ended Gaddafi's rule. This critical mass never formed over Syria. The hope that regime change would come to Damascus, as it had to Cairo, Tunis, and Tripoli, without the need for significant US effort, was misplaced. The protests, beginning in March 2011, which looked like a carbon copy of those that had formed in the other nations of the Arab Spring, were met with a violent response by the Syrian government. Its fierce repression in the face of initially peaceful civil protest was to be a defining feature of the Syrian Civil War, which lasted through and beyond the Obama presidency.

George Bush Sr. did not send US troops into a disintegrating Yugoslavia, because he had "no dog in the fight." This refusal, eventually reversed by Bill Clinton, was sustained for a similar reason by Barack Obama, as Syria descended into chaos through his second term. By the close of his administration, an estimated half a million civilians had been killed, a number almost as great as those dying in the

---

[55] See Louis Fisher, Military Initiatives by President Obama, in Richard S. Conley, ed., *Presidential Leadership and National Security: The Obama Legacy and Trump Trajectory* (New York: Routledge, 2018), pp. 74–92.

[56] See Gunar Olsen, Add Trump's Yemen Veto to Obama's Spotty War Legacy, *New Republic*, April 20, 2019.

Iraq War.[57] The war itself had as many sides as it had causes. The Obama administration, much like Bush Sr. when he surveyed the Balkans, was to rely on this complexity as a reason to do little. Worse still was his tacit emulation of the elder Bush's approach to Iraq in 1991. After banishing Saddam Hussein from Kuwait, the United States refused to honor a commitment to support a subsequent rebellion against him. The Iraqi dictator was to stay in power for another twelve years.

Bashar al-Assad, the Syrian leader, despite a caricature of him as a weak and Westernized version of his hardline father, turned out to be a wise student of American foreign policy. He had three key case studies on which to draw. The first was the American reluctance to act decisively against Saddam Hussein, his fellow Ba'athist, through the 1990s – despite his repressive rule. Assad reasoned that if he was brutal in defense of his regime, Obama would fret, but otherwise not much care. And so it largely proved. Second, Assad observed the fate of Gaddafi. This might have induced in him a wariness of US power, but the collapse of Libya after Gaddafi's execution convinced the Syrian leader that Obama would not repeat the experience. And he was right to be convinced; Obama did not. Third, Assad had confidence that eventually the United States would see his fight against al-Qaeda and ISIS as part of its own war on terror. Again, he was to be proved partially correct on this. Even Syria hawks within the Obama administration – and John McCain outside of it – were concerned that targeting Assad would, by default, advantage opponents America had been fighting since September 11, 2001. If there were mujahedeen among the Syrian rebels, which might have allowed Obama to emulate Reagan's approach to 1980s Afghanistan, they were now either transformed into al-Qaeda or lost in a complex tapestry of anti-Assad forces. With no obvious dog in the fight, to the consternation of Samantha Power, whose prominence came from condemning that attitude and who held a human rights portfolio in the NSC, Obama's Syria strategy was a repeat of Bush Sr.'s "Yellowstone theory" in Yugoslavia: let this brush fire burn itself out.

Options for some sort of intervention in 2011–2012 were canvassed by the CIA director, David Petraeus. None was able to identify a rebel group around which US action might cohere. Obama feared any arms sent to "moderates" would find their way into the hands of extremists; the

---

[57] Possibly 600,000 died in Iraq. See Megan Specia, How Syria's Death Toll Is Lost in the Fog of War, *New York Times*, April 13, 2018; and Philip Bump, 15 Years after the Iraq War Began, the Death Toll Is Still Murky, *Washington Post*, March 20, 2018.

moderates were left to source them any way they could. Syria's descent from street protests to civil war in 2011 also coincided with the withdrawal of US troops from Iraq. Obama was unwilling to leave one theater only to go next door. In November 2012 he would face reelection. A Syrian quagmire would not, he reasoned, help him win. The paradox of this position, as was to become clear after Obama's reelection, was that quitting Iraq created the conditions necessary for the rise of al-Qaeda in Syria – and its opportunistic evolution into ISIS. But even in 2011 the portents were strong. With no moderating American influence in Iraq after December, the Shia-dominated al-Maliki government in Baghdad ratcheted up its sectarianism. Sunnis were targeted as enemies of the state. With no US protection to be had, they increasingly looked to whatever forms were available. Al-Qaeda, along with assorted Sunni Islamist groups, were to become the protectors of last resort – with profound consequences for Obama's efforts to remain above the fray in his second term.

In several important respects, the centrality of the Middle East in Obama's foreign policy, despite his attempts to pivot 'away from it, was a product of the Cold War. That conflict had moved, seemingly inexorably, decade on decade, around the world. It had begun in late 1940s Europe. In the 1950s, it moved to Northeast Asia, and then to Southeast Asia in the 1960s. Africa became a key region of ideological contestation in the 1970s, Latin America in the 1980s. The Cold War did not quite skip the Middle East – Israel remained a bulwark for Washington's efforts to halt Soviet penetration, and the Afghanistan War after 1979 allowed Reagan to engage in a proxy war with Moscow – but the region was not a key front. After the Cold War, conflict within Islam, long suppressed by the Cold War, inviting greater levels of US, and eventually Russian, intervention, made the region central to American foreign policy. By 2010, observed Michael Mandelbaum, the Middle East was "the heart of geopolitics" – the one region of the world still immune to the ideas that victory in the Cold War had helped propagate: "peace, democracy, and the free market."[58] After Iraq and Afghanistan, from which he expended much energy extricating US personnel, Obama wanted to move along and deal with the rise of China and the threat of climate change. If US ideals were to spread, they would have to do so without the Obama administration forcing them. The people of the Middle East made this difficult.

---

[58] Michael Mandelbaum, *The Frugal Superpower: America's Global Leadership in a Cash-Strapped Era* (New York: PublicAffairs, 2010), p. 138.

There were distinct echoes of Ronald Reagan in Obama's Middle East strategy. In October 1983, 241 US Marines were killed in their Beirut barracks by a terrorist bomb. Reagan quickly removed the remaining forces from Lebanon. While rhetorically hawkish on counterterrorism, the Republican president was willing to cede the country to a range of terrorist groups. The ensuing Lebanese civil war cost 10,000 lives. Obama, like Reagan, similarly calculated that withdrawing US troops from Afghanistan would hand terrorists a significant victory. The human rights of thousands of Afghans, especially women, would be put in jeopardy. Yet he withdrew them to a token force, nonetheless. The words, thirty years earlier, of Robert McFarlane, Reagan's national security advisor, proved eerily prescient: "One could draw several conclusions from this episode ... the most telling was the one reached by Middle Eastern terrorists, that the United States had neither the will nor the means to respond effectively to a terrorist attack." The Lebanese retreat, said Reagan's NSA, was "one of the most tragic and costly policy defeats in the brief modern history of American counterterrorism operations."[59] The often uncomfortable mismatch between rhetoric and realism did not die with the end of the Cold War.

RUSSIAN RESET

A complicating feature of the Arab Spring was the Russian response. The revolutionary upheaval filled Vladimir Putin with trepidation. He was said to have watched Gaddafi's gruesome execution on a YouTube loop. If autocracies could be ended, with only a little Western nudging, why not his? The Obama administration had begun its Russia policy more hopefully. In March 2009, US Secretary of State Hillary Clinton famously presented her Russian counterpart, Sergei Lavrov, with a big red "reset" button – symbolizing Obama's hopes that misunderstandings over Serbia (in 1999) and Georgia (in 2008) could be forgotten. "Reset" was mistranslated by the US team as "перегрузка," which actually means "overcharge," as Lavrov observed at the time. Mistranslations were to bedevil Obama's Russian policy throughout this term. When US–Russia cooperation (over nuclear weapons, for example) or disputes (as over Ukraine and Syria) occurred, both were framed within a Cold War

---

[59] Peter Wehner, The Unintended Consequences of a Retreat, *Commentary*, June 21, 2011.

shadow. By 2017, US troops were training for war with Russia using a Cold War manual.[60]

But, as in 2001, relations with Moscow started positively. A year after the red button was pressed another Strategic Arms Reduction Treaty (START) agreement was signed. A Russo–American strategic engagement rooted in the Cold War continued. The original idea for a comprehensive arms control agreement had been Ronald Reagan's in the early 1980s. George H. W. Bush signed it in 1991. Obama was the third president to adopt and extend its framework. Indeed, Obama's START drew criticism for being overly rooted in "a Cold War mentality."[61] Rather than pursue more aggressive antiproliferation efforts – against Iran and North Korea, for example – Obama fell back on a traditional measure of diplomatic success: arms control treaties with Russia. The discomforting Chinese propensity to leak nuclear technology to Pakistan was left essentially unchecked by the Obama administration. With no Cold War precedent to draw on, the United States found formal arms agreements with China hard to come by.

Despite the change he was meant to embody, Obama pursued a traditional foreign policy. This complicated more than it advanced US interests. START was an example of this. President Obama invested significant diplomatic as well domestic political capital in the deal with Russia. And yet it was not clear how a renewed rapprochement with Moscow would solve problems like North Korean nuclear games-manship; the Iranian penetration of Lebanon, Iraq, and Syria; and, compounded by the latter, the capture of the Palestinian West Bank by Hamas. Nor, indeed, was it clear that agreements with Putin could do much to restrain his territorial ambitions in his backyard. Rather than confront these issues, Obama returned to the vision of a nuclear-free world. This may have motivated his student activism in the early 1980s, but it was a second-tier priority in 2010.[62] Pursuing START also meant confronting a Republican Party in Congress newly energized by sweeping gains in the 2010 midterm elections. The deference of the legislature to the White House in the Cold War and post–9/11 crisis environments no

---

[60] Eric Schmitt, U.S. Troops Train in Eastern Europe to Echoes of the Cold War, *New York Times*, August 6, 2017.

[61] See John Noonan, Ending Obama's Cold War Mentality, *Weekly Standard* [blog], April 12, 2010.

[62] Jackson Diehl, Obama's Foreign Policy Needs an Update, *Washington Post*, November 22, 2010.

longer applied. Obama's Russia policy obliged him to fight a battle on Capitol Hill he might otherwise have avoided.

His Nobel Peace Prize, awarded in December 2009, before he had much opportunity to make peace, was ostensibly to reward his promise rather than his performance. The START agreement with Russia had made the Prize committee optimistic of further successes – perhaps the ratification of a binding antinuclear treaty. But START was hardly a revolution in arms control, merely ratifying a Russian warhead decrease that was already largely under way. As with continuity in the War on Terror, Obama displayed a preference for the pursuit of Cold War diplomacy – getting Russia to sign agreements to limit its nuclear stockpiles, using NATO to contain its expansionism – that any number of US presidents had pursued. Bill Clinton, like Obama, wanted to move beyond Cold War anachronisms, but delivered a traditional arms control agenda; Obama, in pursuing nuclear weapons modernization, was complicit in a new arms race with Moscow.[63]

Obama's reset resembles that promised by Jimmy Carter in 1977. Carter and Zbigniew Brzezinski, his national security advisor, wanted to rid American political discourse of the "inordinate fear of communism." Obama maintained that the threat posed by Islam and Islamism was similarly overstated. Carter wanted to get beyond the Cold War, Obama to move beyond the War on Terror. Both objectives, in their time, were widely applauded. Each president was given credit for attempting to transcend the discredited foreign policy of his predecessor. And yet both men experienced qualified failure in seeking to recast American political psychology, which remains skeptical of the claim that the terrorist threat emanating from the Middle East is only coincidentally Islamist, and skeptical of changing the nature of the threat itself. For Carter, downplaying the Soviet menace did little to ameliorate Soviet behavior. In 1979, Soviet troops invaded Afghanistan. For Obama, removing Islam from his national security calculus did not stop terrorists claiming the imprimatur of the Prophet from attacking US interests at home and abroad.

The reliance on "soft power" was also common to the Carter and Obama administrations. Carter set great store in soft power and, by using a variation of it, enjoyed considerable success in peace talks between Israel and Egypt. Obama explicitly grounded his foreign policy in a nexus

---

[63] William J. Broad and David E. Sanger, As U.S. Modernizes Nuclear Weapons, "Smaller" Leaves Some Uneasy, *New York Times*, January 11, 2016.

of soft and "smart" power. The results were more mixed. It is not clear that the Russian governing elite was impressed by this emphasis. The START agreement with Moscow was hailed as a victory for Obama's approach, but also was criticized by his opponents as an empty gesture of little strategic importance. If the treaty was a validation of soft power, it was a very thin one.

The failure of Obama's "open hand" to make the Syrian regime less brutal suggests another Cold War explanation. The Russian (and Chinese) veto of a UN resolution calling on Assad to resign in February 2012 is explicable at a number of levels. Certainly, Putin had no interest in seeing another autocracy overthrown by people power – the veto coincided with popular demonstrations in Moscow against Putin's government. But to understand his defense of Assad more fully, we need to recall Syria's place in Russia's Cold War strategy. When Egypt took a US turn after a disastrous war against Israel in 1973, Syria was Moscow's sole ally in the Middle East. The utility of the alliance, for both parties to it, did not evaporate when the USSR fell. Much contemporary discourse on Syria and the wider Arab Spring forgets this history.[64]

Obama's Russian reset assumed America was at fault for tensions in the US–Russian relationship. The application of an American humility would solve this, said Obama's advisors. This effort to transcend the Cold War standoff by increasing the latitude (President Obama's word was "flexibility") Moscow was to enjoy, did not transform Vladimir Putin's assessment of Russia's national interest. As his detractors argued, Obama did not consign "to history's dustbin the writings of Thucydides, the venerable Athenian historian who, roughly 2,300 years ago, observed that nations, like men, pursue what they perceive as their interests."[65] Engaging Russia with American soft power realized possibly less advantage than confronting it with hard. If Obama sought to forget the Cold War, Putin persisted in its shadow.

In Syria and Iran, Russia stuck to Cold War diplomacy. Rather than facilitate Obama's isolation of these regimes, Putin offered diplomatic cover and arms to the embattled Assad regime in Damascus. Russian technology was sold to Tehran as it moved toward a nuclear weapons capacity. Putin's motivations in both cases were not only to advance Russian interests, but to stymie Obama's. In August 2011, to demonstrate

---

[64] See Dmitri Trenin, Russia's Line in the Sand on Syria, *Foreign Affairs*, February 5, 2012.
[65] Douglas J. Feith and Seth Cropsey, How the Russian "Reset" Explains Obama's Foreign Policy, *Foreign Policy*, October 16, 2012.

how little he cared about the purported reset, he labeled Americans the "parasites" of the global economy.[66] A year later, he banished the US Agency for International Development from his country. Putin's posturing was a direct echo of the words of Nikita Khrushchev, the Soviet leader who claimed he would "bury" American capitalism. As a *Washington Post* editorial concluded, "Mr. Obama's apparent faith that Mr. Putin is ready to do business with him is at odds with the strongman's recent behavior."[67]

President Obama claimed the legacy of several Cold War administrations. His liberal vision came from JFK and LBJ – though Obama's contribution to Libyan freedom was mild in comparison to that underlining their defense of South Vietnam. His realism was rooted in a combination of the approaches of Eisenhower and Bush Sr. While his desire to limit US military exposure in the Middle East copied something from George H. W. Bush, his use of Ike was more problematic. The "new look" President Eisenhower did not retreat and was never as unpopular at home as Obama came to be. Obama may have articulated a public preference for a more passive foreign policy, but at the cost of strategic dissonance. In this last respect, he broke with Cold War precedent.

CONGRESS'S WAR ON OBAMA

If Obama was joined at the hip to Bush when it came to counterterrorism, he had more in common with Bill Clinton when it came to his travails with Congress.[68] Both men had to fight hard for domestic political advantage, and this carried over into foreign policy. Clinton fought his most controversial war against Serbia, in 1999, in the face of an explicit refusal to fund it by Congress, the institution that had done its best to impeach him for his sexual transgressions in the buildup to that war. Obama's success in getting Obamacare (the Patient Protection and Affordable Care Act) passed, on a strict partisan vote, in March 2010, provoked a Republican resistance movement to all and everything he tried to do abroad. Obama's national popularity in 2009 was inversely

---

[66] Maria Tsvetkova, Putin says U.S. Is "Parasite" on Global Economy, *Reuters*, August 2, 2011.

[67] Time for U.S. Leadership on Syria, *Washington Post*, May 29, 2012.

[68] See Elizabeth Drew, *Showdown: The Struggle between the Gingrich Congress and the Clinton White House* (New York: Touchstone, 1996); and David Corn, *Showdown: The Inside Story of How Obama Battled the GOP to Set Up the 2012 Election* (New York: HarperCollins, 2012).

proportionate to his popularity with legislators in Congress. Bad throughout his time in office, relations between Obama and Capitol Hill reached
a new low in 2011.[69] As the Democrats had suffered significant losses in
the November 2010 midterm elections, Obama was weakened, and his
Republican opponents emboldened. Brinkmanship over a possible debt
default that summer was replicated in foreign policy too.

Obama had to run his Libyan intervention with a congress skeptical
that it could work *and* openly contemptuous that Obama had the courage
to see it through. As a consequence, he decided against seeking a congressional authorization for the use of force. This decision was to haunt him
in 2013 when he made an attack on Syria contingent on congressional
(and Russian) approval. Over both wars, as in the long deliberations over
the Afghan surge, Republicans chided him for lacking the gumption to
use overwhelming military force. This backdrop meant efforts to pass
meaningful climate change legislation – and to ratify climate treaties –
became impossible. Obama's concerted efforts at the Paris climate
conference in 2015 produced only an executive agreement back home
and was easily repealed by his successor. Obama's hope that he could
point his foreign policy toward this global challenge, in his second term,
was stymied by the polarization between Democrats and Republicans and
between himself and the Congress, in his first.

THE 2012 ELECTION

The hardline realism of the 2012 campaign stood in contrast with the
"hope and change" mantra of 2008. Obama won reelection by touting
clear national and economic security gains. In killing Osama bin Laden,
he succeeded where Bush had not. He had put in place an economic
plan that had negated the worst of the recession he had inherited. Obama
could also run on having fulfilled his 2008 promise to quit Iraq. In
important and unpredictable ways, his staunch counterterrorism – killing
more terrorists by drones than had Bush – and his unwillingness to close
Guantánamo Bay burnished his national security credentials.

He was also lucky in his opponent. Mitt Romney, a former Republican
governor of a very Democratic state, Massachusetts, was unable to
energize the conservative grassroots. He looked and sounded like the
establishment figure that Donald Trump was to define himself against

---

[69] See Bob Woodward, *The Price of Politics* (New York: Simon & Schuster, 2012).

four years later. Obama won 332 electoral college votes to 206 and
51.1 percent of the popular vote. Ominously for Hillary Clinton's prospects in 2016, 4 million voters that turned out for Obama in 2008 failed
to do so a second time. Counties that Obama turned blue, about
240 of them, were to turn red and stay that way in 2016.

One of the three presidential debates, on October 22, in Florida,
was given over to foreign policy. Obama mocked Romney for his
Russophobia (see this chapter's epigraph). The next presidential term
would not be a retread of the Cold War, said Obama, but an opportunity
to face modern challenges by "organiz[ing] the international community." He told Romney that "when it comes to our foreign policy, you
seem to want to import the foreign policies of the 1980s."[70] But it was
Obama who would recycle Cold War approaches when Russian revanchism presented itself in his second term. Indeed, Russia would feature
prominently in the next election in 2016.[71]

CONCLUSION

Obama had begun his term confident that his own unique personal
attributes – from race to temperament – would render the world more
receptive to America's power. This claim was found wanting. Despite
considerable excitement that his newness would be transformative, it did
not shift the national interest calculations of foreign capitals. Russia's
concerns with its near abroad were immune to the cosmopolitanism of the
man in the Oval Office. The challenges US power faced, and the means
chosen to face them, from 2009 to 2013, were much the same as they
were from 2001 to 2009: the negation of terrorism, the quieting of the
Taliban, the liberation of Muslim populations, the containment of China
and Russia. Obama's character seems to have altered the dynamics of
each hardly at all.

By the close of his first term, "the rise of the rest" had stalled or failed
to live up to expectations. The problem was that the rising others did not
fill the gaps left by the withdrawal of US manpower and willpower.
Indeed, that withdrawal was more rhetorical than it was real. In 2012,
the global public goods provided by the United States remained in

[70] Presidential debate, Lynn University, Boca Raton, Florida, October 22, 2012.
[71] See the Report on the investigation into Russian interference in the 2016 election ("The
Mueller Report," March 2019; released April 2019); at https://apps.npr.org/documents/
document.html?id=5955997-Muellerreport.

demand. It continued to police the world's shipping lanes. Its defense budget, even after a trimming by Obama, was still larger than the next eight highest-spending nations. The European Union could spend more on welfare because American taxpayers subsidized its defense. The US military was key to the maintenance of peace and the balance of power in Western Europe and South Korea. US counterterrorism meant a surge of troops into Afghanistan that no other nation, in the absence of an American commitment, would undertake. The Arab Spring, despite Obama's attempt to stand on its sidelines, received significant direction from his administration, as the fates of Egypt and Libya demonstrated. His refusal to deploy significant military force into Syria helped deepen that conflict. When this vacuum was belatedly filled, as we will see next, it was by Moscow.

Obama's first-term foreign policy offers a study in both liberalism and realism. A key strength offered to the electorate in 2008 was his common sense. Obama would avoid the "dumb" wars of George W. Bush and instead return to a foreign policy of the national interest. This claim was an important way to address concerns about his leftish origins. Every Democratic president since John F. Kennedy has had to find a way to pursue a moral foreign policy – consistent with his progressivism – without obliging overextension, which resulted in the Vietnam quagmire. Obama's solution was to retain a degree of flexibility in his foreign policy. This was a more tenable proposition in his first term, than in his second, when Cold War geostrategy reimposed itself more fully.

7

Barack Obama's Soft Containment, 2013–2017

The contest of ideas [with Moscow] continues.
—*President Obama, speech in Brussels, March 26, 2014*[1]

BIN LADEN IS DEAD. GENERAL MOTORS IS ALIVE
—*Obama–Biden bumper sticker, 2012*

The battle between Obama the realist and Obama the liberal bent toward the former in his second term. His approach to the world became even less interventionist, if it had ever been that, and his reliance on negotiations with US opponents increasingly displaced harder forms of power. In the Cold War, containment had relied on an explicit military threat. In Obama's reworking of it, threats were replaced by appeals to get on the "right side of history." He assured Americans that the "United States military doesn't do pinpricks."[2] But 2013–2017 were years of military minimalism and retrenchment. After the apparently hyperactive militarism of the Bush years, Obama claimed to have restored pragmatism to US foreign policy.

Successes, as we will see, were claimed for his outreach to Cuba and Iran and his activism on climate change. His detractors, however, observed how meager these gains were when Russian aggression, Libyan collapse, Chinese emboldenment, and the Syrian Civil War were set

---

[1] In Michael D. Shear and Peter Baker, Obama Renewing U.S. Commitment to NATO Alliance, *New York Times*, March 26, 2014.
[2] Remarks by the president in address to the nation on Syria, September 10, 2013.

against them. These protracted issues were to complicate claims that Obama's softer realism had worked. Candidate Obama had made much hay condemning Bush's downgrading of Afghanistan to pursue "his vendetta" against Saddam Hussein in 2002–2003, just as Eisenhower condemned Truman in 1952 for "losing" Eastern Europe and China to communism. Obama became open to a similar charge over Ukraine, Syria, and Libya. He may well have disavowed pinpricks and yet much of his military legacy will reside is just such actions: his reliance on drone strikes to kill individual terrorists rather than on the significant deployment of troops to advance US security and/or humanitarian imperatives.

THE SECOND-TERM TEAM

As with the first-term team, Obama chose individuals in the expectation of some sort of creative tension. He wanted old mixed with young and hawks with doves. The confirmation of John Kerry as Obama's second (and final) secretary of state renewed the connection between contemporary foreign policy and the Cold War. Kerry had risen to national prominence as a vocal critic of the Vietnam War, having been a decorated navy lieutenant in it from 1966–1970. In his meet-and-greet address at Foggy Bottom, he joked whether it was possible for "a man to run the State Department" – he was the first since Colin Powell (2001–2005).[3] Susan Rice departed the UN to become the new national security advisor. A former Clinton administration official, she had been scarred by its failure to stop the Rwanda genocide. Samantha Power, whose profile was built on indicting these sins of omission, replaced her at the UN.[4] Together, both women represented a potentially hawkish humanitarian axis within Obama foreign policy – but one which largely failed to materialize. Ben Rhodes, who had joined the Obama team as a 29-year-old think tanker in 2007, gradually grew in proximity to and influence over the president. In the second term, Rhodes, technically a speechwriter, became "the single most influential voice shaping American foreign policy aside from POTUS himself," and the president's "foreign policy guru."[5]

---

[3] John Kerry, address to State Department employees, Washington DC, February 4, 2013.
[4] See Samantha Power, *"A Problem from Hell": America and the Age of Genocide* (New York: Basic Books, 2002), pp. 329–390.
[5] David Samuels, The Aspiring Novelist Who Became Obama's Foreign-Policy Guru, *New York Times*, May 5, 2016. Rhodes was officially deputy national security advisor for strategic communications and speechwriting.

He was to represent a consistent voice of caution – of "don't do stupid stuff" – as the various crises of 2013–2017 unfolded.

The bad-tempered confirmation of the new defense secretary, Chuck Hagel, was an early indication that congressional Republicans would renew partisan warfare in foreign policy. As a Republican senator himself (from Nebraska, 1997–2009), Hagel had earned the abiding suspicion of his party for coming out against the Iraq War. It was a "new Vietnam" he had said in 2005; Bush's surge was folly. This won him Obama's respect, but in 2013 made his confirmation harder.[6] Like Kerry, Hagel was a Vietnam veteran and shared a similar caution about American military adventurism. Unlike Kerry, however, he did not see out the Obama administration. In 2015, he was replaced by the former Harvard professor Ash Carter. Where Hagel had been soft, Carter was to be more hardline, particularly on Russia, China, and Iran. He was confirmed unanimously by the same Senate that had tried to sink Hagel.

The new team, despite concessions, such as the elevation of Power to the UN and Rice to national security advisor, had a decidedly realist flavor. Unlike Bill Clinton, who, in the exuberance of his second term, was to use military force frequently, Barack Obama, freed from the need to win reelection, grew more cautious. This played itself out in Syria, but was also evident in the counsel he sought within the White House. Ben Rhodes had a basic refrain about the "inherent limits" of American power. The United States could not solve for foreigners, he argued often, what the foreigners lacked the will to solve themselves. A troika of top national security aides deepened this innate caution. Tom Donilon, John Brennan, and Denis McDonough, "the grim Irishmen," were consistent voices of negation.[7]

THE RISE OF THE ISLAMIC STATE

The rise of the jihadist fighters who called themselves the Islamic State of Iraq and Syria (ISIS) – one of the most successful terrorist groups in modern history – was intimately connected to the blowback from

---

[6] See Elisabeth Bumiller, Hagel Has Rough Outing before Ex-colleagues, *New York Times*, January 31, 2013.

[7] See Mark Landler, *Alter Egos: Hillary Clinton, Barack Obama, and the Twilight Struggle over American Power* (New York: Random House, 2016), p. 106.

America's withdrawal from Iraq at the end of 2011.[8] Obama, like Bush before him, had wanted to retain a residual force in the country to help consolidate democratic gains. But the Iraqi government would not agree, seeing any American presence as proof that it could not govern without colonial oversight – a position its prime minister was to regret by 2013. Nouri al-Maliki turned out to be no Nelson Mandela. When the South African was handed the reins of power, he attempted reconciliation; al-Maliki pursued vendettas. Fearful to the point of paranoia, the Shia al-Maliki attempted to purge prominent Sunnis from the Iraqi government and society. The new Iraqi army was especially subject to this sectarianism. Al-Maliki, says Kenneth Pollack, filled it with "knuckleheads."[9]

This led many Sunnis to embrace extremists. With little US presence to moderate al-Maliki's sectarianism, groups like al-Qaeda and the al-Nusra Front suddenly found a market among Sunnis for their protective services. A similar logic applied across the border in Syria. America was not about to step in and save the Syrian middle class from the depredations of an Alawite (and thus nominally Shia) government. Groups that were willing to defend Sunnis began to seize territory in northern Iraq and Syria. Calling themselves the Islamic State, they had aspirations not merely to challenge the governments in Baghdad and Damascus, but to establish a "caliphate," which would mobilize jihadists across the world. If war is a real-estate business, ISIS was spectacularly successful at it. By the fall 2013, they controlled an area the size of Oregon, making Raqqa, in northern Syrian, their de facto capital. A dozen years after 9/11, the terrorists inspired by that attack had achieved something approaching statehood.

Again, the United States' attempt to quit the Middle East created the conditions that had necessitated its going there in the first place. The half-hearted counterterrorism of Bill Clinton, which kept Osama bin Laden on the run without ever containing him, allowed the 9/11 plot to proceed. George W. Bush's refusal to send enough troops into Iraq in 2003 created the conditions for al-Qaeda's insurgency there. Barack Obama was now continuing this tradition. While tough on terrorism, his unwillingness to

---

[8] The Obama administration preferred "ISIL": the Islamic State of Iraq and the Levant. The distinction between ISIS and ISIL was more geographic than theological, the latter dominating the Syrian parts of the "caliphate." The Arab acronym for ISIS is Da'ish.

[9] Kenneth M. Pollack, *Armies of Sand: The Past, Present, and Future of Arab Military Effectiveness* (New York: Oxford University Press, 2019), p. 167.

back a side in Syria allowed ISIS – the heirs to bin Laden – to prosper. Obama's initial excuse was the complexity of the Syrian battlefield.

THE SYRIAN CIVIL WAR

Syria (a nation about 1.5 times the size of Pennsylvania with a population about the size of New York State) tipped over into civil war in late 2011. By early 2013, it was developing into a conflict as vicious as any in the history of the modern Middle East. Obama's inaction during this descent was made worse by a rhetoric suggesting its opposite. In August 2012, to the surprise of his aides, he said the use of chemical weapons would constitute "a red line" for military action. When the Assad regime used chemical weapons against its own civilians, beginning that December, Obama said it constituted "a game changer." Chemical attacks, several confirmed as such by US intelligence and the United Nations, killing thousands of Syrians, took place from late 2012 to summer 2013. In August 2013, Obama threatened a military strike unless Assad desisted. On August 30, his secretary of state, John Kerry, made it seem that that strike was imminent. American and French planes were combat-ready in the Mediterranean, waiting for a green light. On August 31, the president announced in the White House Rose Garden, "I have decided that the United States should take military action against Syrian regime targets."[10]

Then Obama pulled back. In an ill-conceived TV address, on September 10, Obama attempted to combine his realism and his liberalism. Obama, the liberal hawk, seemed to be announcing an attack only to then turn back from it for realist reasons. If the speech was not quite schizophrenic, it did display an approach internally divided against itself. Obama spoke of his rage at seeing children dying in their parents' arms. He cited analogies enabling a US military response – the use of poison gas in World War I and the Holocaust. He then changed tack. The nation was "sick and tired of war,'" he said. Afghanistan was cited as a reason to avoid conflict. The line that must have caused Assad to breathe more easily then followed: "I don't think we should remove another dictator with force – we learned from Iraq that doing so makes us responsible for all that comes next."[11] Instead, he would defer to Congress and Russia – perennial opponents of many American presidents – in finding

[10] Statement by the president on Syria, White House, August 31, 2013.
[11] Obama statement on Syria, White House, September 10, 2013.

a nonmilitary solution. "If you say you're going to strike," said Hillary Clinton, "you have to strike. There's no choice." The usually supportive Gideon Rose described the climb down as "a case study in embarrassingly amateurish improvisation."[12]

The Obama team was to claim success. According to Derek Chollet, this was a well-calibrated response to a bafflingly complicated situation. Obama had used soft power – the outreach to Russia – and the US Constitution – in demanding that Congress share in the burden of the decision – to get chemical weapons removed from the Syrian battlefield.[13] Obama later said it was one of the decisions of which he was "most proud."[14] Again, this retrospection befits a realist rather than a progressive. Obama's foreign policy managed an uncomfortable fusion of both. The killing, of course, continued. Hundreds and thousands were to die by the use of conventional weapons. Obama's deference to a Russian solution had the unintended consequence of inviting Putin into the Syrian theater. In September 2015, two years after Obama erased his red line, Russia entered the conflict on the side of the Syrian government. By 2017, Assad had resumed sporadic chemical attacks. By 2019, he remained determinedly in power.

The Vietnam War is more often compared to the Iraq War. The similarities are many and compelling. However, it can be argued that America's abandonment of South Vietnam in 1975 finds a more compelling analogue in Syria. The consequences of both decisions were profound and enduring. The whole of Vietnam fell to communism. The USSR observed that American resolve, if tested, would be found wanting. Soviet communism grew more confident; its penetration of Africa, Latin America, and Afghanistan followed. China learned that American military ambitions in Asia were limited. Iranian revolutionaries saw how easily America could desert its friends. Omer Aziz, a scholar of the Syrian conflict, described Obama's failure in these terms:

The Syrian uprising was ignited by children who spray painted anti-Assad slogans on their school's wall.
    They were arrested and tortured the next day. Their fellow citizens, who had lost their innocence long ago, took to the streets to demand their dignity.

---

[12] Gideon Rose, What Obama Gets Right, *Foreign Affairs* 94, 5 (September/October 2015): 2–12.
[13] See Derek Chollet, *The Long Game: How Obama Defied Washington and Redefined America's Role in the World* (New York: PublicAffairs, 2016), pp. 1–26.
[14] In Jeffrey Goldberg, The Obama Doctrine, *Atlantic* (April 2016).

They chanted, "One, one, one, the Syrian people are one." They threw flowers on [US] Ambassador Ford's car when he went to their rally. They thought the Americans were with them. But the U.S. was nowhere to be found.[15]

Obama's approach to Syria had large and enduring consequences similar to Vietnam. These would condition the remainder of his term and beyond. The humanitarian catastrophe inspired assorted jihadists around the world to "punish" the West for doing little to stop it; terrorist attacks in the Middle East and Europe increased in frequency and severity. His chosen solution to Assad's use of chemical weapons opened the door to Russian intervention in the conflict, specifically, and emboldened Putin, generally. It convinced Obama that Iran, like Syria, could be denuded of its weapons via multilateral diplomacy. European politics was greatly affected by the refugee crisis generated by the Syrian Civil War; demands for greater control of immigration, as we shall see, was a key Brexit platform. Finally, it demonstrated to China, much as had Nixon's withdrawal from Vietnam, that America had no stomach to defend distant foreigners with military force.

OBAMA'S WAR ON TERROR, PART II

In September 2013, al-Shabab, an Islamist terrorist group based in Somalia, attacked a shopping mall in Nairobi, Kenya, killing more than 60 people. In January and November 2015, nearly 150 people were massacred in Paris by Islamic State terrorists in revenge for, among other things, Western ignorance of Syria's suffering. Summer 2016 saw a series of high-casualty terrorist attacks by ISIS, or those inspired by it – most notably in Bangladesh, Nice, Saudi Arabia, and Turkey – that further undermined Obama's claims that the War on Terror was over. An attack on a gay nightclub in Orlando, Florida, in June that year, by a killer claiming an Islamic State affiliation, the largest mass shooting, to that point, by a lone gunman in American history (killing 49), was characterized as a "hate crime" rather than an act of terrorism. Instead, Democrats used it as a reason to try and increase federal gun-control. All the time Syria continued to bleed red.

---

[15] Omer Aziz, How Barack Obama Betrayed the Syrian People, Aljazeera, August 22, 2015, at www.aljazeera.com/indepth/opinion/2015/08/barack-obama-betrayed-syrian-people-150822084544918.html.

Episodic terrorism, argued Obama, did not add up to a reason to change his approach to the Syrian Civil War or to countenance a new surge of US troops into Iraq. The beleaguered Iraqi government had asked for US military assistance when the consequences of its sectarianism became apparent in October 2013. Obama responded with only token support. George W. Bush had intended "the expansion of freedom in all the world" and "an end to evil." Obama's ambition was more measurable and precise. Since 2007, when he began his presidential campaign, he had defined "the most urgent threat" to American security as "the spread of nuclear weapons, material, and technology and the risk that a nuclear device will fall into the hands of terrorists." By 2016, by this definition, lone-wolf attacks and the crude bomb makers of ISIS demonstrated that Obama's counterterrorism had worked; deaths by conventional terrorism and war revealed how distant the enemy was from a deployable, mass-casualty weapon. State failure, as in Iraq and Syria, while an affront to Obama's claims about "a common humanity," at least assured their technological backwardness.

This was scant consolation, of course, for a presidency that was billed as the healer of the Muslim divide. By withdrawing from Muslim-on-Muslim conflict, the United States guaranteed safety for its troops, but at the price of bloodshed for those men and women trapped within the zones of conflict. Henry Kissinger had surveyed the catastrophic Iran–Iraq War (1980–1988) and had willed both sides to lose. Obama did something similar in the face of the Syrian Civil War. His supporters called this realism, but it was some distance from the progressive vision that Obama hoped his foreign policy would fulfill. Obama committed US military force to Syria and Iraq, but under the explicit rationale of "counterterrorism" – special forces, military contractors, and air strikes allowed for pinpricks, but not for civic renewal. Degrading and destroying ISIS left no room for the nation-building projects that might have followed. Indeed, the president's declaiming of a more interventionist role in the Syrian Civil War created the conditions for the rise of ISIS and his subsequent counterterrorist campaign against it. A UN official working in Syria observed how, by 2014, "the Syrian vacuum had become filled with black flags."[16] Obama's abandonment of a humanitarian role in the conflict also invited Russia into the theater.

---

[16] Omer Aziz, How Barack Obama Betrayed the Syrian People.

RUSSIAN REVANCHISM

When a computer is reset, the same operating system comes back. A relationship with Russia, supposedly reset by the Obama administration, had by 2014 assumed a familiar Cold War pattern.[17] Obama's refusal to strike at Syria convinced the Kremlin that he had an aversion to military force. In March of that year, Russian troops invaded Ukraine. Vladimir Putin, on a similar pretext to his war on Georgia six years earlier, and echoing Hitler's claim on the Sudetenland in 1938, declared he was acting in defense of an oppressed ethnic minority. In a popular uprising, days before, the pro-Russian Viktor Yanukovych had been toppled. The new regime looked westward, with muted confidence, to the protection of the European Union.[18] When this was not forthcoming, Putin annexed Crimea, in Ukraine's south. President Obama watched, much as George W. Bush had done, as Moscow rolled tanks into its near abroad. "Russia," said Obama, "was on the wrong side of history" but was on the right side, according to Putin, of the Crimean border.

And yet it was a Cold War history that was repeating itself – both in terms of Russian action and US response. Presidents to whom Obama had compared himself favorably had also been impotent in the face of Russian aggression toward its neighbors. Harry Truman could do little to protect Eastern Europe from Soviet domination in the late 1940s. Dwight Eisenhower had threatened a harder line against global communism, but could do nothing as Russian troops crushed an anti-Soviet uprising in Hungary in 1956. Lyndon Johnson could only bluster when Leonid Brezhnev invaded Czechoslovakia in 1968. Jimmy Carter's substantive response to the Soviet invasion of Afghanistan in 1979 was to boycott the Moscow Olympics. Even the great Cold Warrior Ronald Reagan went no further than a rhetorical commitment to the liberation of Eastern Europeans; by his second term he was cutting deals with their oppressor.

If these men could not resist Russian military power on their eastern front, how might a president wedded far more to the concepts of soft power and diplomatic engagement, of withdrawal from war, do so when Ukrainian independence was threatened? Obama's critics made much of his impotence, but it mirrored that of his predecessors. American options

---

[17] See Michael McFaul, *From Cold War to Hot Peace: An American Ambassador in Putin's Russia* (New York: Houghton Mifflin Harcourt, 2018).
[18] See Rajan Menon and Eugene B. Rumer, *Conflict in Ukraine: The Unwinding of the Post–Cold War Order* (Boston: MIT Press, 2015), pp. 107–144.

for repelling Russian power in the lands of the former Soviet Union remain very limited. This was reflected in an aversion to deeper conflict with Russia. During the spring 2014 crisis in Ukraine, for example, a poll found that, by a margin of 56 percent to 29 percent, Americans favored steering clear of a more forceful response.[19] In July, the shooting down by Russian-backed rebels of a Malaysian passenger plane (MH17) over eastern Ukraine, killing all 298 passengers, caused international outrage, but it did not shift Obama's approach.

US presidents, like Nixon and Reagan, while they cut important deals with the Kremlin, kept the Russians guessing as to their true intentions. Would their anticommunism lead to nuclear belligerence? Was their red-baiting more rhetorical than real? Richard Nixon deliberately sought to convey the impression that he was unhinged. He called it his "Madman Theory":

I want the North Vietnamese to believe I've reached the point where I might do anything to stop the war. We'll just slip the word to them that, "for God's sake, you know Nixon is obsessed about communism. We can't restrain him when he's angry – and he has his hand on the nuclear button," and Ho Chi Minh himself will be in Paris in two days begging for peace.[20]

Barack Obama traded on an opposite persona. In the face of Russian Cold War revanchism, he projected a cool modernity. Obama's supporters welcomed this; his detractors observed that it merely made him predictable. The effect was to telegraph to Putin a deep-seated aversion to military confrontation and even to hard talking. Ronald Reagan's "new Cold War," in the early 1980s, was accompanied by a significant defense buildup (from 4.9 percent of GDP to 6.2 percent) and a rhetoric of moral clarity. In 1983, Reagan called the USSR "the focus of evil in the modern world." When Soviet air defenses shot a South Korean passenger plane (KAL007) out of the sky later that year, killing all 269 passengers and crew, Reagan redoubled his moral outrage. In 1984, he joked into a radio microphone he thought was off that he was about to begin bombing Russia. Obama's Russia policy was conducted in an era of defense sequestration (from 4.6 percent of GDP to 4.2 percent) and, if not in the language of moral relativism, it employed a vocabulary of soft power,

---

[19] Most Say U.S. Should "Not Get Too Involved" in Ukraine Situation, Pew Research Center, March 11, 2014.

[20] H. R. Haldeman, *The Ends of Power* (New York: Times Books, 1977), p. 122. See also James Rosen and Luke A. Nichter, Madman in the White House, *Foreign Policy*, March 25, 2014.

preferring economic sanctions to military bluster. One Turkish official ridiculed Obama's academic dithering over the Syrian Civil War: "The Americans color-coded; the Russians invaded."[21] One of the president's own advisors later conceded that the United States "should have bombed Assad."[22]

Obama made concerted attempts to frame Russian adventurism as a Cold War throwback, but refused to countenance a hard-line, Cold-War style response himself. He had ridiculed his 2012 presidential opponent when Romney designated Russia a key threat to the United States. The 1980s, said Obama, were "calling to ask for their foreign policy back." Fareed Zakaria later noted, "It's ironic that Mitt Romney has been passed over for secretary of state [by Donald Trump] just as his key foreign policy judgment is being vindicated."[23] This dismissal of Cold War thinking was an implicit appeal to Obama's hero of that conflict: President John F. Kennedy. The last senator to become president until Obama in 2009, Kennedy had resolved the 1962 Cuban Missile Crisis not by military threat, but by empathy with Nikita Khrushchev – and a willingness to compromise.

Even as Obama sought to transcend the Cold War, he found himself adapting its strategic lessons. Kennedy's "flexible response" gave him cover to both make war against Soviet interests – Kennedy began the military escalation in Vietnam, for example – and to bargain short of war, as the resolution in Cuba showed. Obama sought similar room for maneuver. Kennedy, though, had framed his Russia policy as a balance between hard and soft power. His rhetoric and his decision-making reveal a calibration of the two. Violence was to be used if necessary, but not if negotiation could achieve the same end. Critics of Obama charged him with a misplaced place faith in the efficacy of soft power – moving the United States, according to Elliott Abrams, from being the world's "arsenal of democracy" to its "linen closet," a charge not easily leveled at Kennedy.[24]

[21] In Richard Cohen, The High Cost of Avoiding War in Syria, *Washington Post*, October 5, 2015.
[22] Philip Gordon in Jeffrey Goldberg, Obama's Former Middle East Adviser: We Should Have Bombed Assad, *Atlantic*, April 20, 2016.
[23] Fareed Zakaria, Vladimir Putin Wants a New World Order: Why Would Donald Trump Help Him? *Washington Post*, December 15, 2016.
[24] Elliott Abrams, Blankets for Ukraine, Council on Foreign Relations [blog], February 5, 2015. As with Cuba in 1962, the US missed the Moscow-led buildup in Ukraine in 2014 and Syria in 2015; see Greg Miller and Karen DeYoung, Despite Signs of Russia's Syria Buildup, U.S. Seemed to Be Caught Flat-Footed, *Washington Post*, October 9, 2015.

And yet both men in their different eras recognized the limits of US power in Russia's sphere of influence. We will never know if Kennedy really would have gone to nuclear war over West Berlin. He treated the Soviet occupation of Eastern Europe as an accomplished fact, seeking little revision to it. Rather, he and his immediate successors chose to fight Russia by proxy, in what is now called the Global South. Obama, likewise, showed no stomach for a military confrontation over Crimea (part of Russia until 1954 and then again after 2014). Like Kennedy, his substantial tools were rhetorical. "In the 21st century," he said, "the borders of Europe cannot be redrawn with force; ... international law matters; and ... people and nations can make their own decisions about their future." Unlike Kennedy, Obama did not commit to "pay any price, bear any burden, meet any hardship," in order to negate Russian meddling. His response was tangentially military – sending extra US fighter jets to Lithuania and Poland, for example – and largely economic and diplomatic.

Whether US presidents ever had a decisive impact on Soviet/Russia behavior and/or caused the demise of the USSR remains an enduring historiographical debate. Obama's foreign policy should be seen within the terms of that debate. Criticism of his alleged passivity in the face of Russian expansion tends to ignore the straitjacketing that geography forces on every US president. Russia's backyard affords the US commander in chief few realistic options. In 1944–1947, Roosevelt and Truman acknowledged that the parts of Europe under Soviet occupation were likely to stay that way – as they did for the next forty-five years. Ronald Reagan increased his moral support of Solidarity in Poland, when the Kremlin ordered a crackdown on it, but did not make military threats. George W. Bush was arguably more forceful in his denunciation of Putin's invasion of Georgia in 2008, but, like his successor, recognized the limits of a military solution. Such evidence points to the relative autonomy Moscow has, and will continue to enjoy to its west, irrespective of who sits in the White House. Russia does what it does for largely endogenous reasons and can get away with it for geographic ones. As Angela Stent has argued, Russian foreign policy embodies continuities as great as those of the United States.[25]

And yet this free pass for Obama relies on a selective reading of US–USSR relations. Other scholars argue that the American posture has been

---

[25] See Angela Stent, *Putin's World: Russia against the West and with the Rest* (New York: Twelve Books, 2019).

crucial in altering Russian calculations – and thus find reason to chide Obama's passivity. Conservative commentators blamed the president squarely for a pusillanimous response to Russia – a rerun of Carter's moral dithering.[26] The historian John Lewis Gaddis noted that "hanging tough paid off" for Ronald Reagan, whose defense buildup forced the USSR to compete and lose.[27] Daniel Deudney and G. John Ikenberry dispute this interpretation.[28] The Soviet Union fell as a consequence of its own internal decrepitude.

Debate about Obama's Russia policy is framed in similar fashion. It is possible to construct a narrative, drawn from the Cold War, that US disinterestedness, exampled in Obama's pivoting toward Asia, emboldened Putin to seize Crimea. Obama's "weakness," his "abandonment" of a missile shield with Poland and the Czech Republic, and his embrace of soft power invited the Kremlin to revert back to Cold War type, to threaten its neighbors and restore a pride wounded by Cold War defeat (a defeat that Putin never accepted had happened).

But such an interpretation necessarily overlooks the seriousness with which Obama took the Ukrainian crisis. Indeed, one could argue his reaction to Putin's annexation of Crimea was more vociferous than that of George W. Bush over the invasion of Georgia. Bush had a need to keep Putin onside in his larger War on Terror. Obama did not feel a similar constraint. Importantly, his framing of the Ukraine situation drew direct Cold War parallels. Having dismissed Romney's anachronistic approach to Russia in 2012, by 2014, Obama was articulating it. "The contest of ideas [with Moscow] continues," he told an audience in Brussels. "For 20 years," one historian noted, "nobody has thought about how to "contain" Russia. Now they will."[29] Obama increased US military cooperation with Eastern Europe and reassured NATO allies of US support. The rotation of more US ground troops through the Baltic States was a clear signal that countries Putin regarded as within Russia's sphere (and which had been colonized by the USSR) were now firmly in the American camp. Remarkably, for those who fondly recalled his

---

[26] See James Kirchick, *The End of Europe: Dictators, Demagogues, and the Coming Dark Age* (New Haven, CT: Yale University Press, 2017).

[27] John Lewis Gaddis, *The United States and the End of the Cold War* (New York: Oxford University Press, 1992), pp. 119–132.

[28] Daniel Deudney and G. John Ikenberry, Who Won the Cold War? *Foreign Policy* (Summer 1992), pp. 123–138.

[29] Anne Applebaum, A Need to Contain Russia, *Washington Post*, March 20, 2014.

2008 presidential campaign, Obama *defended* Bush's Iraq War as indicative of America's desire "to work within the international system. We did not claim or annex Iraq's territory. We did not grab its resources for our own gain."[30]

After Ukraine, Obama's foreign policy was to reside firmly in the Cold War's shadow. In February 2016, to help contain Russian ambitions, he quadrupled US military aid to Europe.[31] "Moving past the last fifteen years," noted Dave Majumdar, "the United States military is once again focusing on great power conflict."[32] Like Bill Clinton, Obama attempted to sweep away the "old-think" of that bipolar conflict and adapt to the sunny uplands of liberal democratic progress. But ideological conflict did not end with the collapse of the Soviet project. Gangster capitalism gave way to a new authoritarianism in Moscow, founded on long-standing notions of Russian exceptionalism that drew a striking parallel to the style and tone of Soviet propaganda. Vladimir Putin exercised a censorious power over Russian society in a manner not even his Soviet counterparts had been able to match. They had presided over economic penury; Putin exploited Russia's natural resources.

The US government targeted that wealth in its response to Putin's Ukrainian machinations. Instead of relying exclusively on the traditional tools of military containment, Obama went after the financial assets of the men and women in Putin's inner circle. As Karen Dawisha observed:

After fourteen years of dealing with [Putin] as a legitimate head of state, the US government has finally admitted publicly what successive administrations have known privately – that he has built a system built on massive predation on a level not seen in Russia since the tsars.[33]

Corruption was not only a way to realize personal gain, but a way of restoring Russian greatness. Putin replicated the suppression of free speech of the old Soviet Union. Independent media disappeared. Internal dissenters, even pop singers, were jailed. As it had in the Cold War, the United States found itself facing a regime riven with corruption, prepared

---

[30] Obama speech in Brussels, March 26, 2014.
[31] See Mark Landler and Helene Cooper, U.S. Fortifying Europe's East to Deter Putin, *New York Times*, February 1, 2016.
[32] Dave Majumdar, America Reveals "Great Power" Plans against Russia and China, *National Interest*, February 3, 2016.
[33] Karen Dawisha, *Putin's Kleptocracy: Who Owns Russia?* (New York: Simon & Schuster, 2014), p. 1.

to destabilize its neighbors, and wedded to pervasive (and state-enforced) nostalgia about a great Russian past.

THE IRAN NUCLEAR DEAL

The apparently successful removal of chemical weapons from Bashar al-Assad's arsenal, even though it relied on Russian diplomacy and bolstered Putin's regional ambitions, was taken as proof that diplomatic engagement could work. Its next application would be in Iran. In July 2015, President Obama announced what he believed to be his legacy-defining nuclear deal with the Iranian government: The Joint Comprehensive Plan of Action (JCPOA). The deal lifted US and European sanctions on Iran, in return for its compliance with nuclear weapons inspections. The more Tehran agreed to limit, and have verified, its nuclear ambitions, the more access to previously frozen funds it would enjoy. The JCPOA was to last a mere thirty-six months. Obama used an executive order to pass it; his successor used an executive order to repeal it. Donald Trump canceled it on November 4, 2018 – the thirty-ninth anniversary of the start of the US Embassy hostage siege in Tehran. But Republican opposition to the JCPOA began as soon as negotiations with Iran restarted under Obama. Knowing Obama could never get a formal treaty ratified by a highly skeptical Republican House, Senate Democrats sought to have the plan approved by blocking passage of a House resolution disapproving of it. On September 10, 2015, despite strenuous efforts by Republicans, the plan passed. "For conservatives," noted Julian Zelizer,

The deal fulfills every negative view that they have about President Obama and the way Democrats handle foreign threats. The narrative is built for the campaign trail – a Democratic president agrees to drop sanctions on a horrible regime that even most Democrats agree shows little signs of reform.[34]

Debate in Congress was nearly as protracted as the P5+1 negotiations themselves.[35] Obama positively beamed at his success in both.[36] Given the lows of the US–Iran relationship over the preceding decades, he was justified in counting the deal as a high.

For Obama, engaging with Tehran was a way of healing a weeping – sometimes gaping – wound, untreated since the Cold War. Iranian politics

[34] In Jennifer Steinhauer, Democrats Hand Victory to Obama on Iran Nuclear Deal, *New York Times*, September 11, 2015.
[35] P 5 + 1 means permanent 5 members of the UN Security Council plus Germany.
[36] See Obama press conference, White House, July 16, 2015.

In the Shadow of the Cold War

have been framed by a distrust of the United States since CIA involvement in a plot that ousted Iran's leader, Mohammad Mosaddeq, in 1953. The Iranian revolution, twenty-six years later, was both revenge for that interference as well as the declaration of a religious war against America, the "great Satan."[37] From November 1979 until January 1981, student activists held hostage fifty-four American diplomats inside the US embassy in Tehran. President Carter's botched attempt to rescue them was a primary reason for his failure to win reelection in 1980. In the years after, the US government veered from secret negotiation (under Ronald Reagan) to open opposition (under George W. Bush). The Sunni Taliban and al-Qaeda are sworn enemies of Shia Iran. The Taliban executed eight of its diplomats in Afghanistan in 1998. In the wake of 9/11, despite the enemy-of-my-enemy-is-my-friend logic, Iranian attempts at rapprochement were rebuffed by Washington.

Obama did not transcend this pattern; he confirmed it. Ever since 1979, American presidents have sought a way to bring Tehran back into the pro-American orientation it had before the Islamic Revolution. Hard and soft power, the threat of force and diplomatic cajolement, have each alternated since that time. Jimmy Carter's presidency became consumed with forging a covert diplomatic channel that would move the new regime away from its public anti-Americanism. It foundered not just in the Tabas Desert in April 1980 – when US rescue aircraft crashed en route to the embassy – but in the complexities of diplomacy in a moment of revolutionary turmoil.[38]

Ronald Reagan followed this pattern. Like Obama, he entered into an arms agreement with Tehran. And, like Obama's, it was met by congressional outrage. His covert efforts to sell arms to the Iranians, to raise cash to support counterrevolutionaries in Nicaragua, nearly led to his impeachment. President Obama did not take a covert route. He chose instead to operate through a coalition of nations (the P5+1) to get Tehran to sign up. Although it raised Republican hackles, this approach continued that of his predecessor. George W. Bush, despite calling the Iranian regime "evil" in 2002, had made the United States part of the P5 negotiations in 2006. As Obama saw it, he was fulfilling a diplomatic objective long-sought by the presidents that came before

---

[37] See Ali M. Ansari, *Confronting Iran: The Failure of American Foreign Policy and the Next Great Crisis in the Middle East* (New York: Basic Books, 2006).

[38] See Gary Sick, *All Fall Down: America's Tragic Encounter with Iran* (New York: Random House, 1986).

him.[39] He had been criticized in 2009 for failing to support a nascent uprising against the regime. But this coolness toward the Iranian opposition was of long standing.

The price paid for the 2015 Iran deal was a high one. Aside from skepticism that the JCPOA could actually work, there was the discontent it stoked in the Arab Middle East. Saudi Arabia, Iran's traditional opponent, detested the deal. Riyadh had initially hoped Obama could be dissuaded from its pursuit. When the president visited the kingdom in March 2014, he was feted as a world statesman. Huge US flags lined his route from the airport. King Abdullah left his deathbed to meet with him. Two years later, the Iran deal in place, Obama returned to the city. A tattered flag flew in the hot breeze and the lowly governor of Riyadh welcomed him. The leverage the Obama administration thought it had accrued in its outreach to the Sunni Arab world was lost. What multilateral diplomacy gave with one hand, it took with the other.

A particularly heavy price was paid by the people of Yemen. The Houthi rebellion in that nation-state, beginning in 2015, because of its Iranian backing, was attacked relentlessly and carelessly by Saudi Arabia. As some sort of compensation for the Iran nuclear deal, the Obama administration chose to appease Riyadh, doing little to rein in the Saudi bombing of Yemeni civilians. The US actually provided limited logistical support to the Saudi coalition – continued by Donald Trump.[40] US support for Saudi Arabia, despite its excesses, has been a constant across the post–Cold War years. By 2019, Yemen was a smaller version of Syria – the other conflict Obama had studiously tried to avoid. Thousands of men and women had been killed – often by US-made munitions – and many more (about 20 million according to the UN), most of them children, were starving.[41] Obama had attempted a neutral path in an increasingly entrenched cold war between Iran and Saudi Arabia. This meant, in effect, the de facto support of Saudi Arabia, to balance his warming to Iran. The Houthi rebels, for their part, explicitly embraced the tactics of

---

[39] See Kumuda Simpson, *U.S. Nuclear Diplomacy with Iran: From the War on Terror to the Obama Administration* (Lanham, MD: Rowman and Littlefield, 2016) and Steven Hurst, *The United States and the Iranian Nuclear Programme: A Critical History* (Edinburgh: Edinburgh University Press, 2018).

[40] See Gunar Olsen, Add Trump's Yemen Veto to Obama's Spotty War Legacy, *New Republic*, April 20, 2019.

[41] See Karoun Demirjian, With Vote to End U.S. Involvement in Yemen's War, House Sets Up Trump's Second Veto, *Washington Post*, April 4, 2019. Trump's veto duly followed.

the Cold War Viet Cong. John Kerry, a veteran of the American war fought against the Viet Cong, was unable to broker any sort of lasting cease-fire.

CONTAINING CHINA?

Despite an early attempt to pivot toward Asia, in his entire eight years in office President Obama never made a significant speech to an American audience about US policy toward China. He determined to deal with Beijing pragmatically rather than emotionally, as a problem of power politics rather than as an ideological opportunity. In doing so, he mimicked the approach of Cold War realists:

> One thing I will say about China ... is you also have to be pretty firm with them, because they will push as hard as they can until they meet resistance. They're not sentimental, and they are not interested in abstractions, and so simple appeals to international norms are insufficient.[42]

Even the pivot was a continuation of an approach George W. Bush had begun. Both men shared an ambivalence toward China. Despite his lived experience of Indonesia, a large Muslim nation long wary of China's power, Obama lacked animation when it came to Beijing's ambitions. He and Bush each attempted to engage China, especially economically, and to shore up relations with China's neighbors, as a means to retain the existing balance of power in Asia – which favored the United States. There is considerable debate over whether this was achieved.[43] But there is agreement that not much separates the post–Cold War presidents in their approaches to the People's Republic. Jeffrey Bader, Obama's China hand, acknowledged that the Asia policy he inherited from Bush was "generally sound."[44]

Successive US administrations, and Obama's no less than any of the others, have faced three options in dealing with China. They could (1) attempt to constrain or contain its rise; (2) accommodate themselves to that rise; or (3) withdraw from Asia. Variations of the first two frame US China policy from Bush Sr. to Barack Obama. Trump attempted the third, which is assessed in the next chapter. Bush Sr. appeased

---

[42] An Interview with the president, *Economist*, August 2, 2014.
[43] See Hugh White, *Without America: Australia in the New Asia*, *Quarterly Essay*, 68 (2017).
[44] Jeffrey A. Bader, *Obama and China's Rise: An Insider's Account of America's Asia Strategy* (Washington, DC: Brookings, 2012), p. 1.

China over Tiananmen Square. Clinton "locked" it into the World Trade Organization, obliging it to play by international rules, and also made clear his commitment to Taiwanese independence by deploying the US Navy to the island's straits in 1996. Bush Jr. welcomed China's help in the War on Terror, but fought a limited trade war against it in 2002 (steel tariffs – quickly abandoned). Through the end of the Obama presidency, a soft containment of China, via both accommodation and resistance, provided some strategic guideposts. But Obama never fell in love with his own China policy. His attempt to balance (rather than contain) it economically, via the Trans-Pacific Partnership (TPP), lasted only the first few hours of his successor's tenure: Donald Trump withdrew from the TPP on his first full day in office.

In part, Obama was constrained by the same economic realities that faced his immediate predecessors. China's rise constitutes something close to a miracle in modern economics. In 1980, the Chinese had a purchasing power parity that was 10 percent of America's. By 2014, it was 101 percent. Its GDP in 1980 was 7 percent of America's; in 2014, it was 60 percent. China's exports were a meager 6 percent of America's in 1980, but were 106 percent thirty-four years later. Graham Allison captures the transformation well:

> In a single generation, a nation that did not appear on any of the international league tables has vaulted into the top ranks. In 1980, China's economy was smaller than that of the Netherlands. [In 2014], the increment of growth in China's GDP was roughly equal to the entire Dutch economy.[45]

Given China's rise, "containing" it was always a nonstarter; indeed, the United States was to benefit significantly from its transformation. China was to become the lender of first resort as Americans borrowed in order to compensate for a stagnation in their own wages. Moreover, restricting any nation so woven into the fabric of the global system would have been "hopeless," as Jeffrey A. Bader observes.[46]

This dynamic was reinforced by the Great Recession. US posturing on China's human rights record counted for very little when set against its economic power, especially after the collapse of the American housing market in 2008. This crisis left Beijing emboldened and Western

---

[45] Graham Allison, The Thucydides Trap: Are the U.S. and China Headed for War? *Atlantic*, September 24, 2015. He offers the statistics cited.
[46] Bader, *Obama and China's Rise*, p. 69.

governments chastened.[47] The governments of North America and Europe found themselves printing money – "quantitative easing" – to maintain financial liquidity. China, in contrast, very quickly invested in large-scale infrastructure projects at home, as a way to stimulate demand. This became a template for its foreign investment strategy: the Belt and Road Initiative (BRI). The "Chinese model of development" now appeared more attractive to regimes keen to develop economically without having to transform politically. The Chinese penetration of Africa continued apace.

From Beijing's perspective, not only did Obama lack the will to save Syrians, he lacked the financial resources too. As China was pumping investment into Africa, Obama was warning Americans that national security must obey the laws of economic reality. When justifying his limited surge of troops in Afghanistan, he cited Dwight Eisenhower: "Each [national security] proposal must be weighed in the light of a broader consideration: the need to maintain balance in and among national programs."[48] The Chinese government was not spendthrift, but could spend with much less constraint and, as the BRI has shown, in the pursuit of geostrategic objectives. There is a cause and effect here. Chinese President Xi Jinping, appointed in 2012 (and for life in 2017), the most powerful leader since Mao, used American dysphoria in the Middle East and the Great Recession to test the waters, literally. His adventurism in the South China Sea, including the construction of islands to facilitate military expansion, correlated with American efforts to extract themselves from Iraq, Afghanistan, Libya, and Syria. While Obama was trying to escape sand, Xi was using it to build naval bases.

In an important respect, Sino–American relations broke free of the Cold War shadow. While the parallels between Russian behavior before and after the Cold War are many, those of the PRC before and after are a study in contrasts. During the Cold War, China was poor; after it, rich. This altered how the United States has related to it. The USSR was contained, the PRC was engaged. However, this is to reduce the relationship to one of economics. What wealth gave the Chinese government was the opportunity to pursue geostrategic and nationalistic ambitions that had been latent during the Cold War. These included attempts to restore sovereignty over islands in the South China Sea and to maintain its goal of

---

[47] See Adam Tooze, *Crashed: How a Decade of Financial Crises Changed the World* (New York: Penguin Random House, 2018).
[48] Obama speech at West Point, December 2, 2009.

ending Taiwanese independence. Crucially, China remains the most important arbiter of North Korea's possible integration into the community of nations. This Cold War hangover remains a central issue in America's national security policy in Asia.

China was an opportunity for Obama to blend his realism and his liberalism. His realism allowed him to appreciate the power China now had. The economic reality of its rise made moralizing about its internal behavior irrelevant to changing it. Obama's agenda toward Beijing was driven by traditional geostrategic concerns, such as maritime disputes in and near its coastal waters and its regional ambitions through the BRI. Stability, not ideology, was the goal of Obama's Asia policy. But Obama the liberal was also present. Despite Chinese objections, he met with China's charismatic opponent, the Dalai Lama, at the White House on four occasions during his presidency. He sided with Japan in its ongoing dispute with China over the Senkaku/Diaoyu Islands because the shared interests *and* values of the relationship with Tokyo mattered. He also embraced a perception at odds with several prominent realists – not least John Mearsheimer – that China was not an inevitable adversary. If its continued rise could be shaped by international law and norms, peace would be more likely than conflict.[49]

BREXIT AND THE 2016 US ELECTION

On June 24, 2016, 51 percent of British voters opted to leave the European Union (EU). Brexit – "British exit" – was to dominate European politics for years. Few experts saw it coming. What was not anticipated at the time was how far this British decision would frame and partly explain the US presidential election that took place five months after. Comparisons between Trump's victory in November and Brexit are prone to exaggeration. But they are present. Obama was responsible for neither, but played a role in both.

Obama's nonintervention in Syria was to have an electoral consequence in Europe. A powerful narrative of both the Brexit and Trump campaigns was the desire to "take back control" of immigration policy. Trump stunned everyone with his anti-Mexican rhetoric. He promised to

---

[49] See John J. Mearsheimer, *The Tragedy of Great Power Politics* (New York: W. W. Norton, 2014), chap. 10, Can China Rise Peacefully? (his answer is a resounding no); and Charles Edel, Limiting Chinese Aggression: A Strategy of Counter-Pressure, *American Interest*, February 9, 2018.

build a wall to check the flow of "illegals" into the United States. Obama was presented as having been soft on the issue. The Vote Leave campaign in Britain fought along similar lines. A long-term antipathy toward a liberal immigration policy was brought into sharp relief in 2015. In August of that year, German chancellor Angela Merkel controversially agreed to settle 890,000 refugees in Germany. The greater proportion of these men and women were Syrians fleeing civil war. The Leave campaign in Britain presented this as evidence of an EU that had lost control of its borders. Posters depicted lines of refugees, with the implication that they would eventually head to the UK. Brexit was about more than immigration, but it was rarely not about this. Obama and Merkel, despite their different reactions to the Syrian Civil War, had inadvertently contrived to offer Brexit a key platform. Obama's sin of omission in Syria in 2013 was to be felt for years to come.

If Brexit in 2016 would have looked unlikely in 2008 or 2012, the prominence of Russia would have looked even more so. Like Bill Clinton, Obama had traduced opponents for exaggerating the threat posed by Moscow. And yet in no election during the Cold War was a Russian presence so keenly felt as it was in 2016. "The Russian government interfered in the 2016 presidential election," declared the official Mueller Report, "in sweeping and systematic fashion."[50] The reverberations of Putin's machinations in Hillary Clinton's defeat lasted across Donald Trump's presidency. In one of his final actions as president of the United States, Obama ordered the expulsion of thirty-five Russian diplomats. This token reprisal was meant to punish Putin for Russian government meddling in the 2016 election. The Kremlin, via its British embassy, mocked the decision on social media:

President Obama expels 35 Russian diplomats in Cold War deja vu. As everybody, incl American people, will be glad to see the last of this hapless Adm.[51]

For a then lame-duck president, believing that he, like his Democratic predecessor, Bill Clinton, had transcended the Cold War, this must have been especially frustrating. Despite his best intentions, Obama ended his term playing by Cold War rules, using Cold War tactics, and speaking in Cold War rhetoric. Vladimir Putin had not been "reset."

[50] Report on the investigation into Russian interference in the 2016 election (The Mueller Report, Washington DC, March 2019; released April 2019), p. 1; at https://apps.npr.org/documents/document.html?id=5955997-Muellerreport
[51] https://twitter.com/RussianEmbassy/status/814564127230271489

Despite nearly every polling organization giving Hillary Clinton a significant lead, and her eventually winning a plurality of votes (48.2 percent to 46.1 percent), Trump won in the electoral college, 306 to 232, and 30 states to her 20. The result was stunning. Widely dismissed as a joke candidate, Trump flipped states Clinton assumed would stay blue: Wisconsin, Iowa, Michigan, Ohio, Pennsylvania, and Florida. About 10 million voters that had turned out for Barack Obama in 2008 failed to do so for Hillary Clinton in 2016. Trump's foreign policy platform was crude but effective: American workers had "been stiffed" by Mexico and China, who had stolen their jobs. The Democrats, who should have been their defenders, had subscribed to a cosmopolitan globalization and been complicit in the defenestration of America's industrial base. At the same time, claimed Trump, Bush and Obama had wasted blood and treasure fighting Muslim wars in the Middle East. Instead of making foreign policy the pursuit of American national interests, the coastal elites had sold out the American middle class, preferring to fund European defense rather than US renewal. He hammered away at these themes and Clinton increasingly found herself having to move toward them – she was compelled to promise the repeal of the Trans-Pacific Partnership, negotiated by the Obama administration, to match Trump – and she alienated crucial swing voters by calling them "deplorables" for warming to his populist message.

On election night, the scale of the defeat left Obama's closest foreign policy advisor and speechwriter, Ben Rhodes, literally speechless.[52]

CONCLUSION: AN OBAMA REVOLUTION?

Obama won the 2012 presidential election able to boast of some significant foreign policy accomplishments. He had ordered the killing of bin Laden and made regime change in Libya possible. He had negotiated a new START agreement with Russia. He had withdrawn from Iraq. He had helped engineer the Paris climate change agreement. By the end of his presidency, in January 2017, however, these achievements were clouded by the Syrian Civil War, a telegraphed withdrawal from Afghanistan, the rise of ISIS, the disaster that post–Gaddafi Libya had become, Russian adventurism, a more assertive China, a Europe fractured by refugee flows,

---

[52] See *The Final Year* movie, directed by Greg Barker (2017).

and a nuclear deal with Tehran that made regime change less likely and that his successor was almost certain to repeal.

If Obama's version of the War on Terror enjoyed some successes, it was on the territory he himself claimed he would bring decisive change that he was, by 2017, most exposed. Peace in Israel/Palestine, a signature issue for Obama early in his term, was no closer as a consequence of his diplomacy. Obama had made not much more progress than George W. Bush and, by the estimates of some, even less. Similarly, and again belying his Peace Prize, his rhetoric of extending open hands to clenched fists in Pyongyang and Damascus led to little improvement in the relationships with these regimes. Obama was far better at removing dictators by hard military power – as in Libya – than by killing them with the kindness of soft power.

His foreign policy had been new or old, effective or ineffective, depending on what one expected of it. American liberalism does not compel a certain kind of foreign policy. Some in his base applauded his troop drawdown from the Middle East. But so did many realists. Likewise, liberal hawks, like Hillary Clinton, were dismayed at Obama's reticence in Libya and Syria, and were joined by several conservative nationalists who indicted his will-o'-the-wisp approach to Russia and China. What these conflicting sources of praise and blame illustrate is the flexibility Obama claimed on behalf of his foreign policy. He refused to be straitjacketed by a doctrinaire approach. This made him inherently reactive and tactical, rather than forward-looking and strategic. But he seemed to like it that way. It could be argued that this afforded him an ambiguity that made him difficult to predict and thus to counter.

The centrality of the Russia issue, despite his initial hopes that Moscow was bending in the right direction, suggests the Cold War shadow was still heavy in the Obama years. Putin's defense of his near abroad and his penetration of the Syrian conflict were behaviors remarkably similar to those of his Soviet predecessors. By the same token, Obama's reaction to Putin's nostalgia for that lost past was to mimic the approach of several Cold War presidents. Obama's inaction when Putin invaded Ukraine was not unlike that of Harry Truman when Stalin seized East Europe, or of Jimmy Carter when Brezhnev invaded Afghanistan. China's rise to economic superpower status, though begun in the 1970s, complicates the imposition of a Cold War template. Beijing prospered by escaping the cul-de-sacs of Cold War Maoism. But with China's increased wealth came the reassertion of its territorial claims and regional ambitions that

were formed in the Cold War. The means Obama chose to counter them –
a combination of balancing and engaging – were positively Kissingerian.
Obama represents continuity not just with his Cold War predecessors
but with George W. Bush too. He did many things better than Bush, but
not necessarily many things different from him. Despite running as the
"un-Bush" candidate in 2008, President Obama pursued a reformulation
of his predecessor's foreign policy – not a revolution away from it. On
Russia, his approach was as straitjacketed as Bush's had been. When
Putin sent troops into Georgia in 2008 and into Ukraine in 2014, Bush
and Obama, respectively, deferred to geographic reality – as all their Cold
War predecessors had done. This was Russia's backyard, which rendered
a US military solution unfeasible. On China, there was little to separate
Bush and Obama. Both men had to adapt to the regional ambitions born
of China's seemingly inexorable economic rise. Both men made better
relations with the PRC a priority but not a demanding necessity. Each
post–Cold War president has inherited a model of wary engagement
begun by Nixon in 1972.

Obama had defined himself as being against the Iraq War – and thus
against Bush and Hillary Clinton, who had supported it. But his interventionism in the Middle East differed in degree, not in kind. Wars
for Muslim liberation were waged by both administrations: in Iraq and
then in Libya. Obama thus continued a trend begun by George H. W.
Bush in Kuwait, and continued by Bill Clinton in the Balkans and by
George W. Bush in Afghanistan and Iraq. Oil was not the motivating
factor behind these interventions. Rather, saving the lives of
Muslims and replacing their leaders was the common theme – realized
imperfectly and inconsistently, but attempted, nonetheless. The chosen
means were also similar. Obama had an aversion to the deployment of
significant military force, of boots on the ground, that was not unlike
Bush's. In 2003, too few troops tried to occupy Iraq. In 2011, that
insufficiency was repeated in Libya. The result was prolonged civil
war in each case. Obama dithered over a surge into Afghanistan but
eventually undertook one. He had reluctantly accepted Bush's Iraq
surge as his template.

The clearest similarity between Bush and Obama was in regard to
counterterrorism. Indeed, there is a case to be made that Obama was
much more aggressive in killing terrorists than was Bush. This was not
simply a function of technology, though drones certainly increased in
their lethality across 2001–2017, but of intent. George W. Bush decided
to wage his war on terror on what he hoped would be clearly demarcated

frontlines in Afghanistan and Iraq. Moving the line from one to the other in 2003 caused a loss of focus on the Taliban. Obama, however, made the war against terrorism central to his actions in the Middle East. He agreed to a surge in Afghanistan because it would advance the fight against terrorists, there and in Pakistan. When he deployed special forces into Iraq and Syria their mission was simple: kill and capture as many jihadists as possible. Nation-building and the freedom agenda were relegated to the point of irrelevance under Obama. His greatest success was arguably the killing of the world's most infamous Islamist: Osama bin Laden. None of his immediate predecessors was able to achieve this.

Paul Miller, a National Security Council director on the Afghanistan and Pakistan desk under George W. Bush, saw Obama's approach as neither a departure nor a failure:

The United States has not failed: It is succeeding at exactly what it set out to do. U.S. strategy – the real strategy, reflected in budgetary and deployment decisions, not the paper strategy reflected in speeches and aspirational documents – aims to sustain an indefinite counterterrorism presence in South Asia to kill or capture militant leaders while avoiding a Taliban takeover in Afghanistan, nothing more. That the United States is still in Afghanistan is not a sign of failure: It is what U.S. policymakers have deliberately chosen, because they will neither accept defeat nor pay the price of a more ambitious campaign to resolve the conflict. Indefinite, low-cost war is a feature, not a bug, of U.S. strategy in Afghanistan. It is not an attractive strategy and not the one I advocated for, but it is successful according to its own terms.[53]

Obama the hard-nosed realist, not Obama the cosmopolitan-in-chief, more often won the battle when it came to US national security. The successes of soft power were much more time-limited. Outreach to Cuba and Iran were to be quickly undone by Donald Trump. Meaningful global cooperation on climate change was similarly prone to domestic negation and international dissensus, not least in China and India. Obama's approach to Africa had none of the humanitarian innovation of Bush's PEPFAR. Rather, by 2016, Obama had made the continent part of his counterterrorism campaign. He deployed US special forces into Somalia (as had Bill Clinton). He used private contractors (as had George W. Bush in Iraq) to fight Islamist militants in the Horn of Africa. In his final full year in office, Obama ordered air strikes in at least seven countries. The

---

[53] Paul D. Miller, Critics Should Stop Declaring Defeat in Afghanistan, *Foreign Policy*, April 12, 2019.

New York Times called it "a blueprint for warfare that President Obama has embraced and will pass along to his successor."[54]

On January 20, 2017, the world, not least Barack Obama himself, with a mixture of incredulity and apprehension, pondered how that successor, whom few ever believed could become president, might change things.

---

[54] Mark Mazzetti, Jeffrey Gettleman, and Eric Schmitt, In Somalia, U.S. Escalates a Shadow War, *New York Times*, October 16, 2016.

Conclusion

Donald Trump and the End of the Cold War Shadow?

> After being dismissed as a phenomenon of an earlier century, great power competition [has] returned ... the United States must prepare for this type of competition.
>
> —*National Security Strategy of the United States of America,*
> *December 2017*[1]

> A New Cold War With Russia? No, It's Worse Than That.
> —New York Times *headline, March 26, 2018*[2]

From 2010 to 2016, the world's highest-ranked game on BoardGame-Geek was *Twilight Struggle: The Cold War, 1945–1989*. Its name is taken from President Kennedy's 1961 call for Americans "to bear the burden of a long twilight struggle." The board game simulates "the forty-five-year dance of intrigue, prestige, and occasional flares of warfare between the Soviet Union and the United States. The entire world is the stage on which these two titans fight to make the world safe for their own ideologies and ways of life."[3] While successive administrations have attempted to transcend the Cold War, the conflict has retained an enduring appeal. More than this, as this book has argued, its lessons have remained central to US policymaking. The Cold War is still needed to understand

---

[1] White House, *National Security Strategy of the United States of America* (Washington, DC, December 2017), p. 27; see http://nssarchive.us/.

[2] Andrew Higginsmarch, *New York Times*, March 26, 2018.

[3] www.boardgamegeek.com/boardgame/12333/twilight-struggle.

contemporary international relations. The actions of President Donald Trump toward Russia appeared so jarring, not because he wanted to get over the Cold War, but because he seemed ignorant of its basic history.

This book started with the collapse of one wall and ends with the building of another. As the British scholars Brendan Simms and Charlie Laderman suggest, "The period 1989–2016 may well become known as the inter-wall era."[4] It began when Russia was central to US foreign policy. It ends with Russia central to American domestic politics. When the Berlin Wall fell in 1989 a supposedly "new world order" was born. With the fitful building of a Mexican wall, we have come full circle. As this book documents, the claim of a new international relations system was more a hopeful prediction than it became an accomplished fact. Instead, we have a trajectory that begins with the end of a movie star presidency in 1989, and ends with the beginning of TV star presidency in 2017. From Reagan to Trump, American foreign policy never transcended the centrality of Russia in its formulation. Despite attempts at "new thinking," the presidents after Reagan each dealt with the world in terms that were more similar than they were different. Efforts were made to transform the US approach toward competitors Russia and China, which had gestated in the Cold War. Successive presidents ended up adapting Cold War strategies. In this concluding chapter we will examine how far Donald Trump was able to escape the shadow of the Cold War.

A TRUMP REVOLUTION?

The style and personality of the newly elected president himself was the first indication of a coming shift in America's global posture. Donald Trump had never held elected office. His leadership skills were honed doing real estate deals and presiding over reality TV shows. Despite running as a Republican, he was not a creature of that party. His political debts, because of this, were few. If he spoke for a vested interest, it was himself, his family, and his supporters. His personality, allied to his unique rise to the presidency, was held to be crucial – by both his admirers and his detractors. Claims that he was unfit for the office became basic to political discourse, nationally and internationally. This all led to both

---

[4] Brendan Simms and Charlie Laderman, *Donald Trump: The Making of a World View* (New York: I. B. Tauris, 2017), p. 17.

confident and fearful expectations that he would transform American foreign policy.

In some respects, those predictions were borne out. Trump's beliefs were of long standing and broadly consistent over time.[5] He thought the United States was recurrently too weak in its prosecution of the Cold War. In 1987, he took out a full-page advertisement in the *New York Times* indicting Ronald Reagan's "weakness." He declared, "There's nothing wrong with America's defense policy that a little backbone can't cure."[6] The ad went onto blame US allies Japan and Saudi Arabia for exploiting American largesse. It was a theme, with the freeloading allies changed, that he took into the 2016 campaign and then into the White House. "We've made other countries rich while the wealth, strength, and confidence of our country has dissipated over the horizon," he said in his inaugural address. "From this day forward, it's going to be only America first. America first."[7]

His downgrading of the alliances central to US success in the Cold War was suggestive of a president who cared little for that conflict. It established an environment that allowed acquisitive foreigners to fleece hard-working Americans. Trump was to travel to several European capitals in 2017–2019, each time berating the opulence of their welfare states and low defense spending, while American wages remained stagnant. His ambivalence toward NATO was a stunning reversal of a Cold War tradition. The transactional emphasis he placed on diplomacy was deliberately crafted to downplay values as the source of Western cohesion. "Let's not let our great country be laughed at anymore," he said in 1987, and it remained a core concern during his presidency.

From Truman to Bush Sr., and from Clinton to Obama, each president had paid homage to, and used, Cold War alliances. Trump seemingly disdained them – and had done so reliably across decades. As a former George W. Bush official observed, "He has been very consistent essentially since the 1980s. He knows very little about the world, about history, about the policy details. But he does have strong convictions and they are remarkably durable and apparently impervious to contrary evidence."[8]

---

[5] This is argued convincingly by Simms and Laderman in *Donald Trump*.
[6] *New York Times*, September 2, 1987.
[7] Donald Trump, inaugural address, January 20, 2017.
[8] Eric S. Edelman in Mark Landler, On Foreign Policy, President Trump Reverts to Candidate Trump, *New York Times*, April 3, 2018.

Trump's embrace of economic nationalism as a means to recapture America's lost wealth also positions him outside of the Cold War shadow. The strength of the West in that conflict and, at least until the Great Recession of 2008, after it, was built on the extraordinary economic engines of free trade and globalization. Trump demurred. These engines had propelled the growth of Tokyo and Beijing, but had left the American middle class denuded of jobs and hope. He renegotiated Bill Clinton's NAFTA because of "the carnage" it had caused at home. He walked away from the Obama-negotiated Trans-Pacific Partnership for similar reasons. His signature foreign policy was the trade war he initiated with China in July 2018. Again, this was a position he had foreshadowed since the 1980s and one at variance with precedent. His embrace of trade as an arena for power politics does not make him unique. But it is illustrative of a president who saw winning in essentially financial terms. The vocabulary of values and ideology, so important to the rhetoric of his predecessors, was largely abandoned. Greatness came from getting the best deal, not from advancing noble causes. George W. Bush, said Trump, was "stupid" for believing in America's power to transform whole civilizations.

The apparent amorality of his foreign policy was evinced by his preference for autocratic leaders. If he made Angela Merkel and Justin Trudeau uncomfortable, he went to great efforts to do the opposite for Vladimir Putin and Kim Jong-un. His early diplomacy was controversially about the cultivation of these autocrats. Trump saw huge transformative power in his personal chemistry with both men. His warm handshakes with Kim in Singapore, Hanoi, and at the DMZ constituted a symbolic revolution away from Cold War constraints. Ronald Reagan had attempted a similarly bold diplomatic breakthrough with Mikhail Gorbachev at Reykjavik in 1986.[9] Trump's validation of Putin's denial of electoral meddling, at an infamous summit in Helsinki (July 2018), was an effort to change great power politics by physical contiguity. By most accounts, this was the first time an American president had sided with a foreign leader against his own intelligence agencies. A former British foreign secretary implied that Trump's diplomacy was unwittingly complicit in "the slow, sinister Russification of Europe."[10]

[9] See Graham Allison, Misunderstanding Trump's "Failed" Hanoi Summit, *National Interest*, March 1, 2019.
[10] William Hague, We Are Failing to Stop the Slow, Sinister Russification of Europe, *Daily Telegraph [London]*, October 8, 2018.

Both substantially and stylistically, then, the Trump administration seemed determined to turn traditional foreign policy upside down. However, there was also in Trump's approach much that illustrates the enduring character of the Cold War. His foreign policy team, despite having three times the churn of Obama's, were from and of that conflict. The way they construed the world relied on a Cold War framing. The centerpieces of foreign policy remained the great powers of the Cold War: China and Russia. Negating their influence meant using strategies previously tested, such as nuclear posture and alliances. When Trump engaged with autocrats, he followed a pattern established by Richard Nixon and Ronald Reagan.

TRUMP AND COLD WAR CONTINUITY

On December 26, 2017, Stephen Bannon, then chief strategist to President-elect Donald Trump, was spotted reading one of the most popular works of Cold War scholarship: David Halberstam's *The Best and the Brightest*.[11] Published in 1972, the book is a brilliant dissection of how academically able men became disastrous foreign policy makers. Bannon's airport reading illustrates how far the Cold War still colors American thinking. Trump had been schooled in political intrigue by Roy Cohn, chief counsel to the notorious 1950s anti-communist Joseph McCarthy. Trump's administration soon became filled with men and women keen to define the world in binary terms. Instead of global communism, the enemy was now "radical Islamic terrorism." Instead of banning communists, Trump moved quickly to limit immigration from "terrorist-exporting" states. He did all this while making Russia central to his foreign policy. Inaugurated at age 70, Trump had spent more of his adult life in the Cold War than any of the three men who preceded him. Trump recast the Cold War, possibly inadvertently; he did not transcend it.

Trump's National Security Strategy (NSS), published in December 2017, applied dynamics central to the Cold War to contemporary international relations. Two areas stand out: the recognition that great-power competition had returned, and that the United States must reestablish the "credible deterrence" it enjoyed during the Cold War. An understanding of the world as a competitive arena was basic to America's rise to

---

[11] See Marc Tracey, Steve Bannon's Book Club, *New York Times*, February 4, 2017.

globalism. Indeed, the United States, as a 230-year political experiment, assumes competition is fundamental to human nature. The US Constitution has been called an "invitation to struggle" for the control of foreign policy.[12] The Trump team claimed the competition of the modern era, especially in the Indo-Pacific, was that "between free and repressive visions of world order."[13] This conceptualization had profound corollaries to the Cold War. That struggle's active theater, as Odd Arne Westad reminds us, was in the developing world.[14] In Europe, again as in the Cold War, there was a "competition for power unfolding" along similarly ideological lines.[15] The Obama administration had attempted to move away from these Cold War loci.[16] Trump reaffirmed them. "With its language about national resurgence and competition with other states," according to George Lopez, the strategy "sounds a lot like the 1980s revisited."[17]

The 1980s echoed after 2017. Deepening the Cold War logic was Trump's insistence that nuclear weapons remained key to US security. Even as America moved away from the Cold War arms race, as Matthew Kroenig has documented, it retained a faith in nuclear superiority.[18] Trump justified his cultivation of Vladimir Putin with reference to the nuclear monopoly ("over 90 percent") that Russia and the United States enjoyed, necessitating that they get along. Ronald Reagan thought in analogous terms, as his diplomacy with Mikhail Gorbachev attests. Trump has revised, not abandoned, Reagan's Cold War nuclear strategy. In October 2018, to counter a Chinese military buildup in the Pacific, he decided to abandon the 1987 Intermediate-Range Nuclear Forces Treaty (INF Treaty), of which China was not a signatory. The INF Treaty had been deteriorating for several years, largely because of Russia's more threatening approach toward its neighbors, which included the moving of tactical nuclear weapons with the express purpose of intimidating

[12] Edward S. Corwin, *The President: Office and Powers, 1787–1957*, 4th rev. ed. (New York: New York University Press, 1957), p. 171.
[13] National Security Strategy (2017), p. 45.
[14] See Odd Arne Westad, *The Global Cold War: Third World Interventions and the Making of Our Times* (Cambridge, UK: Cambridge University Press, 2007); and *The Cold War: A World History* (New York: Penguin, 2018).
[15] National Security Strategy (2017), p. 50.
[16] See National Security Strategy (Washington, DC, February 2015).
[17] In Julian Borger, U.S. Could Broaden Its Use of Nuclear Weapons, Trump Administration Signals, *Guardian*, December 19, 2017.
[18] See Matthew Kroenig, *The Logic of American Nuclear Strategy: Why Strategic Superiority Matters* (New York: Oxford University Press, 2018).

Western European states.[19] Accordingly, Trump's National Security Strategy reaffirmed the "vital purpose" of nuclear deterrence, a defense posture born in the Cold War.[20]

Trump's approach to China both confounds and confirms Cold War precedent. His predecessors treated the USSR as the central adversary. Even Jimmy Carter, in seeking to shift US foreign policy from its focus on Moscow's intentions, had to acknowledge what those intentions were. The People's Republic of China has not played that analogous role since 1989. US administrations and American political parties have developed no clear narrative of what China wants. In the Cold War, by contrast, what Russia was understood to want was basic to the framing of US foreign policy. This often meant the understanding of the struggle as inescapably ideological. The "conflict" with China has only some of that character. Trump narrowed the focus to trade issues and pursued his China policy accordingly. But this has remained someway short of the grand strategic doctrine that was used to contain Soviet power.

Trump's gambit, made as president-elect in December 2016, was to call Tsai Ing-wen, the Taiwanese president, and offer to give her island nation a renewed priority in his Asia policy. This appalled Beijing. It can be surmised that Trump was not a close reader of Nixon's diplomacy. But what Nixon had achieved, Trump now seemed determine to unravel. In 1972, Nixon and Mao had used Taiwan as a bargaining chip. If the United States weakened its support for Taiwanese independence, the PRC would use its good offices to persuade North Vietnam to make peace with the United States.[21] In important respects, the opening of China, and its remarkable economic rise thereafter, was a product of this deal. For Trump, this Cold War statecraft was at best an anachronism and, at worst, was the basis for the destruction of US manufacturing by China – a factor in Trump's election success in 2016. His trade war with China sought to repeal much of the Nixon legacy. Trump's first National Security Strategy accused China (and Russia) of "attempting to erode American security and prosperity."[22]

And yet, even if he did not fully know his Cold War history, Trump inadvertently followed some of its guideposts. Trump attempted to do on

---

[19] See Esther Owens, Trump Is Right about the INF, *Foreign Policy*, October 24, 2018.

[20] National Security Strategy (2017), p. 30.

[21] See Margaret Macmillan, *Seize the Hour: When Nixon Met Mao* (London: John Murray, 2006), pp. 255–265.

[22] National Security Strategy (2017), p. 2.

tariffs what Reagan did on nuclear weapons. The first term of the Reagan administration saw one of the largest defense buildups in American history. Reagan the hawk was determined to spend the USSR into submission. He was widely derided as a warmonger for doing so. By the second term, however, at a summit with Mikhail Gorbachev in Iceland in 1986, Reagan stunned his opposite number by proposing the complete eradication of their respective nuclear arsenals. The tough initial stance allowed for the later mellowing. Likewise, Trump initiated an early trade war with China. He was stoutly condemned for his economic backwardness, but he offered the tantalizing prospect that this was the path to a tariff-free world.

Lastly, Trump's approach to Iran had an important Cold War genesis. As president, he determined to make the regime his chief nemesis. He had not plucked Tehran from the air. As Simms and Laderman observe, "Like so many Americans of his generation, Trump's world view was shaped by the trauma of the [1979 Iran] hostage crisis and the sense of U.S. decline in the late 1970s and 1980s."[23] There is a plausible argument that one of Trump's key strategic ambitions was to redress this long-standing grievance. The cancellation of the Iran nuclear deal was not ordered to belittle his predecessor. Rather, it was the articulation of a 40-year-old grudge. Trump's Iran policy positively basked in the Cold War's shadow.

TRUMP AND POST–COLD WAR CONTINUITY

Donald Trump, George W. Bush, and Bill Clinton were born in June, July, and August of 1946, respectively. This common starting point offers a clue to their similarities in the White House. Trump's foreign policy continued trends established in the Cold War's shadow, after 1989. Most significant was his embrace of the counterterrorism consensus that George W. Bush had forged, and that Barack Obama had affirmed. Stopping the nexus of terrorism and weapons of mass destruction was central to the national security strategy of all three men. "TARGET WMD TERRORISTS" is how Trump's national security strategy put it: "We will direct counter-terrorism operations against terrorist WMD specialists, financiers, administrators, and facilitators." It is an injunction heard often across the post–9/11 years. "Keeping nuclear materials from terrorists," declared Obama's National Security Strategy (2015) "and

---

[23] Simms and Laderman, *Donald Trump*, p. 22.

preventing the proliferation of nuclear weapons remains a high priority." Trump also shared with Obama a hard-line approach to jihadi terrorists such as ISIS. In the 2016 campaign, he promised to "bomb the shit out of 'em." He was advancing Obama's approach in so doing.[24] He continued Obama's deployment of US special forces in Syria for the first two years of his presidency, announcing in December 2018 that they had beaten ISIS and could now withdraw – a decision that was roundly criticized and that he later backtracked from. The minimalist focus on killing terrorists, rather than any maximalist agenda of nation-building, casts Trump's counterterrorism as a third Obama term rather than as a revolution away from his predecessor.[25]

Trump's approach to Afghanistan recycled options that the Obama administration had long argued over. In his relentless focus on counter-terrorism, using trained Afghan soldiers, coupled with drone strikes and special operations, plus a healthy skepticism for Pakistani machinations in that theater, Trump was implementing a plan Vice-President Joe Biden had advocated. Indeed, his tough stance on Pakistan – withholding the US funding that was crucial to its regime – earned the praise of senior Bush officials like Zalmay Khalilzad.[26] Despite fears among members of the Washington foreign policy establishment, Trump was acting within a long-established national security consensus.

Obama's 2012 bumper sticker – "BIN LADEN IS DEAD. GENERAL MOTORS IS ALIVE" – presaged a rhetorical style and emphasis that would continue under his successor. Trump was to be criticized for his "Islamophobia" and ignorance of climate change. And yet it was Obama who had campaigned on having killed the world's most notorious Islamist and on having kept alive greenhouse gas–emitting industries. Similarly, Trump maintained a post–Cold War pattern of military interventionism in defense of beleaguered Muslims. Twice he attacked Syrian defense facilities in reprisal for Assad's repeated use of chemical weapons against civilians. His justification for so doing was essentially the same as that offered by each of his immediate predecessors in their wars of Muslim liberation:

---

[24] See Luke Mogelson, The Recent History of Bombing the Shit Out of 'Em, *New Yorker*, April 20, 2017.

[25] See, for example, Eric Schmitt, After Tough Talk on ISIS, Trump Hews to Obama's Plan, *New York Times*, March 19, 2017; and Adam Taylor, America's Forgotten War in Syria Isn't Stopping, *Washington Post*, November 28, 2018.

[26] Zalmay Khalilzad, Why Trump Is Right to Get Tough with Pakistan, *New York Times*, August 23, 2017.

Today, the nations of Britain, France and the United States of America have marshaled their righteous power against barbarism and brutality. Tonight, I ask all Americans to say a prayer for our noble warriors and our allies as they carry out their missions. We pray that God will bring comfort to those suffering in Syria. We pray that God will guide the whole region toward a future of dignity and of peace.[27]

If their violence against foreign regimes brings Obama and Trump together, so too, despite predictions, does their engagement with them. Trump did reject Obama's nuclear deal with Iran, but he inadvertently used his predecessor's outreach toward Cuba as the basis for his own toward North Korea. US relationships with both regimes were defined by both men as Cold War anachronisms that should be transcended. Obama became the first US president to visit Cuba, in March 2016. An agreement to unfreeze relations with a rogue state that had threatened nuclear war against America (in 1962) soon followed. Trump became the first US president to meet a leader of North Korea, in June 2018. An understanding to ease tensions with the pariah state that had recurrently threatened America with nuclear missiles soon followed. Both Obama and Trump invested huge faith in the power of their own personality to unlock these Cold War enmities.

REMEMBERING BUT NOT REPEATING THE COLD WAR

Robert Legvold reminds us, "Epic historical eras fade very slowly. Their effects persist long after the period in which they occur. Even longer do historians argue over their causes, essence and significance."[28] As the Cold War starts to assume a place in the popular consciousness akin to the Thirty Years War – as a prolonged struggle fought for shifting ends, begun by adversaries some of whom no longer existed – it seems appropriate to close this book with a call for remembrance. The Cold War cost many lives, ruined many more, and risked a nuclear doomsday. These are all well-documented features of the international landscape from the 1940s to the 1980s, and it would be foolish to wish their repetition. And yet we would compound that foolishness if we continue to insist the Cold War had no strategic lessons to impart today.

First among these was the importance of American hegemony in stabilizing global politics. This was a *cold* war because states were given

[27] Trump address on Syria, White House, April 13, 2018.
[28] Robert Legvold, *Return to Cold War* (Cambridge: Polity Press, 2016), p. 55.

a clear choice: to side with Washington or Moscow. That choice largely conditioned the success and failure of the economies of the choosing state. Those joining the US side got richer and enjoyed levels of prosperity far greater than those joining or emulating the Soviet side. Communism produced greater economic equality, but an equality of privation. Unlike its communist opponents, the United States did not proffer a perfect economic model; the evolution of Western-style capitalism from 1990 to today has hardly been smooth. And yet its economic system, supported by an enormous military machine that was in some ways underused (in Vietnam and Iraq, for example, wars were fought with an eye to quick exits rather than long-term occupation), made alternatives seem meager. The Cold War also supplies a containment doctrine, as Michael Mandelbaum has argued, well-suited to modern adaption rather than to nostalgia:

The contemporary world is similar enough to its mid-twentieth-century predecessor to make that old strategy relevant, but different enough that it needs to be modified and updated. While success is not guaranteed, a new containment policy offers the best chance to defend American interests in the twenty-first century.[29]

Second, the Cold War reinforced the imperative of state character in determining foreign policy success. The West has become increasingly prey to political and cultural relativism – the notion that there is no good and bad in the world, only difference and diversity. This should not lead us to conclude that national characteristics do not matter. If Barack Obama toyed with moral relativism – claiming we are all exceptional now – Donald Trump asserted that American greatness is a moral imperative. The world took a decidedly American turn after the end of the Cold War not just because the United States was economically and militarily powerful, but because it was a powerful liberal democracy. The character of its power mattered. It imbued its foreign policy with a legitimacy bought into by other states. Since their disastrous flirtations with Soviet economics in the Cold War, the rising powers of China and India have moved toward Washington, not away. Both Beijing and New Delhi want to be included in the multilateral institutions that American liberal democracy created, from the United Nations to the World Trade Organization. Indeed, the great issue of future world politics will be how far these states adapt their political systems to meet the expectations

---

[29] Michael Mandelbaum, The New Containment: Handling Russia, China, and Iran, *Foreign Affairs* 98, 2 (March/April 2019): 123–131.

of their people. The test for China, with no history of representative democracy, will likely be especially severe.

Donald Trump leads in a world still far more amenable to American leadership than American leaders sometimes are prepared to admit. Trump claimed he would make his country's friends pay their fair share. More important is the fact that the United States has so many friends, and how concerned those friends were at Trump's cold shoulder. America's enemies – defined as those states whose internal legitimacy rests on their anti-Americanism – are so few and so weak that America's freedom of action remains intact. Iran and Cuba may not now or soon count themselves as US friends, but their regimes can no longer plausibly posture on their hatred of the United States. The same goes for the governments of Venezuela and North Korea. They may be proudly anti-Washington, but how serious is this ideological claim when their own people are so impoverished? States like these hardly constitute a mighty balancing coalition against US power.

All the advantages that gave the United States the edge in the Cold War still obtain. Unlike the European Union, the United States enjoys a national legitimacy that the ups and downs of global economics do not weaken. Its capacity to attract and to assimilate immigrants remains a remarkable strength. A former Kenyan goat herder studies at an American university and forty-seven years later his son becomes president of the United States. A quarter of all the men and women seeking a new home make America their first choice. The US economy creates a society with small pockets of great wealth. But freedom of faith has generated a culture remarkably immune to religious conflict. America has racial conflict and tension, not religious conflict, unlike Europe and the Middle East. In 2019, China was imprisoning nearly a million Muslim Uighurs in "reeducation camps." The United States, in contrast, represents a great religious free market. It also enjoys all the foreign policy advantages of being in possession of the greatest military machine in world history (at the price of only about 3 percent of its wealth, its GDP, each year). And its geography gives it a friendly neighborhood from which to project its power. China and Russia, in comparison, are surrounded by suspicious neighbors.

These advantages do not make the US immune to bad foreign policy decisions, but they make poor choices abroad less severe. Soviet, German, Chinese – even British – foreign policies of the last 100 years have either destroyed or nearly destroyed their makers. American failures – in Vietnam and Iraq, for example – were surmountable. Into the US system is built a certain elasticity and flexibility. In 1835, Alexis de Tocqueville cautioned that this democratic character would eventually be victim to autocrats better able to mobilize national power.[30] But the French observer was wrong. Democracy in America imbued its foreign policy with enormous strengths. Its autocratic challengers fell by the wayside. While America is founded on an idea, it has not developed an ideological foreign policy immune to adaptation. Indeed, the fundamental pragmatism of "the American ideology" makes it subversive of the alternative forms chosen by its opponents – from Imperial Japan to the Islamic State. America does not quite believe in its power – it was, after all, founded in 1787 explicitly to prevent too much power being held in too few hands – and yet has become the most powerful state in world history. Its foreign policy has had something to do with that.

To conclude a book that documents several foreign policy failures – from George H. W. Bush's turning away from Bosnia, Clinton's dereliction in Rwanda, Bush Jr.'s botched occupation of Iraq, Obama's abandonment of Syria, to Trump's appeasement of North Korea – by arguing for general foreign policy success might seem perverse. These post–Cold War presidents clearly made profound mistakes, and many thousands of people died as a consequence. And yet, just as in the Cold War, missteps did not spell the end of American power. Foreign policy since 1989 has done a better job of protecting US interests than of ruining them. The United States remains the most important power in the Middle East – a region from which oil continues to flow, with an Arab–Israeli peace process dependent on American facilitation. There have been no major wars between Israel and its neighbors since the United States assumed a greater role in the region in the middle 1970s. Russia, despite its revanchism, has had to adapt itself to US power in its backyard, not vice versa. China is dependent on the US market to maintain its economic growth and relies on American power to contain Japan and to police the shipping lanes of the Pacific. India seeks a fuller alliance with Washington to balance against its regional foes, just as London, Paris, and Bonn did during the Cold War. Eastern Europe, after a twentieth century of subjugation by Germany and Russia, craves an American security umbrella.

The two greatest foes of US power in the post–Cold War era were terrorism and loose credit. The global reach of the former was negated by

---

[30] See Alexis de Tocqueville, *Democracy in America* (1835), trans. Harvey C. Mansfield and Delba Winthrop (Chicago: University of Chicago Press, 2000), pp. 217–220.

changing some of the regimes that exported it: Afghanistan, Iraq, and Libya. The second, profound though the impact of the Great Recession of 2008 has been, was not a foreign policy failure, but a domestic one. The interests Americans defended in the Cold War largely endured in the decades after it. Indeed, those interests have become more secure and their protection sought by not just America alone but most nations whose own interests coincide with them. The great fear of America's allies is that Donald Trump will withdraw and retrench US power – not that he will overextend it.

Despite an autocratic renaissance, Russia and China, the great supposed balancers of US power, remain beholden to a global capitalist system sponsored by Washington. Separately, their challenge is narrowly regional and territorial. Together, Moscow and Beijing constitute "an axis of weak states;" apart, as they frequently are, they constitute no axis at all.[31] Neither has been able to effect an alliance commensurate with its mutual dissatisfaction with American leadership. Russia, as in the Cold War, continues to be a threat to the United States not because it is strong but because it is weak. Trump's National Security Strategy was hardly controversial in pointing out that:

Allies and partners are a great strength of the United States. They add directly to U.S. political, economic, military, intelligence, and other capabilities. Together, the United States and our allies and partners represent well over half of the global GDP. None of our adversaries have comparable coalitions.[32]

China, even on a steep rise, has far fewer allies than does a supposedly declining United States. Washington still leads NATO – an alliance of some of the most prosperous states in world history. Trump's key complaint against it was that it should thus pay more for its own upkeep. He did not deny its geostrategic utility. Beijing's closest ally, in contrast, is Pyongyang. China has clients rather than friends. It practices a form of "debt-trap diplomacy," funding large infrastructure projects abroad that the debtor state must repay as loans or become subject to Chinese Communist Party suasion. China is derided as a "payday lender." Its Belt and Road Initiative lacks the comity of Bretton Woods and of NATO. Similarly, Russian nostalgia for its Soviet empire has been unable to

---

[31] See Gordon G. Chang, China and Russia: An Axis of Weak States, *World Affairs* 176, 6 (March/April 2014): 17–29.
[32] National Security Strategy (2017), p. 37.

attract wealthy nations into a reformulation of it; Putin's project remains mired in grievance. The pro-US European Union, even allowing for Brexit, commands a geostrategic legitimacy far surpassing any other regional alliance. American foreign policy, on the big questions, has worked far more than it has failed. The international architecture that Washington created in the Cold War remains in place, and the global balance of power that tilted America's way in that struggle continues. Neither Barack Obama nor Donald Trump sought a revolution away from these Cold War precedents.

Suggested Reading

The Foreign Relations of the United States series – "the official documentary historical record of major foreign policy decisions and significant diplomatic activity of the U.S. Government" – will begin releasing post–Cold War official documents in the next few years. Until these and more declassified material is made available, readers are pointed toward the increasing number of personal primary and academic secondary accounts of the post–Cold War period. The respective presidential memoirs are a good starting point: George Bush and Brent Scowcroft, *A World Transformed* (New York: Alfred A. Knopf, 1998); Bill Clinton, *My Life* (London: Hutchinson, 2004); and George W. Bush, *Decision Points* (New York: Crown Publishing, 2010).

Those seeking an introduction to the Cold War, in order to assess this book's claim about its shadow, should consult the work of John Lewis Gaddis, especially *Strategies of Containment: A Critical Appraisal of American National Security Policy during the Cold War,* (Oxford: Oxford University Press, 1982; 2005); *Now We Know: Rethinking Cold War History* (Oxford: Oxford University Press, 1998); and his highly readable overview, *The Cold War: A New History* (New York: Penguin Press, 2005). Campbell Craig and Frederik Logevall, in *America's Cold War: The Politics of Insecurity* (Cambridge, MA: Belknap Press, 2009) provide a terrific account of the conflict that argues for the centrality of American conceptions of and agency in it. They attempt to rescue the Cold War from international historians – the best of which is Odd Arne Westad, *The Global Cold War: Third World Interventions and the Making of Our Times* (Cambridge, UK: Cambridge University Press, 2007) and his brilliant *The Cold War: A World History* (New York: Penguin, 2018).

A strong edited collection of essays by participants and scholars is offered by Michael R. Fitzgerald and Allen Packwood, eds., *Out of the Cold: The Cold War and Its Legacy* (London: Bloomsbury, 2014). Hal Brands, in *Making the Unipolar Moment: U.S. Foreign Policy and the Rise of the Post–Cold War Order* (Ithaca, NY: Cornell University Press, 2016), using recently declassified archival materials, argues that the 1980s and early 1990s set the tone for an American global resurgence during the Clinton years.

Studies deriding or bemoaning US foreign policy since the end of the Cold War dominate the literature. Those seeking a robust counterargument to the one I offer in this book should consult: Michael Mandelbaum, *Mission Failure: America and the World in the Post–Cold War Era* (New York: Oxford University Press, 2016); Stephen M. Walt, *The Hell of Good Intentions: America's Foreign Policy Elite and the Decline of U.S. Primacy* (New York: Farrar, Straus and Giroux, 2018); Barry R. Posen, *Restraint: A New Foundation for U.S. Grand Strategy* (Ithaca, NY: Cornell University Press, 2014); Robert D. Kaplan, *The Coming Anarchy: Shattering the Dreams of the Post Cold War* (New York: Penguin Random House, 2000); and *The Return of Marco Polo's World: War, Strategy, and American Interests in the Twenty-First Century* (New York: Random House, 2018).

Important studies sympathetic to my argument (without sharing all of it) include: Thomas H. Henriksen, *American Power after the Berlin Wall* (New York: Palgrave Macmillan, 2007) and his later *Cycles in U.S. Foreign Policy since the Cold War* (New York: Palgrave Macmillan, 2017); Robert Kagan, *The World America Made* (New York: Vintage Books, 2012); Robert J. Lieber, *Retreat and Its Consequences: American Foreign Policy and the Problem of World Order* (New York: Cambridge University Press, 2016); and Stephen Sestanovich, *Maximalist: America in The World from Truman to Obama* (New York: Penguin Random House, 2014). Robert Legvold's, *Return to Cold War* (Cambridge: Polity Press, 2016) argues persuasively, as his title suggests, that US–Russia relations have reverted to a Cold War setting. Stephen G. Brooks and William C. Wohlforth, in *America Abroad: Why the Sole Superpower Should Not Pull Back from the World* (New York: Oxford University Press, 2016), argue that the end of the Cold War was not a decisive turning point in the United States's basic grand strategy and that the United States is likely to remain the world's sole superpower for some time to come.

Other important studies that range across the post–Cold War era include: Hal Brands, *From Berlin to Baghdad: America's Search for*

Purpose in the Post–Cold War World (Lexington: University Press of Kentucky, 2008); George C. Herring, *From Colony to Superpower: U.S. Foreign Relations since 1776* (Oxford: Oxford University Press, 2008); and (though the focus is wider than foreign policy) Sean Wilentz, *The Age of Reagan: A History 1974–2008* (New York: Harper Collins, 2008). Timothy J. Lynch, ed., *The Oxford Encyclopedia of American Military and Diplomatic History* (New York: Oxford University Press, 2013) contains substantial entries on the key decisionmakers and events of the post–Cold War period. The economic context in which foreign policy had to be made in the post–Cold War era is assessed by Iwan Morgan, in *The Age of Deficits: Presidents and Unbalanced Budgets from Jimmy Carter to George W. Bush* (Lawrence: University Press of Kansas, 2009) and Michael Mandelbaum, *The Frugal Superpower: America's Global Leadership in a Cash-Strapped Era* (New York: PublicAffairs, 2010).

GEORGE H. W. BUSH

Broadly sympathetic accounts of his foreign policy include: Jon Meacham, *Destiny and Power: The American Odyssey of George Herbert Walker Bush* (New York: Random House, 2015); Timothy J. Naftali, *George H. W. Bush* (New York: Times Books, 2007); and Christopher Maynard, *Out of the Shadows: George H. W. Bush and the End of the Cold War* (College Station: Texas A&M Press, 2008). For an account of his foreign policy drawing on the interview testimony of several of its makers see chapters 3–5 of Michael Nelson and Barbara Perry, eds., *41: Inside the Presidency of George H. W. Bush* (Ithaca, NY: Cornell University Press, 2014). A compelling account drawing on numerous classified documents and interviews is offered by Jeffrey A. Engel, *When the World Seemed New: George H. W. Bush and the End of the Cold War* (New York: Houghton Mifflin Harcourt, 2017).

Enduring studies of the first Gulf War include Lawrence Freedman and Efraim Karsh, *The Gulf Conflict, 1990–1991: Diplomacy and War in the New World Order* (Princeton, NJ: Princeton University Press, 1993) and Richard Lowry, *The Gulf War Chronicles: A Military History of the First War with Iraq* (Lincoln, NE: iUniverse, 2008). A fascinating dissection of Bush's decision-making process in the conflict, particularly the use of historical analogies, is offered by Steve A. Yetiv, *Explaining Foreign Policy: U.S. Decision-Making and the Persian Gulf War* (Baltimore, MD: Johns Hopkins University Press, 2011). For a very readable narrative account of the place of Iraq in US strategy, see Steven Hurst, *The*

United States and Iraq since 1979: Hegemony, Oil and War (Edinburgh: Edinburgh University Press, 2009).

Bush's team is explored in Bartholomew Sparrow, *The Strategist: Brent Scowcroft and the Call of National Security* (New York: PublicAffairs, 2015) and Karen DeYoung, *Soldier: The Life of Colin Powell* (New York: Alfred A. Knopf, 2006). See also the new biography of James Baker by Peter Baker and Susan Glasser (in press). The memoirs of key players are also an important resource. See especially Howard A. Baker, *The Politics of Diplomacy* (Putnam Adult, 1995) and Norman Schwarzkopf, *It Doesn't Take a Hero: The Autobiography of General H. Norman Schwarzkopf* (New York: Bantam, 1992). The fall of the Soviet Union is retold by Louis Sell, a US diplomat based in Moscow, in *From Washington to Moscow: U.S.–Soviet Relations and the Collapse of the U.S.S.R.* (Durham, NC: Duke University Press, 2016).

BILL CLINTON

The intellectual context of Clinton's foreign policy was established in two best-selling books: Francis Fukuyama, *The End of History and the Last Man* (New York: Free Press, 1992), and Samuel P. Huntington, *The Clash of Civilizations and the Remaking of World Order* (New York: Touchstone, 1996). Their arguments remain enduringly controversial and still color American attitudes to foreign policy.

An important attempt to codify the Clinton Doctrine is offered by Douglas Brinkley in "Democratic Enlargement: The Clinton Doctrine," *Foreign Policy* 106 (Spring 1997), pp. 110–127. Christopher Layne, "Kant or Cant: The Myth of the Democratic Peace," *International Security* 19, 2 (Fall 1994), pp. 5–49, offers a powerful set of observations in defiance of Clinton's faith in the democratic peace hypothesis. Michael Mandelbaum's critical account was seminal, coining a title that stuck, in "Foreign Policy as Social Work," *Foreign Affairs* 75, 1 (January/February 1996), pp. 16–32. First-term failures and misadventures are compellingly assessed in David Halberstam, *War in a Time of Peace: Bush, Clinton, and the Generals* (New York: Touchstone Books, 2002). Incisive scholarly accounts of Clinton's entire foreign policy include John Dumbrell, *Clinton's Foreign Policy: Between the Bushes, 1992–2000* (Abingdon: Routledge, 2009) and Derek Chollet and James Goldgeier, *America between the Wars, 11/9 to 9/11: The Misunderstood Years between the Fall of the Berlin Wall and the Start of the War on Terror* (New York: PublicAffairs, 2008).

Defenses of Clinton foreign policy are offered by some of the officials that helped make it. See the terrific account of the Bosnian intervention by the man who went on to engineer the later Kosovo War: Richard Holbrooke, *To End a War* (New York: Random House, 1998); Anthony Lake, *6 Nightmares: Real Threats in a Dangerous World and How America Can Meet Them* (Boston: Little, Brown, 2000); and Warren Christopher, *In the Stream of History: Shaping Foreign Policy for a New Era* (Stanford, CA: Stanford University Press, 1998). Contrasting accounts of Clinton administration function and dysfunction are offered, respectively, by two men who served in it: Strobe Talbott, *The Russia Hand: A Memoir of Presidential Diplomacy* (New York: Random House, 2002), and George Stephanopoulos, *All Too Human: A Political Education* (Boston: Little, Brown, 1999). One of the clearest (if critical) accounts of Clinton's major military interventions is Robert C. DiPrizio, *Armed Humanitarians: U.S. Interventions from Northern Iraq to Kosovo* (Baltimore, MD: Johns Hopkins University Press, 2002).

GEORGE W. BUSH

The literature on Bush divides between those who think his response to 9/11 (particularly the Iraq War) was appropriate (or at least explicable) and those who do not. The latter camp is large among academic scholars. Some of its ablest members include Terry H. Anderson, *Bush's Wars* (New York: Oxford University Press, 2011); Jean Edward Smith, *Bush* (New York: Simon & Schuster, 2016); and Robert Jervis, "Why the Bush Doctrine Cannot Be Sustained," *Political Science Quarterly* (Fall 2005). Books that impeach the Iraq occupation, at least in its initial phase, are obviously far more common than those that defend it. Some of the most important indictments include: Andrew J. Bacevich, *America's War for the Greater Middle East: A Military History* (New York: Random House, 2016); Larry Diamond, *Squandered Victory: The American Occupation and the Bungled Effort to Bring Democracy to Iraq* (New York: Times Books, 2005); Thomas E. Ricks, *Fiasco: The American Military in Iraq* (New York: Penguin, 2006); and Emma Sky, *The Unraveling: High Hopes and Missed Opportunities in Iraq* (New York: PublicAffairs, 2015). The country Bush invaded is analyzed brilliantly (and empirically) by Lisa Blaydes, *State of Repression Iraq under Saddam Hussein* (Princeton, NJ: Princeton University Press, 2018). The US occupation is set within the context of Iraq's problematic history of Western interference in Toby Dodge, *Inventing Iraq: The Failure of Nation Building and a History Denied* (New York: Columbia University Press, 2003). The role played by Tony Blair – whom Dodge personally urged to avoid Iraq – is dissected in the mammoth official *Chilcot Report* (2016), which summarizes much of the book-length accounts written since 2003.

Arguments sympathetic to Bush foreign policy are made by Frank P. Harvey, *Explaining The Iraq War: Counterfactual Theory, Logic and Evidence* (New York: Cambridge University Press, 2012); Stephen F. Knott, *Rush to Judgement: George W. Bush, the War on Terror, and His Critics* (Lawrence: University Press of Kansas, 2012); and Robert S. Litwak, *Regime Change: U.S. Strategy through the Prism of 9/11* (Washington, DC: Woodrow Wilson Press, 2007). For a clear analysis of the context in which Bush operated see Robert J. Lieber, *The American Era: Power and Strategy for the 21st Century* (New York: Cambridge University Press, 2007). A balanced, narrative-driven, account is offered by Ivo H. Daalder and James M. Lindsay, *America Unbound: The Bush Revolution in Foreign Policy* (Washington, DC: Brookings Institution Press, 2008). Peter Baker, the *New York Times* White House correspondent during the Bush years, has written a compelling account of them: *Days of Fire: Bush and Cheney in the White House* (New York: Doubleday, 2013).

Books that attempt to place Bush foreign policy within a Cold War tradition include John Dumbrell and David Ryan, eds., *Vietnam in Iraq: Lessons, Legacies and Ghosts* (New York: Routledge, 2006) and Timothy J. Lynch and Robert S. Singh, *After Bush: The Case for Continuity in American Foreign Policy* (New York: Cambridge University Press, 2008). Robert Kagan has written some of the most widely read texts placing the 9/11 response and Iraq War within a historical context. See especially *Paradise and Power: America and Europe in the New World Order* (London: Atlantic Books, 2003). Another short, compelling historical grounding of the 9/11 response is offered by John Lewis Gaddis, *Surprise, Security, and the American Experience* (Cambridge, MA: Harvard University Press, 2004).

Alongside Bush's *Decision Points* are other important memoirs by his vice-president, Dick Cheney, *In My Time: A Personal and Political Memoir* (New York: Threshold Editions, 2011); by George Tenet, *At the Center of the Storm: My Years at the CIA* (New York: HarperCollins, 2007); and by Donald Rumsfeld, *Known and Unknown: A Memoir* (New York: Penguin, 2011). Rumsfeld's role in Iraq has spawned an industry of scholarship dedicated to condemning it. Andrew Cockburn, *Rumsfeld: His Rise, Fall, and Catastrophic Legacy* (New York: Scribner, 2007) is especially strident. Unavoidable in any consideration of Bush foreign policy are books by the *Washington Post* journalist Bob Woodward: *Bush at War* (2002), *Plan of Attack* (2004), *State of Denial*, (2006), and *The War Within: A Secret White House History 2006–2008* (2008), each published by Simon & Schuster, New York.

BARACK OBAMA

The foreign policy context Obama inherited was described by journalists Fareed Zakaria, *The Post-American World* (New York: W. W. Norton, 2008) and David E. Sanger, *The Inheritance: The World Obama Confronts and the Challenges to American Power* (London, Bantam Press, 2009), the latter informing Sanger's *Confront and Conceal: Obama's Secret Wars and Surprising Use of American Power* (New York: Crown Publishers, 2012). Bob Woodward's *Obama's Wars* (New York: Simon & Schuster, 2010) was the first "insider account" of Obama's delay in committing troops to Afghanistan. Other influential accounts by journalists include Ryan Lizza, "The Consequentialist: How the Arab Spring Remade Obama's Foreign Policy," *New Yorker*, May 2, 2011, and David Samuels, "The Aspiring Novelist Who Became Obama's Foreign-Policy Guru," *New York Times*, May 5, 2016. The first Obama team is dissected by James Mann, *The Obamians: The Struggle Inside the White House to Redefine American Power* (Viking: New York, 2012).

Memoirs worth consulting include: Robert M. Gates, *Duty: Memoirs of a Secretary at War* (New York: Alfred A. Knopf, 2014); Leon Panetta, *Worthy Fights: A Memoir of Leadership in War and Peace* (New York: Penguin Press 2014); and Michael McFaul, *From Cold War to Hot Peace: An American Ambassador in Putin's Russia* (New York: Houghton Mifflin Harcourt, 2018). Struggles with Hillary Clinton are recounted in Mark Landler, *Alter Egos: Hillary Clinton, Barack Obama, and the Twilight Struggle over American Power* (New York: Random House, 2016).

David Milne, *Worldmaking: The Art and Science of American Diplomacy* (New York: Farrar, Strauss and Giroux, 2015) argues persuasively that Obama was a pragmatist and the heir of a Cold War realist tradition, as opposed to a liberal foreign policy tradition. This interpretation rejects studies that ground his world view and subsequent diplomacy in a leftish moral relativism. These include: Colin Dueck, who offers a concise and especially compelling indictment of Obama's failures, *The Obama Doctrine: American Grand Strategy Today* (New York: Oxford University Press, 2015); Mark Moyar, *Strategic Failure: How President*

Obama's Drone Warfare, Defense Cuts, and Military Amateurism Have Imperiled America (New York: Threshold Editions, 2015); Robert Singh, *Barack Obama's Post–American Foreign Policy: The Limits of Engagement* (London: Bloomsbury, 2012); and Bret Stephens, *America in Retreat: The New Isolationism and the Coming Global Disorder* (New York: Sentinel, 2015).

A seminal account by a sympathetic critic of Obama's foreign policy, who also had a role in making it (as advisor to Richard Holbrooke, 2009–2010), is Vali Nasr, *The Dispensable Nation: American Foreign Policy in Retreat* (New York: Random House, 2013). A more understanding account by a key Obama aide is Ben Rhodes, *The World As It Is: Inside the Obama White House* (London: Bodley Head, 2018). Defenses of Obama are also offered by Martin S. Indyk, Kenneth G. Lieberthal, and Michael E. O'Hanlon, *Bending History: Barack Obama's Foreign Policy* (Washington, DC: Brookings, 2012), and Derek Chollet, *The Long Game: How Obama Defied Washington and Redefined America's Role in the World* (New York: PublicAffairs, 2016).

DONALD TRUMP

The best short introduction is Brendan Simms and Charlie Laderman, *Donald Trump: The Making of a World View* (New York: I. B. Tauris, 2017). The foreign policy inheritance of the Trump administration is considered by Richard Haass, *A World in Disarray: American Foreign Policy and the Crisis of the Old Order* (New York: Penguin 2017) and Hal Brands, *American Grand Strategy in the Age of Trump* (Washington, DC: Brooking Institution Press, 2018). Brands argues convincingly that there is more success than failure in post–Cold War US grand strategy – the work is a collection of articles published elsewhere. The chaotic transition of 2016–2017 is told in worrying and readable detail by Michael Lewis, *The Fifth Risk* (New York: W. W. Norton, 2018). Melvyn Leffler, "Trump's Delusional National Security Strategy," *Foreign Policy* (December 21, 2017); James Mann, "The Adults in the Room," *New York Review of Books* (October 26, 2017); and Barry Posen, "The Rise of Illiberal Hegemony: Trump's Surprising Grand Strategy," *Foreign Affairs* (March/April 2018) offer powerful critiques of early Trump foreign policy.

Patrick Porter, "Why America's Grand Strategy Has Not Changed: Power, Habit, and the U.S. Foreign Policy Establishment," *International Security* (Spring 2018) argues that Trump does not represent a revolution in American foreign policy. He expands on this theme in *The False Promise of Liberal Order* (Polity, forthcoming). Robert Kagan describes the dreadful portents of Trump foreign policy in *The Jungle Grows Back: America and Our Imperiled World* (New York: Knopf, 2018). Thomas J. Wright also offers a clear assessment of the global order Trump disrupted and chaotically tried to reshape in *All Measures Short of War: The Contest for the Twenty-First Century and the Future of American Power* (New Haven, CT: Yale University Press, 2017). Excellent multi-author volumes include Jon Herbert, Trevor McCrisken, and Andrew Wroe, *The Ordinary Presidency of Donald J. Trump* (Basingstoke, UK: Palgrave Macmillan, 2019) and Robert Jervis, Francis J. Gavin, Joshua Rovner, and Diane Labrosse, eds., *Chaos in the Liberal Order: The Trump Presidency and International Politics in the Twenty-First Century* (New York: Columbia University Press, 2018). Accessible early, book-length studies include Carl Unger *House of Trump, House of Putin: The Untold Story of Donald Trump and the Russian Mafia* (Dutton, 2018) and Bob Woodward, *Fear: Trump in the White House* (New York: Simon & Schuster, 2018). Angela Stent's *Putin's World: Russia against the West and with the Rest* (New York: Twelve Books, 2019) offers a very readable account of where Trump fits in the long history of US–Russia relations.

Index

Abdullah, King, 213
Abkhazia. *See* Russia: war with Georgia
Abrams, Elliot, 207
Abu Ghraib, 133, 179
Adams, Gerry, 74
Afghanistan
  Islamism in, 73
  Soviet Union and, 18, 21, 58, 101, 174
Afghanistan War, 112–114
  as "good war," 104, 113
  longest in US history, 158
  Obama surge in, 173–175
  prioritized over democratic universalism, 140
  too few US troops in, 142
  Vietnam War compared to, 173
Agenda, The (Bob Woodward), 53
al-Assad, Bashar. *See* Syrian Civil War
al-Maliki, Nouri, 143–144, 188, 200
al Qaeda. *See also* September 11, 2001
  in Afghanistan, 174
  in Bosnia, 73
  in Iraq, 133–134, 143
  Khobar Towers bombing, 76
al Shabab, 203
Albright, Madeleine, 9, 61, 78–79, 91
Allende, Salvador. *See* Chile
Allison, Graham, 215
American dream, 3
American Enterprise Institute, 141
Anderson, Terry, 114
Anglo-American special relationship, 94
Arab–Israeli conflict
  October 1973 War, 82, 183

peace process, 236, *see also* Camp David II
Arab Spring, 146, 160, 179–181, 186
Arafat, Yasser, 96–98
Aristide, Jean-Bertrand, 62
Ash, Timothy Garton, 30
Aspin, Les, 53–54
Attlee, Clement, 45
Australia, 103, 117, 125, 146
Australia, New Zealand and United States
  Security (ANZUS) Treaty, 103
Aziz, Omer, 202

Bader, Jeffrey, 214–215
Baker, James, 23, 43
Baltic states, 147–148
Bangladesh, 203
Bannon, Stephen, 228
Begin, Menachem, 95
Berger, Samuel ("Sandy"), 78
Berlin, 208
Berlin Airlift, 163
Berlin Wall, 1, 4, 10, 21, 30, 41, 225
Berlusconi, Silvio, 146
Biden, Joe, 232
bin Laden, Osama, *see also* September 11,
    2001
  attacks of 9/11 and, 108–112
  background of, 109
  death of, 152, 176, 194, 197, 222
  Somalia and, 65
  Soviet Union and, 77
Black Hawk Down incident, 62, 185
Blackwill, Robert, 151